A
PREFACE
TO
MORALS

Walter Lippmann

# A
# PREFACE
# TO
# MORALS

*with a new introduction*
*by Sidney Hook*

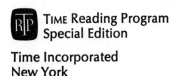

TIME Reading Program
Special Edition

Time Incorporated
New York

## TIME-LIFE BOOKS

EDITOR *Norman P. Ross*
TEXT DIRECTOR *William Jay Gold*
ART DIRECTOR *Edward A. Hamilton*
CHIEF OF RESEARCH *Beatrice T. Dobie*
ASSISTANT TEXT DIRECTOR *Jerry Korn*

EDITOR, TIME READING PROGRAM *Max Gissen*
RESEARCHER *Ann S. Lang*
DESIGNER *Lore Levenberg*

PUBLISHER *Rhett Austell*
GENERAL MANAGER *John A. Watters*

## TIME MAGAZINE

EDITOR *Roy Alexander*
MANAGING EDITOR *Otto Fuerbringer*
PUBLISHER *Bernhard M. Auer*

COVER: "Mercurious in the Vessel" *by Richard Anuszkiewicz*
Courtesy The Contemporaries

# Contents

Part Three

THE GENIUS OF MODERNITY

# Editors'
# Preface

Most Americans, it seems likely, know the author of this book principally as an eminent newspaper columnist. Walter Lippmann has been writing the widely syndicated *Today and Tomorrow* column since 1931 and has left his imprint on just about every issue of consequence that newspaper readers have been obliged to consider in these years. He has sometimes been wrong, but it has never been possible to ignore his views; they have always been part of any dialogue on contemporary problems. Their force has derived from Lippmann's cool reason, his historical perspective and his insistence on relating the day's headlines to the eternal themes of philosophy. His column has always commanded the respect even of those it enraged—of whom, over the years, there have been quite a few.

Older Americans will recall that the pre-1931, precolumnist Lippmann was also a force to be reckoned with. He first came into the public's view before World War I, as an imposing young intellectual, plainly a man of genius, who had raced through Harvard in three years, then remained to serve as a teaching assistant to the famous Professor George Santayana, had written a well-received book called *A Preface to Politics* (among those who reviewed it with admiration was Theodore Roosevelt) and had gone to work for the Wilson Administration. During the war, while still less than 30, he helped to draft President Wilson's famous Fourteen Points program for postwar peace. In the 1920s his principal occupation was writing editorials for the New York *World*. And it was toward the end of that decade that he began work on *A Preface to Morals,* which was published in 1929.

The critic Edmund Wilson hailed the work. "In style," he said, "it is a long way from the sometimes tiresome Chestertonisms of his early political books; and in thought, it shows a new competence, a new inspiration even, in fields where he has never before ventured. It is beautifully organized, beautifully clear; and it is both outspoken and persuasive in bringing news which has been uneasily awaited." *A Preface to Morals* is still widely regarded as Lippmann's most important book. It is, in any case, the most eloquent expression of the philosophy of scientific humanism that structures his thinking and still informs his newspaper columns.

Lippmann's earlier works had addressed themselves to political questions and had proposed political answers. In writing *A Preface to Politics,* he afterward recalled, he had "assumed without question that in a regime of personal liberty each nation could by the increasing exercise of popular sovereignty create for itself gradually a spaciously planned and intelligently directed social order." Later Lippmann became persuaded that, while democracy was necessary to the good life, it was not sufficient. The problem he wrestles with in *A Preface to Morals* plainly requires a nonpolitical solution.

The heart of the problem is modern man's loss of faith. Lippmann puts the case succinctly in the first few lines of the book:

> Among those who no longer believe in the religion of their fathers some are proudly defiant, and many are indifferent. But there are also a few, perhaps an increasing number, who feel that there is a vacancy in their lives. . . .
>
> When such men put their feelings into words they are likely to say that, having lost their faith, they have lost the certainty that their lives are significant, and that it matters what they do with their lives.

The loss of faith took place over a period of several hundreds of years but became a critical matter only in the 19th Century. Lippmann's reconstruction of this developing crisis is fascinating. He begins by observing that although the devout have always had the problem of the Bible's seeming absurdities and contradictions, for many generations this problem could be solved by the practice of construing certain passages allegorically. In times when modes of thought were less precise, the devout did not make the distinction—which forces itself on men today—between symbolic and literal truths. "We must be careful," Lippmann cautions, "not to misunderstand this method of thought. When they said that the beautiful woman in the Song of Solomon was the Church, they were not conscious, as we are, that this is a figure of speech." Thus a passage could be read allegorically, which got the reader past any difficulties it might entail, and could still be regarded as literally true. But eventually the method of allegory had to break down, not only because men began to distinguish different kinds of truth but because the method, by encouraging multiple interpretations of critical passages, led to multiple heresies.

Allegory was succeeded by the so-called Higher Criticism, i.e., by the efforts of serious Christian scholars to determine what the original authors of the Bible actually had meant to say. The effect of these efforts, Lippmann believes, was to make the problem of faith more critical than ever for modern readers. "When they read the Bible as allegory," he writes, "they found in it unending confirmation of what they already believed. But when they read it literally, as history, as astronomy, and biology, and as a code of laws, it contradicted at many crucial points the practical working convictions of their daily lives." What was to be done then?

The most important of several attempted solutions was to take the Bible as a message that is, so to speak, in cipher; it must be "decoded" so as to get at the profound and enduring meanings that reside in certain crucial passages. But in this effort to modernize religion, some of Christianity's central concepts had to be restated—and, in effect, replaced. Christians were still promised an eternal life after death but the promise no longer meant what it once had, for the word "eternal" now referred, mystically, to a realm independent of time and space. The achievement of this modernist religion was to reconstruct a body of doctrine that was intellectually respectable and rooted in the noblest traditions of the faith. Yet the new religion was beyond the power of a mass audience to grasp; beyond that, it was not the kind of religion that could command unquestioning faith even from those who had studied and absorbed its doctrines. What it lacked, principally, was authority; what it had lost was certainty. It was too plainly the work of scholars—and the work of scholars, even of the most devout and perceptive scholars, is no substitute for divine revelation.

Lippmann writes:

> Religious professions will not work when they rest merely on a kind of passive assent; or on intricate reasoning, or on fierce exhortation, or on a good-natured conspiracy to be vague and highflown. A man cannot cheat about faith. Either he has it in the marrow of his bones, or in a crisis, when he is distracted and in sorrow, there is no conviction there to support him. Without complete certainty religion does not offer genuine consolation.

With its loss of certainty and authority, religion had also lost its relevance to most of the activities that men are concerned with in their daily lives. Ministers may still address themselves to contemporary issues, but they are apt to speak in the accents of earnest and conscientious men, not in the accents of authority. If they have anything to say about business practices, for example, or sexual morality or art, they are apt to say it (unless they are preaching in church) without bringing the will of God into the discussion.

Thus, Lippmann indicates, business, the family and the other preoccupations of men's daily lives are, in effect, religion's "lost provinces." This loss has inevitably made life seem less meaningful to many men. For with each province now autonomous, each having its own standards and its own modes of thought, there is no longer any strong central theme in men's lives; nothing seems to be organically related to anything else, and so nothing seems to be terribly important. But even that is not the worst of it.

The greater challenge to the view that it matters what men do has been the insistent evidence of modern science that the universe is "neutral." In the "constitution of the universe," as Lippmann calls it, there is no preamble about men's destinies. "The prestige, which once adhered to those who spoke by revelation, has passed to scientists. But science, though it is the most reliable method of knowledge we now possess, does not provide an account of the world in which human destiny is the central theme. . . . It enables us to realize some of our hopes. But it offers no guarantees that they can be fulfilled."

There are a number of possible responses to the human predicament outlined in the first section of *A Preface to Morals*. In the second section, Lippmann describes some of these. He argues persuasively against several of them and then concludes that the only workable philosophy for modern men is a new humanism, and in the final section of the book he takes up its immediate applications. The term "humanism" has often been used to denote an irreligious philosophy, on grounds that it is derived from men's own needs rather than God's commandments. Lippmann's humanism conforms to this definition; and yet its content, he argues, is akin to the "high religion" of history's great teachers—of Jesus, Buddha and Confucius. At the same time his humanism is responsive to the imperatives of modern science. Indeed, Lippmann suggests a relationship between the teachings of high religion and the findings of modern psychology.

Perhaps that is as much as an editors' preface should say about this author's conclusions. Readers might better follow Lippmann's own learned and logical route to them —and that is a pleasure no reader should be allowed to miss.

—THE EDITORS OF TIME

# Introduction

Were the reader to chance upon this volume unidentified by title or author, he would surely believe, if he disregarded some illustrative details, that it was published yesterday, not 35 years ago, and that it addressed itself to him in his present condition and not to a generation now grown old. *A Preface to Morals* was written at a time when a crisis of confidence was beginning to undermine the support which ancestral religion had given to public and private morality. This crisis of confidence had spread from the intellectual leaders of the age to the opinion makers in popular art and thought. The voices of Clarence Darrow and H. L. Mencken, of Sinclair Lewis and Aldous Huxley were being heard in the land.

Sophistication rode high but it was uneasy in the saddle, for the familiar signposts were gone. Roads ran in all directions, some in circles. The world had become more exciting and uncertain, and yet lonelier and more unfamiliar. It was as if one had moved from a small, well-kept and well-lit home, in which everything seemed to have its appointed place, into a huge house which never could be seen

completely in perspective, and whose vast cellars and endless corridors sent back ominous echoes.

Modern science had dethroned an anthropomorphic
God from his ontological eminence. But what followed is
not unusual in many revolutions. After the first flush of
emancipation and tingling sense of liberation had subsided,
a feeling of emptiness and loneliness stole over those newly
released from their bonds. It could not be banished by
episodic and frenetic outbursts of self-expression through
bootleg liquor or bootleg sex. For the person who is un-
attached to ideal objects of allegiance soon tires of sensuous
athleticism. If one can gorge on fruit at any time, there is
no pleasure in stealing it.

The loss of the ordered certainties of religion, then as
now, gave rise to a popular unreflective relativism according
to which no objective moral principles of any kind could
be justified. Once religious authority was abandoned, it was
assumed that the only alternative authority was that of
raw desire. From this it seemed to follow that any mode of
life was as good as any other, that all experiences had equal
value and significance. Order and discipline were equated
with Puritanical restraint of the kind which condemned
bearbaiting not because it gave pain to the bear but because
it gave pleasure to the spectators. Among the bright young
men, moral judgments tended to be dismissed as pronouncements of sour virtue, handed down by those secretly envious
of joys which were beyond their courage or their power to
experience.

It was in the cultural atmosphere of the Roaring 20s,
during the dizzy months which preceded the Great Depression that was soon to be heralded by the Wall Street crash,
that Walter Lippmann published this book of his middle
years. It was a simple but noble work with a profound

central insight, and it was dramatically appropriate to the intellectual needs of the time. Yet seen in retrospect, it was nevertheless touched by innocence. Its great achievement was to give a popular and felicitous expression to the philosophy of humanism in opposition to the ritualistic orthodoxies of the past and the threatening barbarisms, red and black, which sat on the threshold of the future. Its voice and its message reminded one of the Stoic sages who lived and taught the life of reason in the last days of the Roman Empire before it was destroyed by the fanatics from within and the barbarians from without. That the foundations of this humanism, but not its applications, had been laid by George Santayana and John Dewey detracts not at all from the significance of Lippmann's achievement. For Santayana and Dewey were primarily teachers of teachers, while Lippmann taught in the marketplace. In the decade which witnessed the last losing fight between traditional religion and science, Lippmann wrote:

> When men can no longer be theists, they must, if they are civilized, become humanists. They must live by the premise that whatever is righteous is inherently desirable because experience will demonstrate its desirability. They must live, therefore, in the belief that the duty of man is not to make his will conform to the will of God but to the surest knowledge of the conditions of human happiness.

This makes morals man-centered, not God-centered. It removes a benign cosmic support from the human adventure. The standing difficulty in this view is to explain how experience can generate its own standards of the desirable without a guide from outside of experience. How can man live with his finitude except in the shadow and worship of the Infinite? The humanist answer is that the rhythms and patterns of human life, the needs and wants of human nature, the duties and obligations of an ordered society furnish a basis on which it is possible to build a reasonable moral economy, at once objective and yet relative to the specific possibilities history offers in this place and in this time. The moral life is autonomous with reference to any transcendent principle but is bound, not by logic but by wisdom, to the nature of man and his reflective choices.

It is this central principle in the philosophy of humanism which retains its perennial validity throughout all its deviant forms. For if they agree on this principle, humanists of all varieties have a common method of reference and control by which they can settle their other differences, a method which is conspicuously absent in the clash of religious absolutes.

That man does not need God to become truly man, or even a better one, runs counter to weighty religious traditions from time immemorial. Yet its validity can be established by many considerations. The most powerful one, implicit in what Lippmann says, is that even in their religious worship men cannot escape their own natures, that they create their gods in their own moral image and have always done so. That is why the history and development of human religion has reflected the history and development of human morality. Moral commands are invested with the awful authority of the Creator of the Universe, who is presumed to be their source. The result is that moral growth is hampered by the residual moral principles of another age which seem to be the powerful decrees of Heaven because men have not yet penetrated to the secret of their origins on earth and in their own human past.

The growth of science reveals that the natural order is

not a moral order, that the cosmos is neutral to good and evil, and thereby makes man alone responsible for his own moral destiny in the world of which he is a part. He can live the life of a beast outside of society or the life of miserable man within society—as Thomas Hobbes described it, "poor, nasty, ugly, brutish and short." He can also live like a rational man in a rational society, if in human affairs he follows the guide not of conventional or traditional religion but of modern science. In this way, he will at least find human experience more tolerable than it has ever been in the past. Lippmann claims that the modernist liberal religion of his day, in its struggles against religious fundamentalism, had actually emptied religious rituals and practices of their religious significance and thereby acknowledged, albeit halfheartedly, the primacy of the moral dimension. But modernist liberal religion, according to Lippmann, had not gone far enough. Because its vocabulary was systematically ambiguous, it confused our minds and made our emotions discordant.

Since the original publication of Lippmann's *A Preface to Morals*, there have been some surprising developments in religious thinking, completely unanticipated by the author's rather sanguine expectations that the growth of the scientific attitude would eclipse the religious outlook. There may be some who interpret this impressive phenomenon of religious revival as a challenge to Lippmann's position. Something therefore must be said of it in the way of assessment.

Largely in consequence of the Depression years and World War II—which many individuals attributed to the impact of science on society, rather than to the failure to apply the rationale of scientific inquiry to social problems—religious thought, including theology, has undergone a renaissance. Inspired by the writings of Kierkegaard and

Barth abroad and the work of Niebuhr and Tillich in this country, God and the principle of transcendence have been restored to the central place from which the religion of the social gospel and various forms of religious liberalism and modernism had displaced them. Battening on the inadequacies of some shallow formulations of social liberalism, and ignoring the depths of a naturalism that built firmly on the tragic facts of life, the new theology defined God (in Tillich's words) as the object of man's "ultimate concern." God is no longer the highest Being or Power or Personality —He is not even a Being at all—but the unconditioned source of everything which is or may be conceived, Being-as-such. Conceived in this way, God functions to curb man's absolute demands, to bring home to him a proper sense of his finitude, partiality and humility.

Although Lippmann has not discussed the newer movements in religion and theology, it is not difficult to see the kind of objections he would raise to them. For with some modifications, they are implied in his criticism of modernist, liberal religion as represented by Dr. Harry Emerson Fosdick. Like the modernists, the new existentialist theology rejects the literal inspiration of the Bible and the entire conception of God as lawgiver, judge and father of human life. It is even further removed from the simple religious faith and pieties of the plain man and his churches. It substitutes a moral attitude for religious knowledge. Everything it says about man and his nature, if true, is better warranted by the empirical study of man than by insights expressed in the misleading language of religious myth. It is basically inadequate because although it is careful not to encroach on science, it nonetheless gives man an assurance of cosmic support for a *leap of faith* which cannot be justified either by reason or experience.

Lippmann wishes to separate out the ethical ideals from the great historical religions. When all the vestiges of superstition and magic and wish thinking have been pruned away, he finds that the values exhibited in the lives of some of the great protagonists of historical religion represent the genuine moral discoveries of the human spirit. They remain part of the permanent moral legacy of the human race. They are historically embedded in religious practices and beliefs but not logically dependent on them. Lippmann insists, however—and rightly it seems to me—that maturity requires the dissociation of this moral heritage from the framework of distinctively religious belief of any kind, if for no other reason than that the ethical insights of the past, once fortified by the divine and awesome authority of God, the all-powerful and invisible King, are no longer subject to the tests and checks of new experience. They become cruel and constricting dogmas supporting fetishistic practices. The history of medicine, the history of political morality, the history of sexual morality illustrate this.

The great religious spirits of the past, on this view, were great humanists, too. For the essence of humanist morality, according to Lippmann, is self-understanding in the light of the order of nature, the reconstruction of desires and self to bring them into harmony with the true nature of things, the development of habits of reasonable expectation, the unillusioned perception of man's modest yet glorious place in nature. This is the wisdom of Jesus, of Buddha and of Confucius, who is quoted in the *Analects* as having achieved salvation (alas! only at 70!): "I could follow what my heart desired, without transgressing what was right."

This morality of maturity Lippmann calls "high religion." The core of high religion is "disinterestedness." It is obviously not found in the community of saints who struggled against the flesh, against scientific knowledge, against the natural fact of death. It is found only in the rare few among the spiritually elect of the world. "High religion," he writes, "is a prophecy and an anticipation of what life is like when desire is in perfect harmony with reality." And Lippmann recommends that this religion of the elite now become, in our age of science, technology and democracy, the religion of man.

At this point certain questions arise. Lippmann has assumed that the transformation of human desires to bring them into harmony with the world is the surest way to happiness. But does this not depend on the character of the desires and the character of the world at the time? Happiness may sometimes be achieved by transforming the world to bring it into harmony with human desires, rather than by transforming the self to bring it into harmony with the world. We can find happiness in getting what we want or in learning to want what we've got. In a world in which the legacy of Hitler and Stalin still prevails in large areas, in which in our own culture millions are still excluded from the kingdom of democratic ends, in which there is still want and deprivation, in which neither peace nor freedom are secure, humanism must find its inwardness through multiple activities designed to make the world worthier of man.

Still, the difference between such a humanism and the humanism of Lippmann is perhaps a difference only of nuance. In either case a humanist philosophy will not only tolerate but encourage a plurality of ways of looking at the world that are compatible with one another, that are engaged in fruitful dialogue, not bloody combat, in the hope that by pooling our multiple ignorance and weakness we may win more knowledge and strength and less unhappiness.

—SIDNEY HOOK

Part One

# THE DISSOLUTION OF THE ANCESTRAL ORDER

*"Whirl is King, having driven out Zeus."*

ARISTOPHANES.

# I The Problem of Unbelief

## 1. WHIRL IS KING

Among those who no longer believe in the religion of their fathers, some are proudly defiant, and many are indifferent. But there are also a few, perhaps an increasing number, who feel that there is a vacancy in their lives. This inquiry deals with their problem. It is not intended to disturb the serenity of those who are unshaken in the faith they hold, and it is not concerned with those who are still exhilarated by their escape from some stale orthodoxy. It is concerned with those who are perplexed by the consequences of their own irreligion. It deals with the problem of unbelief, not as believers are accustomed to deal with it, in the spirit of men confidently calling the lost sheep back into the fold, but as unbelievers themselves must, I think, face the problem if they face it candidly and without presumption.

When such men put their feelings into words they are likely to say that, having lost their faith, they have lost the certainty that their lives are significant, and that it matters what they do with their lives. If they deal with young people they are likely to say that they know of no

compelling reason which certifies the moral code they adhere to, and that, therefore, their own preferences, when
tested by the ruthless curiosity of their children, seem to
have no sure foundation of any kind. They are likely to
point to the world about them, and to ask whether the
modern man possesses any criterion by which he can measure the value of his own desires, whether there is any
standard he really believes in which permits him to put a
term upon that pursuit of money, of power, and of excitement which has created so much of the turmoil and the
squalor and the explosiveness of modern civilization.

These are, perhaps, merely the rationalizations of the
modern man's discontent. At the heart of it there are
likely to be moments of blank misgiving in which he finds
that the civilization of which he is a part leaves a dusty
taste in his mouth. He may be very busy with many
things, but he discovers one day that he is no longer sure
they are worth doing. He has been much preoccupied;
but he is no longer sure he knows why. He has become
involved in an elaborate routine of pleasures; and they do
not seem to amuse him very much. He finds it hard to believe that doing any one thing is better than doing any
other thing, or, in fact, that it is better than doing nothing
at all. It occurs to him that it is a great deal of trouble to
live, and that even in the best of lives the thrills are few
and far between. He begins more or less consciously to
seek satisfactions, because he is no longer satisfied, and
all the while he realizes that the pursuit of happiness was
always a most unhappy quest. In the later stages of his
woe he not only loses his appetite, but becomes excessively miserable trying to recover it. And then, surveying
the flux of events and the giddiness of his own soul, he
comes to feel that Aristophanes must have been thinking

of him when he declared that "Whirl is King, having driven out Zeus."


## 2. FALSE PROPHECIES

The modern age has been rich both in prophecies that men would at last inherit the kingdoms of this world, and in complaints at the kind of world they inherited. Thus Petrarch, who was an early victim of modernity, came to feel that he would "have preferred to be born in any other period" than his own; he tells us that he sought an escape by imagining that he lived in some other age. The Nineteenth Century, which begat us, was forever blowing the trumpets of freedom and providing asylums in which its most sensitive children could take refuge. Wordsworth fled from mankind to rejoice in nature. Chateaubriand fled from man to rejoice in savages. Byron fled to an imaginary Greece, and William Morris to the Middle Ages. A few tried an imaginary India. A few an equally imaginary China. Many fled to Bohemia, to Utopia, to the Golden West, and to the Latin Quarter, and some, like James Thomson, to hell where they were

> gratified to gain
> That positive eternity of pain
> Instead of this insufferable inane.

They had all been disappointed by the failure of a great prophecy. The theme of this prophecy had been that man is a beautiful soul who in the course of history had somehow become enslaved by

> Scepters, tiaras, swords, and chains, and tomes
> Of reasoned wrong, glozed on by ignorance,

and they believed with Shelley that when "the loathsome mask has fallen," man, exempt from awe, worship, degree, the king over himself, would then be "free from guilt or pain." This was the orthodox liberalism to which men turned when they had lost the religion of their fathers. But the promises of liberalism have not been fulfilled. We are living in the midst of that vast dissolution of ancient habits which the emancipators believed would restore our birthright of happiness. We know now that they did not see very clearly beyond the evils against which they were rebelling. It is evident to us that their prophecies were pleasant fantasies which concealed the greater difficulties that confront men, when having won the freedom to do what they wish—that wish, as Byron said:

> which ages have not yet subdued
> In man—to have no master save his mood,

they are full of contrary moods and do not know what they wish to do. We have come to see that Huxley was right when he said that "a man's worst difficulties begin when he is able to do as he likes."

The evidences of these greater difficulties lie all about us: in the brave and brilliant atheists who have defied the Methodist God, and have become very nervous; in the women who have emancipated themselves from the tyranny of fathers, husbands, and homes, and with the intermittent but expensive help of a psychoanalyst, are now enduring liberty as interior decorators; in the young men and women who are world-weary at twenty-two; in the multitudes who drug themselves with pleasure; in the crowds enfranchised by the blood of heroes who cannot be persuaded to take an interest in their destiny; in the millions, at last free to think without fear of priest or policeman, who have made the moving pictures and the popular newspapers what they are.

These are the prisoners who have been released. They ought to be very happy. They ought to be serene and composed. They are free to make their own lives. There are no conventions, no tabus, no gods, priests, princes, fathers, or revelations which they must accept. Yet the result is not so good as they thought it would be. The prison door is wide open. They stagger out into trackless space under a blinding sun. They find it nerve-racking. "My sensibility," said Flaubert, "is sharper than a razor's edge; the creaking of a door, the face of a bourgeois, an absurd statement set my heart to throbbing and completely upset me." They must find their own courage for battle and their own consolation in defeat. They complain, like Renan after he had broken with the Church, that the enchanted circle which embraced the whole of life is broken, and that they are left with a feeling of emptiness "like that which follows an attack of fever or an unhappy love affair." Where is my *home?* cried Nietzsche: "For it do I ask and seek, and have sought, but have not found it. O eternal everywhere, O eternal nowhere, O eternal in vain."

To more placid temperaments the pangs of freedom are no doubt less acute. It is possible for multitudes in time of peace and security to exist agreeably—somewhat incoherently, perhaps, but without convulsions—to dream a little and not unpleasantly, to have only now and then a nightmare, and only occasionally a rude awakening. It is possible to drift along not too discontentedly, somewhat nervously, somewhat anxiously, somewhat confusedly, hoping for the best, and believing in nothing very much. It is possible to be a passable citizen. But it is not possible to be wholly at peace. For serenity of soul requires some better organization of life than a man can attain by pursuing his casual ambitions, satisfying his hungers, and for the rest accepting destiny as an idiot's tale in which one dumb sensation succeeds another to no known end. And it is not possible for him to be wholly alive. For that depends upon his sense of being completely engaged with the world, with all his passions and all the faculties in rich harmonies with one another, and in deep rhythm with the nature of things.

These are the gifts of a vital religion which can bring the whole of a man into adjustment with the whole of his relevant experience. Our forefathers had such a religion. They quarreled a good deal about the details, but they had no doubt that there was an order in the universe which justified their lives because they were a part of it. The acids of modernity have dissolved that order for many of us, and there are some in consequence who think that the needs which religion fulfilled have also been dissolved. But however self-sufficient the eugenic and perfectly educated man of the distant future may be, our present experience is that the needs remain. In failing to meet them, it is plain that we have succeeded only in substituting trivial illusions for majestic faiths. For while the modern emancipated man may wonder how any one ever believed that in this universe of stars and atoms and multitudinous life, there is a drama in progress of which the principal event was enacted in Palestine nineteen hundred years ago, it is not really a stranger fable than many which he so readily accepts. He does not believe the words of the Gospel but he believes the best-advertised notion. The older fable may be incredible to-day, but when it was credible it bound together the whole of experience upon a stately and dignified theme.

The modern man has ceased to believe in it but he has not ceased to be credulous, and the need to believe haunts him. It is no wonder that his impulse is to turn back from his freedom, and to find some one who says he knows the truth and can tell him what to do, to find the shrine of some new god, of any cult however newfangled, where he can kneel and be comforted, put on manacles to keep his hands from trembling, ensconce himself in some citadel where it is safe and warm.

For the modern man who has ceased to believe, without ceasing to be credulous, hangs, as it were, between heaven and earth, and is at rest nowhere. There is no theory of the meaning and value of events which he is compelled to accept, but he is none the less compelled to accept the events. There is no moral authority to which he must turn now, but there is coercion in opinions, fashions and fads. There is for him no inevitable purpose in the universe, but there are elaborate necessities, physical, political, economic. He does not feel himself to be an actor in a great and dramatic destiny, but he is subject to the massive powers of our civilization, forced to adopt their pace, bound to their routine, entangled in their conflicts. He can believe what he chooses about this civilization. He cannot, however, escape the compulsion of modern events. They compel his body and his senses as ruthlessly as ever did king or priest. They do not compel his mind. They have all the force of natural events, but not their majesty, all the tyrannical power of ancient institutions, but none of their moral certainty. Events are there, and they overpower him. But they do not convince him that they have that dignity which inheres in that which is necessary and in the nature of things.

In the old order the compulsions were often painful, but there was sense in the pain that was inflicted by the will

of an all-knowing God. In the new order the compulsions
are painful and, as it were, accidental, unnecessary, wanton, and full of mockery. The modern man does not make
his peace with them. For in effect he has replaced natural
piety with a grudging endurance of a series of unsanctified
compulsions. When he believed that the unfolding of events
was a manifestation of the will of God, he could say: Thy
will be done. . . . In His will is our peace. But when he believes that events are determined by the votes of a majority,
the orders of his bosses, the opinions of his neighbors, the
laws of supply and demand, and the decisions of quite selfish men, he yields because he has to yield. He is conquered
but unconvinced.

## 3. SORTIES AND RETREATS

It might seem as if, in all this, men were merely going
through once again what they have often gone through before. This is not the first age in which the orthodox religion
has been in conflict with the science of the day. Plato was
born into such an age. For two centuries the philosophers
of Greece had been critical of Homer and of the popular
gods, and when Socrates faced his accusers, his answer to
the accusation of heresy must certainly have sounded un-
responsive. "I do believe," he said, "that there are gods,
and in a higher sense than that in which my accusers believe in them." That is all very well. But to believe in a
"higher sense" is also to believe in a different sense.

There is nothing new in the fact that men have ceased
to believe in the religion of their fathers. In the history of
Catholic Christianity, there has always existed a tradition,
extending from the author of the Fourth Gospel through

Origen to the neo-platonists of modern times, which rejects
the popular idea of God as a power acting upon events, and
of immortality as everlasting life, and translates the popular theology into a symbolic statement of a purely spiritual
experience. In every civilized age there have been educated
and discerning men who could not accept literally and simply the traditions of the ancient faith. We are told that during the Periclean Age "among educated men everything
was in dispute: political sanctions, literary values, moral
standards, religious convictions, even the possibility of
reaching any truth about anything." When the educated
classes of the Roman world accepted Christianity they had
ceased to believe in the pagan gods, and were much too
critical to accept the primitive Hebraic theories of the creation, the redemption, and the Messianic Kingdom which
were so central in the popular religion. They had to do what
Socrates had done; they had to take the popular theology
in a "higher" and therefore in a different sense before they
could use it. Indeed, it is so unusual to find an age of active-
minded men in which the most highly educated are genuinely orthodox in the popular sense, that the Thirteenth
Century, the age of Dante and St. Thomas Aquinas, when
this phenomenon is reputed to have occurred, is regarded
as a unique and wonderful period in the history of the
world. It is not at all unlikely that there never was such an
age in the history of civilized men.

And yet, the position of modern men who have broken
with the religion of their fathers is in certain profound ways
different from that of other men in other ages. This is the
first age, I think, in the history of mankind when the circumstances of life have conspired with the intellectual habits of the time to render any fixed and authoritative belief
incredible to large masses of men. The dissolution of the

old modes of thought has gone so far, and is so cumulative in its effect, that the modern man is not able to sink back after a period of prophesying into a new but stable orthodoxy. The irreligion of the modern world is radical to a degree for which there is, I think, no counterpart. For always in the past it has been possible for new conventions to crystallize, and for men to find rest and surcease of effort in accepting them.

We often assume, therefore, that a period of dissolution will necessarily be followed by one of conformity, that the heterodoxy of one age will become the orthodoxy of the next, and that when this orthodoxy decays a new period of prophesying will begin. Thus we say that by the time of Hosea and Isaiah the religion of the Jews had become a system of rules for transacting business with Jehovah. The Prophets then revivified it by thundering against the conventional belief that religion was mere burnt offering and sacrifice. A few centuries passed and the religion based on the Law and the Prophets had in its turn become a set of mechanical rites manipulated by the Scribes and the Pharisees. As against this system Jesus and Paul preached a religion of grace, and against the "letter" of the synagogues the "spirit" of Christ. But the inner light which can perceive the spirit is rare, and so shortly after the death of Paul, the teaching gradually ceased to appeal to direct inspiration in the minds of the believers and became a body of dogma, a "sacred deposit" of the faith "once for all delivered to the saints." In the succeeding ages there appeared again many prophets who thought they had within them the revealing spirit. Though some of the prophets were burnt, much of the prophesying was absorbed into the canon. In Luther this sense of revelation appeared once more in a most confident form. He rejected the authority not

only of the Pope and the clergy, but even of the Bible itself,
except where in his opinion the Bible confirmed his faith.
But in the establishment of a Lutheran Church the old difficulty reappeared: the inner light which had burned so
fiercely in Luther did not burn brightly or steadily in all
Lutherans, and so the right of private judgment, even in
Luther's restricted use of the term, led to all kinds of heresies and abominations. Very soon there came to be an authoritative teaching backed by the power of the police. And
in Calvinism the revolt of the Reformation became stabilized to the last degree. "Everything," said Calvin, "per-
taining to the perfect rule of a good life the Lord has so
comprehended in His law that there remains nothing for
man to add to that summary."

Men fully as intelligent as the most emancipated
among us once believed that, and I have no doubt that the
successors of Mr. Darrow and Mr. Mencken would come
to believe something very much like it if conditions permitted them to obey the instinct to retreat from the chaos
of modernity into order and certainty. It is all very well to
talk about being the captain of your soul. It is hard, and
only a few heroes, saints, and geniuses have been the captains of their souls for any extended period of their lives.
Most men, after a little freedom, have preferred authority
with the consoling assurances and the economy of effort
which it brings. "If, outside of Christ, you wish by your
own thoughts to know your relation to God, you will break
your neck. Thunder strikes him who examines." Thus
spoke Martin Luther, and there is every reason to suppose
that the German people thought he was talking the plain-
est common sense. "He who is gifted with the heavenly
knowledge of faith," said the Council of Trent, "is free
from an inquisitive curiosity." These words are rasping to

our modern ears, but there is no occasion to doubt that the men who uttered them had made a shrewd appraisal of average human nature. The record of experience is one of sorties and retreats. The search for moral guidance which shall not depend upon external authority has invariably ended in the acknowledgment of some new authority.

## 4. DEEP DISSOLUTION

This same tendency manifests itself in the midst of our modern uneasiness. We have had a profusion of new cults, of revivals, and of essays in reconstruction. But there is reason for thinking that a new crystallization of an enduring and popular religion is unlikely in the modern world. For analogy drawn from the experience of the past is misleading.

When Luther, for example, rebelled against the authority of the Church, he did not suppose the way of life for the ordinary man would be radically altered. Luther supposed that men would continue to behave much as they had learned to behave under the Catholic discipline. The individual for whom he claimed the right of private judgment was one whose prejudgments had been well fixed in a Catholic society. The authority of the Pope was to be destroyed and certain evils abolished, but there was to remain that feeling for objective moral certainties which Catholicism had nurtured. When the Anabaptists carried the practice of his theory beyond this point, Luther denounced them violently. For what he believed in was Protestantism for good Catholics. The reformers of the Eighteenth Century made a similar assumption. They really believed in democracy for men who had an aristocratic training. Jefferson, for example, had an instinctive fear of the urban rabble, that most democratic part of the population. The society of free men which he dreamed about was composed of those who had the discipline, the standards of honor and the taste, without the privileges or the corruptions, that are to be found in a society of well-bred country gentlemen.

The more recent rebels frequently betray a somewhat similar inability to imagine the consequences of their own victories. For the smashing of idols is in itself such a preoccupation that it is almost impossible for the iconoclast to look clearly into a future when there will not be many idols left to smash. Yet that future is beginning to be our present, and it might be said that men are conscious of what modernity means insofar as they realize that they are confronted not so much with the necessity of promoting rebellion as of dealing with the consequences of it. The Nineteenth Century, roughly speaking the time between Voltaire and Mencken, was an age of terrific indictments and of feeble solutions. The Marxian indictment of capitalism is a case in point. The Nietzschean transvaluation of values is another; it is magnificent, but who can say, after he has shot his arrow of longing to the other shore, whether he will find Caesar Borgia, Henry Ford, or Isadora Duncan? Who knows, having read Mr. Mencken and Mr. Sinclair Lewis, what kind of world will be left when all the boobs and yokels have crawled back in their holes and have died of shame?

The rebel, while he is making his attack, is not likely to feel the need to answer such questions. For he moves in an unreal environment, one might almost say a parasitic environment. He goes forth to destroy Caesar, Mammon, George F. Babbitt, and Mrs. Grundy. As he wrestles with these demons, he leans upon them. By inversion they offer him much the same kind of support which the conformer enjoys. They provide him with an objective which enables him to know exactly what he thinks he wants to do. His energies are focussed by his indignation. He does not suffer from emptiness, doubt, and division of soul. These are the maladies which come later when the struggle is over. While the rebel is in conflict with the established nuisances he has an aim in life which absorbs all his passions. He has his own sense of righteousness and his own feeling of communion with a grand purpose. For in attacking idols there is a kind of piety, in overthrowing tyrants a kind of loyalty, in ridiculing stupidities an imitation of wisdom. In the heat of battle the rebel is exalted by a whole-hearted tension which is easily mistaken for a taste of the freedom that is to come. He is under the spell of an illusion. For what comes after the struggle is not the exaltation of freedom but a letting down of the tension that belongs solely to the struggle itself. The happiness of the rebel is as transient as the iconoclasm which produced it. When he has slain the dragon and rescued the beautiful maiden, there is usually nothing left for him to do but write his memoirs and dream of a time when the world was young.

What most distinguishes the generation who have approached maturity since the debacle of idealism at the end of the War is not their rebellion against the religion and the moral code of their parents, but their disillusionment with their own rebellion. It is common for young men and women to rebel, but that they should rebel sadly and without faith in their own rebellion, that they should distrust the new freedom no less than the old certainties—that is something of a novelty. As Mr. Canby once said, at the age of seven they saw through their parents and characterized them in a phrase. At fourteen they saw through education and dodged it. At eighteen they saw through morality and stepped over it. At twenty they lost respect for their home towns, and at twenty-one they discovered that our social system is ridiculous. At twenty-three the autobiography ends because the author has run through society to date and does not know what to do next. For, as Mr. Canby might have added, the idea of reforming that society makes no appeal to them. They have seen through all that. They cannot adopt any of the synthetic religions of the Nineteenth Century. They have seen through all of them.

They have seen through the religion of nature to which the early romantics turned for consolation. They have heard too much about the brutality of natural selection to feel, as Wordsworth did, that pleasant landscapes are divine. They have seen through the religion of beauty because, for one thing, they are too much oppressed by the ugliness of Main Street. They cannot take refuge in an ivory tower because the modern apartment house, with a radio loudspeaker on the floor above and on the floor below and just across the courtyard, will not permit it. They cannot, like Mazzini, make a religion of patriotism, because they have just been demobilized. They cannot make a religion of science like the post-Darwinians because they do not understand modern science. They never learned enough mathematics and physics. They do not like Bernard Shaw's religion of creative evolution because they have read enough to know that Mr. Shaw's biology is literary and evangelical. As for the religion of progress, that is preempted by George F. Babbitt and the Rotary Club, and the religion of humanity is utterly unacceptable to those who have to ride in the subways during the rush hour.

Yet the current attempts to modernize religious creeds

are inspired by the hope that somehow it will be possible to construct a form of belief which will fit into this vacuum. It is evident that life soon becomes distracted and tiresome if it is not illuminated by communion with what William James called "a wider self through which saving experiences come." The eager search for new religions, the hasty adherence to cults, and the urgent appeals for a reconciliation between religion and science are confessions that to the modern man his activity seems to have no place in any rational order. His life seems mere restlessness and compulsion, rather than conduct lighted by luminous beliefs. He is possessed by a great deal of excitement amidst which, as Mr. Santayana once remarked, he redoubles his effort when he has forgotten his aim.

For in the modern age, at first imperceptibly with the rise of the towns, and then catastrophically since the mechanical revolution, there have gone into dissolution not only the current orthodoxy, but the social order and the ways of living which supported it. Thus rebellion and emancipation have come to mean something far more drastic than they have ever meant before. The earlier rebels summoned men from one allegiance to another, but the feeling for certainty in religion and for decorum in society persisted. In the modern world it is this very feeling of certainty itself which is dissolving. It is dissolving not merely for an educated minority but for every one who comes within the orbit of modernity.

Yet there remain the wants which orthodoxy of some sort satisfies. The natural man, when he is released from restraints, and has no substitute for them, is at sixes and sevens with himself and the world. For in the free play of his uninhibited instincts he does not find any natural substitute for those accumulated convictions which, however

badly they did it, nevertheless organized his soul, econo-
mized his effort, consoled him, and gave him dignity in his
own eyes because he was part of some greater whole. The
acids of modernity are so powerful that they do not tolerate
a crystallization of ideas which will serve as a new orthodoxy into which men can retreat. And so the modern world
is haunted by a realization, which it becomes constantly
less easy to ignore, that it is impossible to reconstruct an
enduring orthodoxy, and impossible to live well without the
satisfactions which an orthodoxy would provide.

# II God in the Modern World

## 1. IMAGO DEI

By the dissolution of their ancestral ways men have been deprived of their sense of certainty as to why they were born, why they must work, whom they must love, what they must honor, where they may turn in sorrow and defeat. They have left to them the ancient codes and the modern criticism of these codes, guesses, intuitions, inconclusive experiments, possibilities, probabilities, hypotheses. Below the level of reason, they may have unconscious prejudice, they may speak with a loud cocksureness, they may act with fanaticism. But there is gone that ineffable certainty which once made God and His Plan seem as real as the lamp-post.

I do not mean that modern men have ceased to believe in God. I do mean that they no longer believe in him simply and literally. I mean that they have defined and refined their ideas of him until they can no longer honestly say that he exists, as they would say that their neighbor exists. Search the writings of liberal churchmen, and when you come to the crucial passages which are intended to express their belief in God, you will find, I think, that at just this point their uncertainty is most evident.

The Reverend Harry Emerson Fosdick has written an essay, called "How Shall We Think of God?", which illustrates the difficulty. He begins by saying that "believing in God without considering how one shall picture him is deplorably unsatisfactory." Yet the old ways of picturing him are no longer credible. We cannot think of him as seated upon a throne, while around him are angels playing on harps and singing hymns. "God as a king on high—our fathers, living under monarchy, rejoiced in that image and found it meaningful. His throne, his crown, his scepter, his seraphic retinue, his laws, rewards, and punishments—how dominant that picture was and how persistent is the continuance of it in our hymns and prayers! It was always partly poetry, but it had a prose background: there really had been at first a celestial land above the clouds where God reigned and where his throne was in the heavens."

Having said that this picture is antiquated, Dr. Fosdick goes on to state that "the religious man must have imaginations of God, if God is to be real to him." He must "picture his dealing with the Divine in terms of personal relationship." But how? "The place where man vitally finds God . . . is within his own experience of goodness, truth, and beauty, and the truest images of God are therefore to be found in man's spiritual life." I should be the last to deny that a man may, if he chooses, think of God as the source of all that seems to him worthy in human experience. But certainly this is not the God of the ancient faith. This is not God the Father, the Law-giver, the Judge. This is a highly sophisticated idea of God, employed by a modern man who would like to say, but cannot say with certainty, that there exists a personal God to whom men must accommodate themselves.

## 2. AN INDEFINITE GOD

It may be that clear and unambiguous statements are not now possible in our intellectual climate. But at least we should not forget that the religions which have dominated human history have been founded on what the faithful felt were undeniable facts. These facts were mysterious only in the sense that they were uncommon, like an eclipse of the sun, but not in the sense that they were beyond human experience. No doubt there are passages in the Scriptures written by highly cultivated men in which the Divine nature is called mysterious and unknowable. But these passages are not the rock upon which the popular churches are founded. No one, I think, has truly observed the religious life of simple people without understanding how plain, how literal, how natural they take their supernatural personages to be.

The popular gods are not indefinite and unknowable. They have a definite history and their favorite haunts, and they have often been seen. They walk on earth, they might appear to anyone, they are angered, they are pleased, they weep and they rejoice, they eat and they may fall in love. The modern man uses the word 'supernatural' to describe something that seems to him not quite so credible as the things he calls natural. This is not the supernaturalism of the devout. They do not distinguish two planes of reality and two orders of certainty. For them Jesus Christ was born of a Virgin and was raised from the dead as literally as Napoleon was Emperor of the French and returned from Elba.

This is the kind of certainty one no longer finds in the utterances of modern men. I might cite, for example, a typically modern assertion about the existence of God, made by Mr. W. C. Brownell, a critic who could not be reproached with insensitiveness to the value of traditional beliefs. He wrote that "the influence of the Holy Spirit, exquisitely called the Comforter, is a matter of actual experience, as solid a reality as that of electro-magnetism." I do not suppose that Mr. Brownell meant to admit the least possible doubt. But he was a modern man, and surreptitiously doubt invaded his certainty. For electro-magnetism is not an absolutely solid reality to a layman's mind. It has a questionable reality. I suspect that is why Mr. Brownell chose this metaphor; it would have seemed a little too blunt to his modern intelligence to say that his faith was founded not on electro-magnetism, but as men once believed, on a rock.

The attempts to reconstruct religious creeds are beset by the modern man's inability to convince himself that the constitution of the universe includes facts which in our skeptical jargon we call supernatural. Yet as William James once said, "religion, in her fullest exercise of function, is not a mere illumination of facts already elsewhere given, not a mere passion, like love, which views things in a rosier light. . . . It is something more, namely, a postulator of new *facts* as well." James himself was strongly disposed toward what he so candidly described as "overbeliefs"; he had sympathy with the beliefs of others which was as large and charitable as any man's can be. There was no trace of the intellectual snob in William James; he was in the other camp from those thin argumentative rationalists who find so much satisfaction in disproving what other men hold sacred. James loved cranks and naifs and sought them out for the wisdom they might have. But withal he was a modern man who lived toward the climax of the revolutionary period. He had the Will to Believe, he argued eloquently for the Right to Believe. But he did not wholly believe. The utmost that he could honestly believe was something which he confessed would "appear a sorry underbelief" to some of his readers. "Who knows," he said, "whether the faithfulness of individuals here below to their own poor overbeliefs may not actually help God in turn to be more effectively faithful to his own greater tasks?" Who knows? And on that question mark he paused and could say no more.


## 3. GOD IN MORE SENSES THAN ONE

But even if there was some uncertainty as to the existence of the God whom William James described, he was at least the kind of God with whom human beings could commune. If they could jump the initial doubt they found themselves in an exciting world where they might live for a God who, like themselves, had work to do. James wrote the passage I have quoted in 1902. A quarter of a century later Alfred North Whitehead came to Harvard to deliver the Lowell Lectures. He undertook to define God for modern men.

Mr. Whitehead, like William James, is a compassionate man and on the side of the angels. But his is a wholly modernized mind in full command of all the conceptual instruments of scientific logic. By contrast with the austerity of Mr. Whitehead's thinking, James, with his chivalrous offer of fealty to God, seems like one of the last of the great romantics. There is a God in Mr. Whitehead's philosophy, and a very necessary God at that. Unhappily, I am not enough of a logician to say that I am quite sure I understand what it means to say that "God is not concrete, but He is the ground for concrete actuality." There have been moments when I imagined I had caught the meaning of this, but there have been more moments when I knew that I had not. I have never doubted, however, that the concept had meaning, and that I missed it because it was too deep for me. Why then, it may be asked, do I presume to discuss it? My answer is that a conception of God, which is incomprehensible to all who are not highly trained logicians, is a possible God for logicians alone. It is not presumptuous to say of Mr. Whitehead's God what he himself says of Aristotle's God: that it does "not lead him very far toward the production of a God available for religious purposes."

For while this God may satisfy a metaphysical need in the thinker, he does not satisfy the passions of the believer. This God does not govern the world like a king nor watch over his children like a father. He offers them no purposes to which they can consecrate themselves; he exhibits no image of holiness they can imitate. He does not chastise them in sin nor console them in sorrow. He is a principle with which to explain the facts, if you can understand the explanation. He is not himself a personality who deals with the facts. For the purposes of religion he is no God at all; his universe remains stonily unaware of man. Nothing has happened by accepting Mr. Whitehead's definition which changes the inexorable character of that destiny which Bertrand Russell depicted when he wrote that

> we see, surrounding the narrow raft illumined by the flickering light of human comradeship, the dark ocean on whose rolling waves we toss for a brief hour; from the great night without, a chill blast breaks in upon our refuge; all the loneliness of humanity amid hostile forces is concentrated upon the individual soul, which must struggle alone, with what of courage it can command, against the whole weight of a universe that cares nothing for its hopes and fears.

It is a nice question whether the use of God's name is not misleading when it is applied by modernists to ideas so remote from the God men have worshiped. Plainly the modernist churchman does not believe in the God of Genesis who walked in the garden in the cool of the evening and called to Adam and his wife who had hidden themselves behind a tree; nor in the God of Exodus who appeared to Moses and Aaron and seventy of the Elders of Israel, standing with his feet upon a paved walk as if it were a sapphire stone; nor even in the God of the fifty-third chapter of Isaiah who in his compassion for the sheep who have gone astray, having turned everyone to his own way, laid on the Man of Sorrows the iniquity of us all.

This, as Kirsopp Lake says, is the God of most, if not all, the writings in the Bible. Yet "however much our inherited sentiments may shrink from the admission, the scientists are to-day almost unanimous in saying that the universe as they see it contains no evidence of the existence of any anthropomorphic God whatever. The experimentalist (*i.e.,* modernist) wholly agrees that this is so. Nevertheless he refuses as a rule, and I think rightly—to abandon the use of the word 'God.'" In justification of this refusal to abandon the word 'God,' although he has abandoned the accepted meaning of the word, Dr. Lake appeals to a tradition which reaches back at least to Origen who, as a Christian neo-platonist, used the word 'God' to mean, not the King and Father of creation, but the sum of all ideal values. It was this redefinition of the word 'God,' he says, which "made Christianity possible for the educated man of the third century." It is this same redefinition which still makes Christianity possible for educated churchmen like Dr. Lake and Dean Inge.

Dr. Lake admits that although this attractive bypath

of tradition "is intellectually adorned by many princes of thought and lords of language" it is "ecclesiastically not free from reproach." He avows another reason for his use of the word 'God' which, if not more compelling, is certainly more worldly. 'Atheist' has meant since Roman times an enemy of society; it gives a wholly false impression of the real state of mind of those who adhere to the platonic tradition. They have been wholly without the defiance which 'atheism' connotes; on the contrary they have been a few individuals in each age who lived peaceably within the shelter of the church, worshiping a somewhat different God inwardly and in their own way, and often helping to refresh the more mundane spirit of the popular church. The term 'agnostic' is almost as unavailable. It was invented to describe a tolerant unbelief in the anthropomorphic God. In popular usage it has come to mean about the same thing as atheist, for the instinct of the common man is sound in these matters. He feels that those who claim to be open-minded about God have for all practical purposes ceased to believe in him. The agnostic's reply that he would gladly believe if the evidence would confirm it, does not alter the fact that he does not now believe. And so Dr. Lake concludes that the modernist must use the word 'God' in his own sense, "endeavoring partly to preserve Origen's meaning of the word, and partly shrinking from any other policy as open to misconstruction."

I confess that the notion of adopting a policy about God somehow shocks me as intruding a rather worldly consideration which would seem to be wholly out of place. But this feeling is, I am sure, an injustice to Dr. Lake who is plainly and certainly not a worldling. He is moved, no doubt, by the conviction that in letting 'God' mean one thing to the mass of the devout and another to the educated minority, the loss of intellectual precision is more than compensated by the preservation of a community of feeling. This is not mere expediency. It may be the part of wisdom, which is profounder than mere reasoning, to wish that intellectual distinctions shall not divide men too sharply.

But if it is wisdom, it is an aristocratic wisdom. And in Dean Inge's writings, this is frankly avowed. "The strength of Christianity," he says, "is in transforming the lives of individuals—of a small minority, certainly, as Christ clearly predicted, but a large number in the aggregate. To rescue a little flock, here and there, from materialism, selfishness, and hatred, is the task of the Church of Christ in all ages alike, and there is no likelihood that it will ever be otherwise."

But in other ages, one thing was otherwise. And in this one thing lies the radical peculiarity of the modern difficulty. In other ages there was no acknowledged distinction between the ultimate beliefs of the educated and the uneducated. There were differences in learning, in religious genius, in the closeness of a chosen few to God and his angels. Inwardly there were even radical differences of meaning. But critical analysis had not made them overt and evident, and the common assumption was that there was one God for all, for the peasant who saw him dimly and could approach him only through his patron saint, and for the holy man who had seen God and talked with him face to face. It has remained for churchmen of our era to distinguish two or more different Gods, and openly to say that they are different. This may be a triumph of candor and of intelligence. But this very consciousness of what they are doing, these very honest admissions that the God of Dean Inge, for example, is only in name the

God of millions of other protestants—that is an admission, when they understand it, which makes faith difficult for modern men.

## 4. THE PROTEST OF THE FUNDAMENTALISTS

Fundamentalism is a protest against all these definitions and attenuations which the modern man finds it necessary to make. It is avowedly a reaction within the Protestant communions against what the President of the World's Christian Fundamentalist Association rather accurately described as "that weasel method of sucking the meaning out of words, and then presenting the empty shells in an attempt to palm them off as giving the Christian faith a new and another interpretation." In actual practice this movement has become entangled with all sorts of bizarre and barbarous agitations, with the Ku Klux Klan, with fanatical prohibition, with the "anti-evolution laws," and with much persecution and intolerance. This in itself is significant. For it shows that the central truth, which the fundamentalists have grasped, no longer appeals to the best brains and the good sense of a modern community, and that the movement is recruited largely from the isolated, the inexperienced, and the uneducated.

Into the politics of the heated controversy between modernists and fundamentalists I do not propose here to enter. That it is not merely a dispute in the realm of the spirit is made evident by the President of the Fundamentalist Association when he avers that "nothing" holds modernists and fundamentalists together except "the billions of dollars invested. Nine out of ten of these dollars, if not ninety-nine out of every hundred of them, spent to construct the great denominational universities, colleges, schools of second grade, theological seminaries, great denominational mission stations, the multiplied hospitals that bear denominational names, the immense publication societies and the expensive societies were given by fundamentalists and filched by modernists. It took hundreds of years to collect this money and construct these institutions. It has taken only a quarter of a century for the liberal bandits to capture them. . . ."

Not all the fundamentalist argument, however, is pitched at this level. There is also a reasoned case against the modernists. Fortunately this case has been stated in a little book called *Christianity and Liberalism* by a man who is both a scholar and a gentleman. The author is Professor J. Gresham Machen of the Princeton Theological Seminary. It is an admirable book. For its acumen, for its saliency, and for its wit this cool and stringent defense of orthodox Protestantism is, I think, the best popular argument produced by either side in the current controversy. We shall do well to listen to Dr. Machen.

Modernism, he says, "is altogether in the imperative mood," while the traditional religion "begins with a triumphant indicative." I do not see how one can deny the force of this generalization. "From the beginning Christianity was certainly a way of life. *But how was the life to be produced?* Not by appealing to the human will, but by telling a story; not by exhortation, but by the narration of an event." Dr. Machen insists, rightly I think, that the historic influence of Christianity on the mass of men has depended upon their belief that an historic drama was enacted in Palestine nineteen hundred years ago during the reign of the Emperor Tiberius. The veracity of that story was fundamental to the Christian Church. For while all the ideal values may remain if you impugn the historic record set forth in the Gospels, these ideal values are not certified to the common man as inherent in the very nature of things. Once they are deprived of their root in historic fact, their poetry, their symbolism, their ethical significance depend for their sanction upon the temperament and experience of the individual believer. There is gone that deep, compulsive, organic faith in an external fact which is the essence of religion for all but that very small minority who can live within themselves in mystical communion or by the power of their understanding. For the great mass of men, if the history of religions is to be trusted, religious experience depends upon a complete belief in the concrete existence, one might almost say the materialization, of their God. The fundamentalist goes to the very heart of the matter, therefore, when he insists that you have destroyed the popular foundations of religion if you make your gospel a symbolic record of experience, and reject it as an actual record of events.

The liberals have yet to answer Dr. Machen when he says that "the Christian movement at its inception was not just a way of life in the modern sense, but a way of life founded upon a message. It was based, not upon mere feeling, not upon a mere program of work, but on an account of facts." It was based on the story of the birth, the life, the ministry, the death, and the resurrection of Jesus Christ. That story set forth the facts which certify the Christian experience. Modernism, which in varying degree casts doubt upon the truth of that story, may therefore be defined as an attempt to preserve selected parts of the experience after the facts which inspired it have been rejected. The orthodox believer may be mistaken as to the facts in which he believes. But he is not mistaken in thinking that you cannot, for the mass of men, have a faith of which the only foundation is their need and desire to be-

lieve. The historic churches, without any important exceptions, I think, have founded faith on clear statements
about matters of fact, historic events, or physical manifestations. They have never been content with a symbolism
which the believer knew was merely symbolic. Only the sophisticated in their private meditations and in esoteric
writing have found satisfaction in symbolism as such.

Complete as was Dr. Machen's victory over the Protestant liberals, he did not long remain in possession of
the field. There is a deeper fundamentalism than his, and
it is based on a longer continuous experience. This is the
teaching of the Roman Catholic Church. From a priest of
that church, Father Riggs, has come the most searching
criticism of Dr. Machen's case. Writing in the *Commonweal* Father Riggs points out that "the fundamentalists
are well-nigh powerless. They are estopped, so to speak,
from stemming the ravaging waters of agnosticism because
they cannot, while remaining loyal to the (Protestant) reformers . . . set limits to destructive criticism of the Bible
without making an un-Protestant appeal to tradition."
Father Riggs, in other words, is asking the Protestant
fundamentalists, like Dr. Machen, how they can be certain
that they know these *facts* upon which they assert that
the Christian religion is founded.

They must reply that they know them from reading
the Bible. The reply is, however, unsatisfying. For obviously there are many ways of reading the Bible, and therefore
the Protestant who demands the right of private judgment
can never know with absolute certainty that his reading
is the correct one. His position in a skeptical age is, therefore, as Father Riggs points out, a weak one, because a
private judgment is, after all, only a private judgment.
The history of Protestantism shows that the exercise of

private judgment as to the meaning of Scripture leads not to universal and undeniable dogma, but to schism within schism and heresy within heresy. From the point of view, then, of the oldest fundamentalism of the western world the error of the modernists is that they deny the facts on which religious faith reposes; the error of the orthodox Protestants is that although they affirm the facts, they reject all authority which can verify them; the virtue of the Catholic system is that along with a dogmatic affirmation of the central facts, it provides a living authority in the Church which can ascertain and demonstrate and verify these facts.

## 5. IN MAN'S IMAGE

The long record of clerical opposition to certain kinds of scientific inquiry has a touch of dignity when it is realized that at the core of that opposition there is a very profound understanding of the religious needs of ordinary men. For once you weaken the belief that the central facts taught by the churches are facts in the most literal and absolute sense, the disintegration of the popular religion begins. We may confidently declare that Mr. Santayana is speaking not as a student of human nature, but as a cultivated unbeliever, when he writes that "the idea that religion contains a literal, not a symbolic, representation of truth and life is simply an impossible idea." The idea is impossible, no doubt, for the children of the great emancipation. But because it is impossible, religion itself, in the traditional popular meaning of the term, has become impossible for them.

If it is true that man creates God in his own image, it

is no less true that for religious devotion he must remain unconscious of that fact. Once he knows that he has created the image of God, the reality of it vanishes like last night's dream. It may be that to anyone who is impregnated with the modern spirit it is almost self-evident that the truths of religion are truths of human experience. But this knowledge does not tolerate an abiding and absorbing faith. For when the truths of religion have lost their connection with a superhuman order, the cord of their life is cut. What remains is a somewhat archaic, a somewhat questionable, although a very touching, quaint medley of poetry, rhetoric, fable, exhortation, and insight into human travail. When Mr. Santayana says that "matters of religion should never be matters of controversy" because "we never argue with a lover about his taste, nor condemn him, if we are just, for knowing so human a passion," he expresses an ultimate unbelief.

For what would be the plight of a lover, if we told him that his passion was charming?—though, of course, there might be no such lady as the one he loved.

# III The Loss of Certainty

## 1. WAYS OF READING THE BIBLE

It is important to an understanding of this matter that we should not confuse the modern practice of redefining God with the ancient use of allegory.

From the earliest days the words of the Bible have been embroidered with luxuriant and often fantastic meanings. In Leviticus it says, for example, that the meal offering may be baked in an oven, fried in a pan, or toasted on a plate. This passage, says Origen, proves that Scripture must have three meanings. It came to have any number of meanings. Thus St. Augustine explained that Eden meant the life of the blessed, and its four rivers the four virtues; farther on in the same chapter he declares that Eden is the Church, and that its four rivers are the four Gospels.

In the same manner Wyclif in a later age preached a sermon explaining the parable of the Good Samaritan. The man who went down from Jerusalem to Jericho represents Adam and Eve; the robbers are the fiends of hell; the priest and Levite who went by on the other side are the patriarchs, saints, and prophets who failed to bring salvation;

the Good Samaritan is Jesus; the wine which he pours into his wounds is sharp words to prick men from sin, and the oil is hope. . . . Savonarola, we are told, preached during the whole of Lent, 1492, taking as his text Noah's Ark and "giving each day a different interpretation of the ten planks of which the Ark was composed."

By this method of interpretation the devout adapted the Bible to their own uses, smoothing away its contradictions and explaining away passages, like the command in Genesis to kill uncircumcised children, which, read literally, would have seemed to them barbarous and immoral. We must be careful, however, not to misunderstand this method of thought. When they said that the beautiful woman in the Song of Solomon was the Church, they were not conscious, as we are, that this is a figure of speech. There had not entered into their habits of thought the kind of analytical precision in which one thing can mean only one thing. It is no contradiction to say that the allegory was taken literally; certainly there was no sense of unreality about it, as there is for us. "These and similar allegorical interpretations may be suitably put . . ." says St. Augustine, speaking here to the educated minority, "without giving offense to anyone, while yet we believe the strict truth of the history confirmed by its circumstantial narrative of facts."

But at last men became too analytical and too self-conscious to accept the naive use of allegory. They realized that allegory was a loose method of interpretation which lent itself easily to the citing of scripture in order to justify heresy. If the ten planks in Noah's Ark could mean a different set of truths on each day in Lent, there was no telling what they might come to mean in the end. It was clear, therefore, that allegory was dangerous and might, as Luther said, "degenerate into a mere monkey game"; it was wanton, like "a sort of beautiful harlot who proves herself spiritually seductive to idle men."

This danger was a result of the general loosening of organic faith which was already evident in Luther's day. To men who had the unconscious certainties about God and his universe, allegory was a perfectly safe method of interpreting the Bible because all the interpretations, however fantastic, were inspired by the same prejudgments and tended therefore to confirm the same convictions. The allegories of simple men are like many-colored flowers in one garden, growing from the same soil, watered by the same rains, turning their faces toward the same sun. But as men became emancipated from their ancestral way of life, their convictions about God and destiny and human morality changed. Then the method of allegory ceased to be the merely exuberant expression of the same ancient truths, and became a confusing method of rationalizing all kinds of new experiments. It promoted heresy because men had become heretical, where once, while men were devout, it had only embroidered their devotions.

"To allegorize is to juggle with Scripture," said Luther. The Protestant Reformers could not tolerate that. For they lived in an age when faith was already disintegrating, and they had themselves destroyed the authority of an infallible source of religion. "We must," wrote Calvin, "entirely reject the allegories of Origen, and of others like him, which Satan, with the deepest subtlety, has endeavored to introduce into the Church, for the purpose of rendering the doctrine of Scripture ambiguous and destitute of all certainty and firmness."

The insistence of the Reformers on a literal interpretation of the Bible had, as Dr. Fosdick points out, two unforeseen results. It led to the so-called Higher Criticism which in substance is nothing but a scientific attempt to find out what the Bible did mean literally to those who wrote it. And this in turn made it practically impossible for modern men to believe all that the Bible literally says. When they read the Bible as allegory they found in it unending confirmation of what they already believed. But when they read it literally, as history, as astronomy, and biology, and as a code of laws, it contradicted at many crucial points the practical working convictions of their daily lives. "The consequence is," says Dr. Fosdick, "that we face the Biblical world made historically vivid over against the modern world presently experienced, and we cannot use the old method (*i.e.* allegory) of accommodating one to the other."

## 2. MODERNISM: IMMORTALITY AS AN EXAMPLE

This predicament forced modern churchmen to seek what Dr. Fosdick calls "a new solution." They could not believe that the Bible was taken down, as John Donne put it, by "the Secretaries of the Holy Ghost." Yet they believed, as every sane man does, that the Bible contains wisdom which bears deeply upon the conduct of human life. Their problem was to find a way of picking and choosing passages in the Scriptures, and then of interpreting those which were chosen in such a way as to make them credible to modern men. They had to find some way of setting aside the story that God made Eve out of Adam's rib, that God commanded the massacre of whole populations, and that he enjoyed the slaughter of animals at the sacrifice; but they had at the same time to find a way of preserving for the use of modern men the lessons of the ministry of Jesus and the promise of life everlasting.

The method they employ is based on a theory. It is a theory that the Bible contains "abiding messages" placed in a "transient setting." The Bible, for example, is full of stories about devils and angels. Now, modern men do not believe in devils and angels. These are "categories" which they have outgrown. But what the devils and angels stood for are evils and blessings which modern men still encounter. We have, therefore, only to "decode" the Bible, and where it speaks of devils to see temptations, sin, disease, pain, and suffering, which have a psychic origin; where it speaks of angels to remember that sense of unseen friendliness which may help us at a crisis in our lives. The old wine is still good, but it needs to be put in new bottles. "The modern preacher's responsibility is thus to decode the abiding meanings of Scripture from outgrown phraseology."

This is not so difficult a thing to do for the devils and the angels. But a little reflection will show, I think, that in dealing with the major themes of religion, the solution is not so easy. The real difficulty appears when Dr. Fosdick attempts to decode the biblical promise of immortal life.

He begins by rejecting completely the resurrection of the flesh and any kind of immortality which is imagined as the survival of the physical person. Yet he believes in "the persistence of personality through death." For he maintains that without this belief the final victory of death would signify "the triumphant irrationality of existence"; not to believe in immortality is to submit to "mental confusion." Speaking quite frankly, however, he cannot easily imagine "a completely disembodied existence." Yet it is obviously not easy to imagine the persistence of personality through death once you have made up your mind not to imagine a concrete heaven inhabited by well-defined persons.

Modern churchmen, like Dean Inge for example, who have faced the difficulty more boldly than Dr. Fosdick does, arrive at an intelligible explanation of what they mean by immortality. But they mean something which is not only very difficult to understand, but extremely difficult for most men to enjoy when they have understood it. They inject intelligible meaning into the word "eternal" by employing it in a sense which is wholly different from that which the common man employs. By immortality he means life that goes on age after age without stopping. But the modern churchmen who have really clarified their minds are platonists. They apply the word "eternal" to that which is independent of time and existence. Between the two conceptions there is the profoundest difference, for in the commonsense of the worldling existence is so precious that he wishes it to continue for ever and ever. But to the platonist existence, or embodiment, is transient, accidental, irrational; only that is permanent which is timeless. Commonsense demands that if we are immortal we should meet our friend again later and continue our friendship; the platonist loves the memory of his friend after death as he loved an ideal image of him during his life. In communing with his memories and his ideals he knows himself to be in touch with eternal things. For not even the gods, says Homer, can undo the past; no accident of mortality can destroy anything which can be represented in the mind. Heroes die, but that such heroic deeds were done is a chapter forever, as Mr. Santayana says, in any complete history of the universe. The thinker dies, but his thoughts are beyond the reach of destruction. Men are mortal; but ideas are immortal.

I do not know whether I have known how to state clearly what is meant by this platonic view to which, in varying degrees of clarity, all emancipated minds turn when they talk of immortality. But, at least, it is clear that it is a conception which calls for a radically different adjustment to life than that to which the worldling is accustomed. He desires objects to love, goods and successes that are perishable, and he wishes them not to perish. Before he can enter the platonic world, before he can even attain to a hint of its meaning, he must abandon the very desires of which his hope of immortality is the expression. He must detach himself from his wish to acquire and possess objects that die; he must learn what it means to possess things not by holding them, but by understanding them, and to enjoy them as objects of reflection. He must not only cease to desire immortality as he conceives it, but the material embodiment of things as well. Then only, when he has renounced his love of existence, can he begin to love the forms of existence, and to live among imperishable ideas. Then, and in this sense only, does he enter into eternal life.

The ordinary man, when he hears this doctrine expounded, is almost certain to say with the Indian sage: "the worship of the Impersonal laid no hold upon my heart." His heart is set on the enjoyment of worldly goods, and the doctrine, for all but a few exceptional spirits, requires a radical change of heart. It is forbidding except to the few in whom "the intellect (is) passionate and the passions cold." For it demands a conversion of their natural desire to possess tangible things into a passion to understand intangible and abstract things. This philosophy is ascetic, unworldly, and profoundly disinterested.

Now it can be argued that this is precisely what the

Gospels teach as to the meaning of salvation. Excellent authority can be cited from the Gospel of St. John and the Epistles of St. Paul to justify this form of the Christian tradition: "Flesh and blood cannot inherit the kingdom of God" . . . "the things that are seen are temporal, but the things that are not seen are eternal" . . . "I see another law in my members, warring against the law of my mind." It can hardly be denied, as Dean Inge says, that "we are able to carry back to the fountain-head that Christian tradition" which may quite accurately be described as the religion of the spirit. But mixed with it in the Scripture, there is the other tradition, the popular tradition which may be called the religion of commonsense. Out of this latter have grown the institutions of the church and the faith of the mass of men. The religion of the spirit has been reserved for a few, "a succession of lives which have been sheltered rather than inspired by the machinery and state-craft of a mighty institution," and while the few who lived the life of the spirit have undoubtedly done much to inspire the popular religion with new insight, they have been, on the whole, a group apart.

Yet those who belonged to these two distinct traditions did use the same churches and the same symbolism. There was an even deeper bond of unity between them. Both believed that renunciation and self-discipline are the way of salvation—in the religion of the spirit as the way to enter now into love of eternal things; in the religion of commonsense as a rather heavy price paid to God in return for everlasting happiness after death. It may be argued, therefore, by churchmen like Dr. Fosdick, that the "abiding message" of the Bible about immortality is that men must renounce the world in order to win eternity. That some men mean by eternity a kind of perpetual motion and others a kind of abstraction is merely a difference in their habits of thought, and does not impair the validity or the importance of the central experience. If they will renounce their worldly passions, they will find what the idea of eternity has to give, no matter what they imagine it to mean.

But although Dr. Fosdick implies that this solves the difficulty, it can be shown, I believe, that it does not. What he has succeeded in doing is to disentangle from the Bible a meaning for immortality which has a noble tradition behind it and is at the same time intellectually possible for a modern man. But the history of religion ought to put us on guard against assuming too easily that a statement of the purest truth is in itself capable of affecting the lives of any considerable number of people. Dean Inge, who is a very much more clear-headed churchman, says quite frankly that "a religion succeeds, not because it is true, but because it suits the worshippers." Merely to tell men, however fervently, that they may conquer mortality by renouncing the flesh, will not go far toward persuading many of them to renounce the flesh. There must be, as there has been in all the historic religions, something more than a statement of the moral law. There must be a psychological machinery for enforcing the moral law.

For those who are suited to the religion of the spirit no machinery is needed. But for the mass of men who are not naturally suited to it, a machinery which compels this conversion is indispensable. Jesus in his time, and Gautama Buddha before him, taught a moral law which was addressed to those who could receive it. They were not many. Buddhism and Christianity became world religions centuries after the death of the founders, and only when there had been added to the central message a great organized method of teaching it.

The essence of such an organization is the title to say with apostolic certainty that the message is true. Churchmen like Dr. Fosdick can make no such claim about their message. They reject revelation. They reject the authority of any church to speak directly for God. They reject the literal inspiration of the Bible. They reject altogether many parts of the Bible as not only uninspired, but false and misleading. They do not believe in God as a lawgiver, judge, father, and spectator of human life. When they say that this or that message in the Bible is "permanently valid," they mean only that in their judgment, according to their reading of human experience, it is a well-tested truth. To say this is not merely to deny that the Bible is authoritative in astronomy and biology; it is to deny equally that it is authoritative as to what is good and bad for men. The Bible thus becomes no more than a revered collection of hypotheses which each man may reject or accept in the light of his own knowledge.

The lessons may still be true. But they are robbed of their certainty. Each man is thrown back upon his own resources; he is denied the support which all popular religion offers him, the conviction that outside himself there is a power on which he can and must lean for guidance. In the ancient faith a man said: "I believe this on the authority of an all-wise God." In the new faith he is in effect compelled to say: "I have examined the alleged pronouncements of an all-knowing God; some of them are obviously untrue, some are rather repulsive, others, however, if they are properly restated, I find to be exceedingly good."

Something quite fundamental is left out of the modernist creeds. At least something which has hitherto been quite fundamental is left out. That something is the most abiding of all the experiences of religion, namely, the conviction that the religion comes from God. Suppose it were true, which it plainly is not, that Dr. Fosdick by his process of selection and decoding has retained "precisely the thing at which the Bible was driving." Still he would be without the thing on which popular religion has been founded. For the Bible to our ancestors was not simply, as he implies, a book of wisdom. It was a book of wisdom backed by the power of God himself. That is not an inconsiderable difference. It is all the difference there is between a pious resolution and a moral law.

The Bible, as men formerly accepted it, contained wisdom *certified* by the powers that govern the universe. It did not merely contain many well-tested truths, similar in kind to those which are to be found in Plato, Aristotle, Montaigne, and Bernard Shaw. It contained truths which could not be doubted because they had been spoken by God through his prophets and his Son. They could not be wrong. But once it is allowed that each man may select from the Bible as he sees fit, judging each passage by his own notions of what is "abiding," you have stripped the Scriptures of their authority to command men's confidence and to compel their obedience. The Scriptures may still inspire respect. But they are disarmed.

## 3. WHAT MODERNISM LEAVES OUT

Many reasons have been adduced to explain why people do not go to church as much as they once did. Surely the most important reason is that they are not so certain that they are going to meet God when they go to church. If they had that certainty they would go. If they really believed that they were being watched by a Supreme Being who is more powerful than all the kings of earth put together, if they really believed that not only their actions but their secret thoughts were known and would be remembered by the creator and ultimate judge of the universe, there would be no complaint whatever about church attendance. The most worldly would be in the front pews, and preachers would not have to resort so often to their rather desperate expedients to attract an audience. If the conviction were there that the creed professed was invincibly true, the modern congregation would not come to church, as they usually do to-day, to hear the preacher and to listen to the music. They would come to worship God.

Religious professions will not work when they rest merely on a kind of passive assent; or on intricate reasoning, or on fierce exhortation, or on a good-natured conspiracy to be vague and highflown. A man cannot cheat about faith. Either he has it in the marrow of his bones, or in a crisis, when he is distracted and in sorrow, there is no conviction there to support him. Without complete certainty religion does not offer genuine consolation. It is without the strength to compensate our weakness. Nor can it sanction the rules of morality. Ethical codes cannot lay claim to unhesitating obedience when they are based upon the opinions of a majority, or on the notions of wise men, or on estimates of what is socially useful, or on an appeal to patriotism. For they depend then on the force which happens to range itself behind them at a particular time; or on their convenience for a moment. They are felt to be the outcome of human, and therefore quite fallible, decisions. They are no necessary part of the government of the universe. They were not given by God to Moses on Sinai. They are not the commandments of God speaking through his Infallible Church.

A human morality has no such sanction as a divine. The sanction of a divine morality is the certainty of the believer that it originated with God. But if he has once come to think that the rule of conduct has a purely human, local, and temporal origin, its sanction is gone. His obedience is transformed, as ours has been by knowledge of that sort, from conviction to conformity or calculated expediency.

Without certainty there can be no profound sense that a man's own purpose has become part of the purpose of the whole creation. It is necessary to believe in a God who is active in the world before a man can feel himself to be, as St. Paul said, "a fellow laborer" with God. Yet this sense of partnership with a Person who transcends the individual's own life, his own ego, and his own capacities, is fundamental in all popular religion. It underlies all the other elements of religion. For in the certainty that he is enlisted with God, man finds not only comfort in defeat, not only an ideal of holiness which persuades him to renounce his immediate desires, but an ecstatic mobilizing of all his scattered energies in one triumphant sense of his own infinite importance.

# IV The
   Acids
   of
   Modernity

## 1. THE KINGLY PATTERN

What I have said thus far can be reduced to the statement
that it is difficult for modern men to conceive a God whom
they can worship. Yet it would be a crude misunderstanding of religious experience to assume that it depends upon
a clear conception of God. In truly religious men the experience of God is much more intensely convincing than
any definition of his nature which they can put into words.
They do not insist on understanding that which they believe, for their belief gives them a consciousness of divinity
which transcends any conviction they could reach by the
understanding. They are not oppressed by the conflict between reason and faith because the testimony of faith is
irresistible. It may become so irresistible that any attempt
to understand is finally held, as it was by John Chrysostom,
to be an impertinence.

St. Chrysostom, who is described by the *Catholic Encyclopedia* as the most prominent doctor of the Greek
Church and the greatest preacher ever heard in a Christian
pulpit, is a striking example of how in other ages a man

who was both learned and devout was able to surmount
the intellectual difficulties which to-day cause so much
trouble for modernists and fundamentalists alike. Chrysostom was born at Antioch in the middle of the Fourth
Century and grew up in a time when the intellectual foundations of Christianity were intensely disputed. The Catholic theology had not yet emerged victoriously, and Antioch was the theatre of fierce struggles between Pagans,
Manichaeans, Gnostics, Arians, Jews, and others. These
struggles turned in considerable measure upon just such
attempts to define and comprehend God as now confuse
the teaching of the Protestant Church. Among the sectarians
there were some who claimed that it was possible "to know
God exactly" and it was against them that Chrysostom
preached that "he insults God who seeks to apprehend His
essential being." For "the difference between the being of
God and the being of man is of such a kind that no word
can express it and no thought can appraise it. . . . He
dwells, says St. Paul, in an unapproachable light." Even
the angels in heaven are stupefied by the glory and majesty
of God: "Tell me," he says, "wherefore do they cover their
faces and hide them with their wings? Why but that they
cannot endure the dazzling radiance and its rays that pour
from the Throne?"

Here in language so eloquent that the author became
known as Chrysostom, "the golden-mouthed," we have the
doctrine that "a comprehended God is no God," that "God
is incomprehensible because He is blessed and blessed because He is incomprehensible." But if we look more closely
at what Chrysostom actually says, it is apparent that he
has a much clearer idea of God than he knows. He conceives
of God as the creator, the ruler, and the judge of the universe. When he says that God is incomprehensible he means

that it is impossible for a human being to imagine what it would be like to be God. But that does not prevent Chrysostom from knowing what it is like to be the creature of the incomprehensible God. He is very definitely on his knees before the throne of a divine king whose radiance is so dazzling that he cannot look his Lord in the face.

There is thus a very solid intellectual conception embedded in the faith of this great teacher who staked everything on the assertion that it is impossible to conceive God. The conception is there but it has not been isolated and realized. It is unconsciously assumed. We find the same thing in Luther when he said: "I venture to put my trust in the one God alone, the invisible and incomprehensible, who hath created Heaven and Earth and is alone above all creatures." For in spite of the fact that Luther calls God incomprehensible, he is able to make a number of extremely important statements about him. He is able to say that God is the only God, that he created the earth, that there is a heaven, that God created heaven, and that God alone is above all his creatures. To know that much about God is to comprehend the function of God if not his nature.

Now if we examine the religious difficulty of modern men, we find, I think, that they do not lack the sense of mystery, of majesty, of terror, and of wonder which overwhelm Chrysostom and Luther. The emotional disposition is there. But it is somehow inhibited from possessing them utterly. The will to believe is checked by something in their experience which Chrysostom did not have. That something is the sense that the testimony of faith is not wholly credible, that the feeling of sanctity is no assurance of the existence of sacred powers, that awe and wonder and terror in the breast of the believer are not guarantees that there exist real objects that are awful and wonderful. The modern man is not incapable of faith, but he has within him a contrary passion, as instinctive and often as intense as faith, which makes incredible the testimony of his faith.

It is that contrary passion, and not the thin argumentation of atheists and agnostics, which lies, I think, at the root of what churchmen call modern irreligion. It is that passion which they must understand if they are ever to understand the modern religious difficulty. For just as men could surmount any intellectual difficulty when their passion to believe was whole-hearted, so to-day, when the passion to disbelieve is so strong, they are unable to believe no matter how perfectly their theological dilemmas are resolved.

We must ask ourselves, then, what there is in modern men which makes the testimony of faith seem more or less incredible to them. We have seen in the citations from Chrysostom and Luther that the testimony of faith really contains a large number of unconscious statements of fact about the universe and how it is governed. It is these statements of fact which we are no longer able to assume unconsciously, and having become conscious of them they are rather incredible. But why are they no longer unconsciously assumed and why are they incredible? The answer is, I think, that they have ceased to be consistent with our normal experience in ordinary affairs.

The faith of Chrysostom and Luther is entangled with, and supported upon, the assumption that the universe was created and is governed by a father and king. They had projected upon the universe an imaginary picture which reflected their own daily experience of government among men. These pictures of how the universe is governed change with men's political experience. Thus it would not have been easy for an Asiatic people to imagine the divine government in any other way but as a despotism, and Yahveh, as he appears in many famous portraits in the Old Testament, is very evidently an Oriental monarch inclined to be somewhat moody and very vain. He governs as he chooses, constrained by no law, and often without mercy, justice, or righteousness. The God of mediaeval Christianity, on the other hand, is more like a great feudal lord, supreme and yet bound by covenants to treat his vassals on earth according to a well-established system of reciprocal rights and duties. The God of the Enlightenment in the Eighteenth Century is a constitutional monarch who reigns but does not govern. And the God of Modernism, who is variously pictured as the *élan vital* within the evolutionary process, or as the sum total of the laws of nature, is really a kind of constitutionalism deified.

Provided that the picture is so consistent with experience that it is taken utterly for granted, it will serve as a background for the religious experience. But when daily experience for one reason or another provides no credible analogy by which men can imagine that the universe is governed by a supernatural king and father, then the disposition to believe, however strong it may be at the roots, is like a vine that reaches out and can find nothing solid upon which to grow. It cannot support itself. If faith is to flourish, there must be a conception of how the universe is governed to support it.

It is these supporting conceptions—the unconscious assumption that we are related to God as creatures to creator, as vassals to a king, as children to a father—that the acids of modernity have eaten away. The modern man's daily experience of modernity makes instinctively incredible to him these unconscious ideas which are at the core of the great traditional and popular religions. He does not wantonly reject belief, as so many churchmen assert. His predicament is much more serious. With the best will in the world, he finds himself not quite believing.

In the last four hundred years many influences have conspired to make incredible the idea that the universe is governed by a kingly person. An account of all of these influences would be a history of the growth of modern civilization. I am attempting nothing so comprehensive or so ambitious. I should like merely to note certain aspects of that revolutionary change which, as Lord Acton says, came "unheralded" and "founded a new order of things . . . sapping the ancient reign of continuity." For that new order of things has made it impossible for us to believe, as plainly and literally as our forefathers did, that the universe is a monarchy administered on this planet through divinely commissioned, and, therefore, unimpeachably authoritative ministers.

## 2. LANDMARKS

In a famous passage at the beginning of *Heretics*, Mr. Chesterton says that "nothing more strangely indicates the enormous and silent evil of modern society than the extraordinary use which is made nowadays of the word 'orthodox.' In former days the heretic was proud of not being a heretic. It was the kingdom of the world and the police and the judges who were heretics. He was orthodox. All the tortures born out of forgotten hells could not make him admit that he was heretical. But a few modern phrases have made him boast of it. He says with a conscious laugh, 'I suppose I am very heretical,' and looks around for applause. The word 'heresy' not only means no longer being wrong; it practically means being clear-headed and courageous."

Mr. Chesterton goes on to explain that this change of attitude has come about because "people care less for whether they are philosophically right than they used to care." It may be so. But if they cared as much or more, it would not help them. To be orthodox is to believe in the right doctrines and to follow the ancient rules of living deduced from a divine revelation. The modern man finds that the doctrines do not fit what he believes to be true, and that the rules do not show him how to conduct his life. For he is confronted at every turn with radical novelties about which his inherited dogma teaches him something which is plainly unworkable, or, as is even more often the case, teaches him nothing at all.

In the old world there were, of course, novelties, too. But the pace of change was so slow that it did not seem to cause radical change. There was ample time to make subtle and necessary revisions of the fundamental assumptions of right and wrong without seeming to challenge the distinction between right and wrong. Looking back at it in long perspective we can see now that there was a constant evolution of the Christian faith from the Apostles to the later councils of the Church. But in relation to the life of any individual the change was so slow that men could honestly believe that the Catholicism of Hildebrand was identical with the Christianity of Paul. Men had few means of reconstructing the past, and few ways of knowing how great was the variety of belief at any one time within the frontiers of Christendom. Within their horizon, change came too slowly to seem like change, because only that seems to move which moves rather fast.

For that reason the large changes which took place were not vividly realized. The small, quick changes, of which men were conscious, could therefore easily be made to seem, especially since men were not too exact and observant, as inevitable deductions from unchanging premises. Even in the great arguments over the nature of Christ, the rights of Church and Empire, the meaning of grace and transubstantiation, both sides appealed in theory to the same premises. Each side asserted that it was following the true revelation. And since ordinary men for the most part never heard the other side, except from their own priests and doctors, they had no reason for doubting that the side on which they happened to find themselves was absolutely right. They did not have to choose between competing creeds; they had merely to defend their creed, which was the true one, against the enemies of God. And so if they were disturbed by the quarrel, they were not disturbed much by doubt.

The grand adjustments were taken for granted, and within that framework men could make the minor adjustments patiently and elaborately, letting them become habitual and well-worn. This, perhaps, is the secret of the charm that an old civilization has for us to-day. We feel that here is a way of life which men have had time to refine and to embellish. The modern man in a progressive community has neither the time nor the energy for this delightful superficiality. He is too busy solving fundamental problems. He is so free to question his premises that he is no longer free to work out his conclusions. His philosophy of life is like the skyscraper; it is nine-tenths structure. So much effort has gone into constructing it, and making it fit to bear the strains, it is so new and yet it will so soon be out of date, that nobody is much interested in the character of it. But a mediaeval cathedral, like the mediaeval philosophy, was built slowly over generations and was to last forever; it is decorated inside and out, where it can be seen and where it cannot be seen, from the crypt to the roof.

The modern man is an emigrant who lives in a revolutionary society and inherits a protestant tradition. He must be guided by his conscience. But when he searches his conscience, he finds no fixed point outside of it by which he can take his bearings. He does not really believe that there is such a point, because he himself has moved about too fast to fix any point long enough in his mind. For the sense of authority is not established by argument. It is acquired by deep familiarity and indurated association. The ancient authorities were blended with the ancient landmarks, with fields and vineyards and patriarchal trees, with ancient houses and chests full of heirlooms, with churchyards near at hand and their ancestral graves, with old men who remembered wise sayings they had heard from wise old men. In that kind of setting it is natural to believe that the great truths are known and the big questions settled, and to feel that the dead themselves are still alive and are watching over the ancient faith.

But when creeds have to be proved to the doubting they are already blighted; arguments are for the unbelievers and the wavering, for those who have never had, and for those who have lost these primordial attachments. Faith is not a formula which is agreed to if the weight of evidence favors it. It is a posture of man's whole being which predisposes him to assimilate, not merely to believe, his creed. When the posture is native to him, in tune with the rhythm of his surroundings, his faith is not dependent upon intellectual assent. It is a serene and whole-hearted absorption, like that of the infant to its mother, in the great powers outside which govern his world. When that union of feeling is no longer there, as it is not there for a large part of our talkative fundamentalist sects, we may be sure that corrosive doubting has begun. The unlovely quality of much modern religiosity is due to these doubts. So much of its belief is synthetic. It is forced, made, insisted upon, because it is no longer simple and inevitable. The angry absurdities which the fundamentalists propound against "evolution" are not often due to their confidence in the inspiration of the Bible. They are due to lack of confidence, to doubt resisted like an annoying tune which a man cannot shake out of his head. For if the militant fundamentalists were utterly sure they are right, they would exhibit some of that composure which the truly devout display. Did they really trust their God, they would trust laws, politicians, and policemen less. But because their whole field of consciousness is trembling with uncertainties they are in a state of fret and fuss; and their preaching is frousy, like the seductions of an old coquette.

### 3. BARREN GROUND

The American people, more than any other people, is composed of individuals who have lost association with their old landmarks. They have crossed an ocean, they have spread themselves across a new continent. The American who still lives in his grandfather's house feels almost as if he were living in a museum. There are few Americans who have not moved at least once since their childhood, and even if they have staid where they were born, the old landmarks themselves have been carted away to make room for progress. That, perhaps, is one reason why we have so much more Americanism than love of America. It takes time to learn to love the new gas station which stands where the wild honeysuckle grew. Moreover, the great majority of Americans have risen in the world. They have moved out of their class, lifting the old folks along with them perhaps, so that together they may sit by the steam pipes, and listen to the crooning of the radio. But more and more of them have moved not only out of their class, but out of their culture; and then they leave the old folks behind, and the continuity of life is broken. For faith grows well only as it is passed on from parents to their children amidst surroundings that bear witness, because nothing changes radically, to a deep permanence in the order of the world. It is true, no doubt, that in this great physical and psychic migration some of the old household gods are carefully packed up and put with the rest of the luggage, and then unpacked and set up on new altars in new places. But what can be taken along is at best no more than the tree which is above the ground. The roots remain in the soil where first they grew.

The sidewalks of a city would in any case be a stony soil in which to transplant religion. Throughout history, as Spengler points out, the large city has bred heresies, new cults, and irreligion. Now when we speak of modern civilization we mean a civilization dominated by the culture of the great metropolitan centers. Our own civilization in America is perhaps the most completely urbanized of all. For even the American farmers, though they live in the country, tend to be suburban rather than rural. I am aware of how dominating a role the population outside the great cities plays in American life. Yet it is in the large cities that the tempo of our civilization is determined, and the tendency of mechanical inventions as well as economic policy is to create an irresistible suction of the country towards the city.

The deep and abiding traditions of religion belong to the countryside. For it is there that man earns his daily bread by submitting to superhuman forces whose behavior he can only partially control. There is not much he can do when he has ploughed the ground and planted his seed except to wait hopefully for sun and rain from the sky. He is obviously part of a scheme that is greater than himself, subject to elements that transcend his powers and surpass his understanding. The city is an acid that dissolves this piety. How different it is from an ancient vineyard where men cultivate what their fathers have planted. In a modern city it is not easy to maintain that "reverent attachment to the sources of his being and the steadying of his life by that attachment." It is not natural to form reverent attachments to an apartment on a two-year lease, and an imitation mahogany desk on the thirty-second floor of an office building. In such an environment piety becomes absurd, a butt for the facetious, and the pious man looks like a picturesque yokel or a stuffy fool.

Yet without piety, without a patriotism of family and place, without an almost plant-like implication in unchangeable surroundings, there can be no disposition to believe in an external order of things. The omnipotence of God means something to men who submit daily to the cycles of the weather and the mysterious power of nature. But the city man puts his faith in furnaces to keep out the cold, is proudly aware of what bad sewage his ancestors endured, and of how ignorantly they believed that God, who made Adam at 9 A.M. on October 23 in the year 4004 B.C., was concerned with the behavior of Adam's children.

## 4. SOPHISTICATED VIOLENCE

Much effort goes into finding substitutes for this radical loss of association. There is the Americanization movement, for example, which in some of its public manifestations has as much resemblance to patriotism as the rape of the Sabine women had to the love of Dante for Beatrice. There is the vociferous nationalism of the hundred-per-centers which is always most eloquent when it is about to be most rowdy. There are the anxious outcries of the sectarians who in their efforts to revive the religion of their fathers show the utmost contempt for the aspirations of their sons. There is Mr. Henry Ford hastily collecting American antiques before his cars destroy the whole culture which produced them. There is Mr. Lothrop Stoddard looking every man in the eye to see whether it is Nordic blue. There are a thousand and one patently artificial, sometimes earnest, often fantastic fundamentalist agitations. They are all attempts to impose quickly by one kind of sophisticated violence or another a posture of faith which can be genuine only when it belongs to the unquestioned memories of the soul. They are a shrill insistence that men ought to feel that which no man can feel who does not already feel it in the marrow of his bones.

Novelties crowd the consciousness of modern men. The machinery of intelligence, the press, the radio, the moving picture, have enormously multiplied the number of unseen events and strange people and queer doings with which he has to be concerned. They compel him to pay attention to facts that are detached from their backgrounds, their causes and their consequences, and are only half known because they are not seen or touched or actually heard. These experiences come to him having no beginning, no middle, and no end, mere flashes of publicity playing fitfully upon a dark tangle of circumstances. I pick up a newspaper at the start of the day and I am depressed and rejoiced to learn that: anthracite miners have struck in Pennsylvania; that a price boost plot is charged; that Mr. Ziegfeld has imported a blonde from England who weighs 112 pounds and has pretty legs; that the Pope, on the other hand, has refused to receive women in low-necked dress and with their arms bare; that airplanes are flying to Hawaii; and that the Mayor says that the would-be Mayor is a liar. . . .

Now in an ordered universe there ought to be place for all human experiences. But it is not strange that the modern newspaper-reader finds it increasingly difficult to believe that through it all there is order, permanence, and connecting principle. Such experience as comes to him from the outside is a dissonance composed of a thousand noises. And amidst these noises he has for inner guidance only a conscience which consists, as he half-suspects, of the confused echoes of earlier tunes.

## 5. RULERS

He cannot look to his betters for guidance. The American social system is migratory, revolutionary, and protestant. It provides no recognized leaders and no clear standards of conduct. No one is recognized as the interpreter of morals and the arbiter of taste. There is no social hierarchy, there is no acknowledged ruling class, no well-known system of rights and duties, no code of manners. There are smart sets, first families, and successful people, to whom a good deal of deference is paid and a certain tribute of imitation. But these leaders have no real authority in morals or in matters of taste because they themselves have few standards that are not the fashions of a season. They exercise, therefore, an almost autocratic power over deportment at the country club. But what they believe about God, salvation, or the destiny of America nobody knows, not even they themselves.

There have been perhaps three ruling classes in America, the Puritan merchants, the Knickerbocker gentry, and the Cavalier planters of the South. Each presided for a few generations over an ordered civilization. But the New Englanders uprooted themselves and went west, and those who have been left behind are marooned in a flood of aliens. The Knickerbocker squirearchy dissolved in the commercial greatness of New York, and the southern aristocracy was overthrown and ruined by a social revolution which culminated in the Civil War. They have left no successors, and unless and until American society becomes stabilized once more somewhere for a few generations, they are not likely to have any successors.

Our rulers to-day consist of random collections of successful men and their wives. They are to be found in the inner circles of banks and corporations, in the best clubs, in the dominant cliques of trade unions, among the political churchmen, the higher manipulating bosses, the leading professional Catholics, Baptists, Methodists, Irish, Germans, Jews, and the grand panjandrums of the secret societies. They give orders. They have to be consulted. They can more or less effectively speak for, and lead some part of, the population. But none of them is seated on an assured throne, and all of them are forever concerned as to how they may keep from being toppled off. They do not know how they happen to be where they are, although they often explain what are the secrets of success. They have been educated to achieve success; few of them have been educated to exercise power. Nor do they count with any confidence upon retaining their power, nor of handing it on to their sons. They live, therefore, from day to day, and they govern by ear. Their impromptu statements of policy may be obeyed, but nobody seriously regards them as having authority.

# V The Breakdown of Authority

## 1. GOD'S GOVERNMENT

The dissolution of the ancestral order is still under way, and much of our current controversy is between those who hope to stay the dissolution and those who would like to hasten it. The prime fact about modernity, as it presents itself to us, is that it not merely denies the central ideas of our forefathers but dissolves the disposition to believe in them. The ancestral tradition still lives in many corners of the world. But it no longer represents for us, as it did for Dante and for St. Thomas Aquinas seven hundred years ago, the triumphant wisdom of the age. A child born in a modern city may still learn to use the images of the theological drama, but more or less consciously he is made to feel that in using them he is not speaking of things that are literally and exactly true.

Its dogma, as Mr. Santayana once said, is insensibly understood to be nothing but myth, its miracles nothing but legend, its sacraments mere symbols, its bible pure literature, its liturgy just poetry, its hierarchy an administrative convenience, its ethics an historical accident, and its whole function simply to lend a warm mystical aureole to human culture and ignorance. The modern man does not take his religion as a real account of the constitution, the government, the history, and the actual destiny of the universe. With rare exceptions his ancestors did. They believed that all their activities on this earth had a sequel in other activities hereafter, and that they themselves in their own persons would be alive through all the stretches of infinite time to experience this fulfilment. The sense of actuality has gone out of this tremendous conception of life; only the echoes of it persist, and in our memories they create a world apart from the world in which we do our work, a noble world perhaps in which it is refreshing to dwell now and then, and in anxiety to take refuge. But the spaces between the stars are so great; the earth is now so small a planet in the skies; man is so close, as St. Francis said, to his brother the ass, that in the daylight he does not believe that a great cosmic story is being unfolded of which his every thought and act is a significant part. The universe may have a conscious purpose, but he does not believe he knows just what it is; humanity may be acting out a divine drama, but he is not certain that he knows the plot.

There has gone out of modern life a working conviction that we are living under the dominion of one supreme ideal, the attainment of eternal happiness by obedience to God's will on earth. This conviction found its most perfect expression in the period which begins with St. Augustine's *City of God* and culminates in the *Divine Comedy* of Dante. But the underlying intuitions are to be found in nearly all popular religion; they are the creature's feeling of dependence upon his creator, a sense that his destiny is fixed by a being greater than himself. At the bottom of it there is a conviction that the universe is governed by superhuman persons, that the daily visible life of the world is constitutionally subject to the laws and the will of an invisible government. What the thinkers of the Middle Ages did was to work out in elaborate detail and in grandiose style the constitutional system under which supernatural government operates. It is not fanciful, and I hope not irreverent, to suggest that the great debates about the nature of the Trinity and the Godhead were attempts to work out a theory of divine sovereignty; that the debates about election and predestination and grace are attempts to work out a theory of citizenship in a divine society. The essential idea which dominates the whole speculation is man's relation to a heavenly king.

As this idea was finally worked out by the legists and canonists and scholastics

> every ordering of a human community must appear as a component part of that ordering of the world which exists because God exists, and every earthly group must appear as an organic member of that *Civitas Dei,* that God-State, which comprehends the heavens and the earth. Then, on the other hand, the eternal and other-worldly aim and object of every individual man must, in a directer or an indirecter fashion, determine the aim and object of every group into which he enters.
>
> But as there must, of necessity, be connection between the various groups, and as all of them must be connected with the divinely ordered Universe, we come by the further notion of a divinely instituted Harmony which pervades the Universal Whole and every part thereof. To every Being is assigned its place in that whole, and to every link between Beings corresponds a divine decree. . . .

There is no need to suppose that everyone in the Middle

Ages understood the theory, as Gierke describes it here, in all its architectural grandeur. Nevertheless, the theory is implicit in the feeling of simple men. It is the logical elaboration of the fundamental belief that the God who governs the world is no mere abstraction made up of hazy nouns and a vague adoration, but that, as Henry Adams says, he is the feudal seigneur to whom Roland, when he was dying, could proffer "his right-hand glove" as a last act of homage, such as he might have made to Charlemagne, and could pray:

> O God the Father who has never lied,
> Who raised up Saint Lazarus from death,
> And Daniel from the lions saved,
> Save my soul from all the perils
> For the sins that in my life I did!

## 2. THE DOCTRINE OF THE KEYS

The theory of divine government has always presented some difficulties to human reason, as we can see even in St. Augustine, who never clearly made up his mind whether the City of God was the actual church presided over by the Bishop of Rome or whether it was an ideal and invisible congregation of the saved. But we may be sure that to plainer minds it was necessary to believe that God governs mankind through the agency of the visible church. The unsophisticated man may not be realistic, but he is literal; he would be quite incapable, we may be sure, of understanding what St. Thomas meant when he asked "why should not the same sacred letter . . . contain several senses founded on the literal?" He would accept all the senses but he would accept them all literally. And taking them literally he would have to believe that if God governs the world, he governs it, not in some obscure meaning of the term, but that he actually governs it, as a king who is mightier than Charlemagne, but not essentially unlike Charlemagne.

The disposition to believe in the rule of God depended, therefore, upon the capacity to believe in a visible church upon earth which holds its commission from God. In some form or other all simple people look to a priestly caste who make visible the divine power. Without some such actualization the human imagination falters and becomes vagrant. The Catholic Church by its splendor and its power and its universality during the Middle Ages must have made easily credible the conception of God the Ruler. It was a government exercising jurisdiction over the known world, powerful enough to depose princes, and at its head was the Pope who could prove by the evidence of Scripture that he was the successor to Peter and was the Vice-gerent of God. To ask whether this grandiose claim was in fact true is, from the point of view of this argument, to miss the point. It was believed to be true in the Middle Ages. Because it was believed, the Church flourished. Because the Church flourished, it was ever so much easier to be certain that the claim was true. When men said that God ruled the world, they had evidence as convincing as we have when we say that the President is head of the United States Government; they were convinced because they came into daily contact with God's appointees administering God's laws.

It is this concrete sense of divine government which modern men have lost, and it may well be that this is where the Reformation has exercised its most revolutionary effect. What Luther did was to destroy the pretensions not only of the Roman Catholic Church, but of any church and of any priestly class to administer God's government on earth.

The Protestant reformers may not have intended to destroy as deeply as they did; the theocracies established by Calvin and Knox imply as much. But, nevertheless, when Luther succeeded in defying the Holy See by rejecting its claim that it was the exclusive agent of God, he made it impossible for any other church to set up the same claim and sustain it for any length of time.

> Now Christ says that not alone in the Church is there forgiveness of sins, but that where two or three are gathered together in His name, they shall have the right and the liberty to proclaim and promise to each other comfort and the forgiveness of sins. . . . We are not only kings and the freest of all men, but also priests forever, a dignity far higher than kingship, because by that priesthood we are worthy to appear before God, to pray for others, and to teach one another mutually the things which are of God.

This denial of the special function of the priesthood did not, of course, originate with Luther. Its historical antecedents go back to the primitive Christians; there is quotable authority for it in St. Augustine. It was anticipated by Wyclif and Huss and by many of the mystics of the Middle Ages. But Luther, possibly because the times were ripe for it, translated the denial of the authority of the priesthood into a political revolution which divided Christendom. When the Reformation was an accomplished fact, men looked out upon the world and no longer saw a single Catholic Apostolic Church as the visible embodiment of God's government. A large part of mankind, and that an economically and politically powerful part, no longer believed that Christ gave to Simon Peter and his successors at the Roman See the Keys of the Kingdom of Heaven with the promise that "whatsoever thou shalt bind on earth shall be bound in heaven: and whatsoever thou shalt loose on earth shall be loosed in heaven."


## 3. THE LOGIC OF TOLERATION

As a result of the great religious wars the governing classes were forced to realize that unless they consented to the policy of toleration they would be ruined. There is no reason to suppose that except among a few idealists toleration has ever been much admired as a principle. It was originally, and in large measure it still is, nothing but a practical necessity. For in its interior life no church can wholly admit that its rivals may provide an equally good vehicle of salvation.

Martin Luther certainly had none of the modern notion that one church is about as good as the next. To be sure he appealed to the right of private judgment, but he made it plain nevertheless that in his opinion "pagans or Turks or Jews or fake Christians" would "remain under eternal wrath and an everlasting damnation." John Calvin let it be known in no uncertain tone that he did not wish any new sects in Geneva. Milton, writing his beautiful essay on liberty, drew the line at Papists. And in our own day the *Catholic Encyclopedia* says in the course of an eloquent argument for practical civic toleration that "as the true God can tolerate no strange gods, the true Church of Christ can tolerate no strange churches beside herself, or, what amounts to the same, she can recognize none as theoretically justified." This is the ancient dogma that outside the church there is no salvation—*extra ecclesiam nulla salus*. Like many another dogma of the Roman church, it is not even in theory absolutely unbending. Thus it appears from the allocution of Pope Pius IX, *Singulari quadam* (1854), that "those who are ignorant of the true religion, if their ignorance is invincible (which means, if they have never had a chance to know the true religion) are not, in this matter, guilty of any fault in the sight of God."

As a consequence of the modern theory of religious freedom the churches find themselves in an anomalous position. Inwardly, to their communicants, they continue to assert that they possess the only complete version of the truth. But outwardly, in their civic relations with other churches and with the civil power, they preach and practice toleration. The separation of church and state involves more than a mere logical difficulty for the churchman. It involves a deep psychological difficulty for the members of the congregation. As communicants they are expected to believe without reservation that their church is the only true means of salvation; otherwise the multitude of separate sects would be meaningless. But as citizens they are expected to maintain a neutral indifference to the claims of all the sects, and to resist encroachments by any one sect upon the religious practices of the others. This is the best compromise which human wisdom has as yet devised, but it has one inevitable consequence which the superficial advocates of toleration often overlook. It is difficult to remain warmly convinced that the authority of any one sect is divine, when as a matter of daily experience all sects have to be treated alike.

The human soul is not so divided in compartments that a man can be indifferent in one part of his soul and firmly believing in another. The existence of rival sects, the visible demonstration that none has a monopoly, the habit of neutrality, cannot but dispose men against an unquestioning acceptance of the authority of one sect. So many faiths, so many loyalties, are offered to the modern man that at last none seems to him wholly inevitable and fixed in the order of the universe. The existence of many churches in one community weakens the foundation of all of them. And that is why every church in the heyday of its power proclaims itself to be catholic and intolerant.

But when there are many churches in the same community, none can make wholly good the claim that it is catholic. None has that power to discipline the individual which a universal church exercises. For, as Dr. Figgis puts it, when many churches are tolerated, "excommunication has ceased to be tyrannical by becoming futile."

## 4. A WORKING COMPROMISE

If the rival churches were not compelled to tolerate one another, they could not, consistently with their own teaching, accept the prevailing theory of the public school. Under that theory the schools are silent about matters of faith, and teachers are supposed to be neutral on the issues of history and science which bear upon religion. The churches permit this because they cannot agree on the dogma they would wish to have taught. The Catholics would rather have no dogma in the schools than Protestant dogma; the fundamentalists would rather have none than have modernist. This situation is held to be a good one. But that is only because all the alternatives are so much worse. No church can sincerely subscribe to the theory that questions of faith do not enter into the education of children.

Wherever churches are rich enough to establish their

own schools, or powerful enough to control the public school, they make short work of the "godless" school. Either they establish religious schools of their own, as the Catholics and Lutherans have done, or they impose their views on the public schools as the fundamentalists have done wherever they have the necessary voting strength. The last fight of Mr. Bryan's life was made on behalf of the theory that if a majority of voters in Tennessee were fundamentalists then they had the right to make public education in Tennessee fundamentalist too. One of the standing grievances of the Catholic Church in America is that Catholics are taxed to support schools to which they cannot conscientiously send their children.

As a matter of fact non-sectarianism is a useful political phrase rather than an accurate description of what goes on in the schools. If there is teaching of science, that teaching is by implication almost always agnostic. The fundamentalists point this out, and they are quite right. The teaching of history, under a so-called non-sectarian policy, is usually, in this country, a rather diluted Protestant version of history. The Catholics are quite right when they point this out. Occasionally, it may be, a teacher of science appears who has managed to assimilate his science to his theology; now and then a Catholic history-teacher will depart from the standard textbooks to give the Catholic version of disputed events during the last few hundred years. But the chief effect of the non-sectarian policy is to weaken sectarian attachment, to wean the child from the faith of his fathers by making him feel that patriotism somehow demands that he shall not press his convictions too far, that commonsense and good-fellowship mean that he must not be too absolute. The leaders of the churches are aware of this peril. Every once in a while they make an effort to combat it. Committees composed of parsons, priests, and rabbis appear before the school boards and petition that a non-sectarian God be worshiped and the non-controversial passages of the Bible be read. They always agree that the present godless system of education diminishes the sanctions of morality and the attendance at their respective churches. But they disagree when they try to agree on the nature of a neutral God, and they have been known to dispute fiercely about a non-controversial text of the Ten Commandments. So, if the sects are evenly balanced, the practical sense of the community turns in the end against the reform.

## 5. THE EFFECT OF PATRIOTISM

Modern governments are not merely neutral as between rival churches. They draw to themselves much of the loyalty which once was given to the churches. In fact it has been said with some truth that patriotism has many of the characteristics of an authoritative religion. Certainly it is true that during the last few hundred years there has been transferred to government a considerable part of the devotion which once sustained the churches.

In the older world the priest was a divinely commissioned agent and the prince a divinely tolerated power. But by the Sixteenth Century Melanchthon, a friend of Luther's, had denied that the church could make laws binding the conscience. Only the prince, he said, could do that. Out of this view developed the much-misunderstood but essentially modern doctrine of the divine right of kings. In its original historic setting this doctrine was a way of asserting that the civil authority, embodied in the king, derived its power not from the Pope, as God's viceroy on earth, but by direct appointment from God himself. The divine right of kings was a declaration of independence as against the authority of the church. This heresy was challenged not only by the Pope, but by the Presbyterians as well. And it was to combat the Presbyterian preachers who insisted on trying to dictate to the government that King James I wrote his *True Law of Free Monarchy,* asserting the whole doctrine of the Divine Right of Kings.

In the Religious Peace of Augsburg an even more destructive blow was struck at the ancient claim of the church that it is a universal power. It was agreed that the citizen of a state must adopt the religion of his king. *Cuius regio ejus religio.* This was not religious liberty as we understand it, but it was a supreme assertion of the civil power. Where once the church had administered religion for the multitude, and had exercised the right to depose an heretical king, it now became the prerogative of the king to determine the religious duties of his subjects. The way was open for the modern absolute state, a conception which would have been entirely incomprehensible to men who lived in the ages of faith.

We must here avoid using words ambiguously. When I speak of the absolute state, I do not refer to the constitutional arrangement of powers within the state. It is of no importance in this connection whether the absolute power of the state is exercised by a king, a landed aristocracy, bankers and manufacturers, professional politicians, soldiers, or a random majority of voters. It does not matter whether the right to govern is hereditary or obtained with the consent of the governed. A state is absolute in the sense which I have in mind when it claims the right to a monopoly of all the force within the community, to make war, to make peace, to conscript life, to tax, to establish and disestablish property, to define crime, to punish disobedience, to control education, to supervise the family, to regulate personal habits, and to censor opinions. The modern state claims all these powers, and in the matter of theory there is no real difference in the size of the claim between communists, fascists, and democrats. There are lingering traces in the American constitutional system of the older theory that there are inalienable rights which government may not absorb. But these rights are really not inalienable because they can be taken away by constitutional amendment. There is no theoretical limit upon the power of the ultimate majorities which create civil government. There are only practical limits. They are restrained by inertia, and by prudence, even by good will. But ultimately and theoretically they claim absolute authority as against all foreign states, as against all churches, associations, and persons within their jurisdiction.

The victory of the civil power was not achieved everywhere at the same time. Spasmodically, with occasional setbacks, but in the long run irresistibly, the state has attained supremacy. In the feudal age the monarch was at no time sovereign. The Pope was the universal law-giver, not only in what we should call matters of faith, but in matters of business and politics as well. As late as the beginning of the Seventeenth Century, Pope Paul V insisted that the Doge of the Venetian Republic had no right to arrest a canon of the church on the charge of flagrant immorality. When, nevertheless, the canon was arrested, the Pope laid Venice under an interdict and excommunicated the Doge and the Senate. But the Venetian Government answered that it was founded on Divine Right; its title to govern did not come from the church. In the end the

Pope gave way, and "the reign of the Pope," says Dr. Figgis, "as King of Kings was over."

It was as a result of the loss of its civil power that the Roman Church evolved the modern doctrine of infallibility. This claim, as Dr. Figgis points out, is not the culmination but the (implicit) surrender of the notions embodied in the famous papal bull, *Unam Sanctam*. The Pope could no longer claim the political sovereignty of the world; he then asserted supreme rights as the religious teacher of the Catholic communion. "The Pope, from being the Lord of Lords, has become the Doctor of Doctors. From being the mother of states, the Curia has become the authoritative organ of a teaching society."

## 6. THE DISSOLUTION OF A SOVEREIGNTY

Thus there has gradually been dissolving the conception that the government of human affairs is a subordinate part of a divine government presided over by God the King. In place of one church which is sovereign over all men, there are now many rival churches, rival states, voluntary associations, and detached individuals. God is no longer believed to be a universal king in the full meaning of the word king, and religious obedience is no longer the central loyalty from which all other obligations are derived. Religion has become for most modern men one phase in a varied experience; it no longer regulates their civic duties, their economic activities, their family life, and their opinions. It has ceased to have universal dominion, and is now held to be supreme only within its own domain. But there is much uncertainty as to what that domain is. In actual affairs, the religious obligations of modern men are often weaker

than their social interests and generally weaker than the
fiercer claims of patriotism. The conduct of the churches
and of churchmen during the War demonstrated that fact
overwhelmingly. They submitted willingly or unwillingly
to the overwhelming force of the civil power. Against this
force many men claim the right of revolution, or at least
the right of passive resistance and conscientious objection.
Sometimes they base their claims upon a religious precept
which they hold sacred. But even in their disobedience to
Caesar they are forced to acknowledge that loyalty in the
modern world is complex, that it has become divided and
uncertain, and that the age of faith which was absolute is
gone for them. However reverent they may be when they
are in their churches, they no longer feel wholly assured
when they listen to the teaching that these are the words of
the ministers of a heavenly king.

# VI    Lost Provinces

## 1. BUSINESS

In any scheme of things where the churches, as agents of God, assert the right to speak with authority about the conduct of life they should be able to lay down rules about the way business shall be carried on. The churches once did just that. In some degree they still attempt to do it. But the attempts have grown feebler and feebler. In the last six hundred years the churches have fought a losing battle against the emancipation of business from religious control.

The early Christian writers looked upon business as a peril to the soul. Although the church was in itself, among other things, a large business corporation, they did not countenance business enterprise. Money-making they called avarice and money-lending usury, just as they spoke of lust when they meant sexual desire. They had sound reasons of their own for this attitude. They knew from observation, perhaps even from introspection, that the desire for riches is so strong a passion that men possessed by it will devote only their odd moments to God. The objection to a business career was like the objection to fornication; it diverted the energies of the soul.

There were, no doubt, worldly reasons as well which account for the long resistance of the mediaeval Church to what we now regard as the highest form of capitalistic endeavor. The Church belonged to the feudal system. The Pope and his bishops were in fact great feudal lords. They thrived best in a social order where men lived upon the land. They had a premonition that the rise of capitalism, with its large cities, its financiers, merchants, and proletarian workers, was bound to weaken the secular authority of the church and to dissolve the influence of religion in men's lives. They failed in their resistance, but surely one can hardly say that their vision was not prophetic. The drastic legislation of the church against business was enacted in the early days of capitalism; it was inspired, like the English corn laws and many another agrarian measure, by a determination to preserve a landed order of society. Thus in discussing whether money might properly be loaned out at interest Pope Innocent IV argued that if this were permitted "men would not give thought to the cultivation of their land, except when they could do naught else . . . even if they could get land to cultivate, they would not be able to get the beasts and implements for cultivating it, since the poor themselves would not have them, and the rich, both for the sake of profit and security, would put their money into usury rather than into smaller and more risky investments." The argument is the same as that which the American farmer makes when he complains that the bankers in Wall Street prefer to lend money to business men and to speculators rather than to farmers.

But the solid reasons which once inspired the church's opposition to business do not concern us here. The opposition was unsuccessful, the reasons were forgotten, and the old pronouncements against usury were looked upon as quaint and unworldly. For the new economic order which displaced feudalism, the Catholic Church, at least, had no program. It did not adapt itself readily to the spirit of commercial enterprise which captured the active minds of Northern Europe. The Protestant churches did adapt themselves and contrived to preach a gospel which encouraged, where Roman Catholicism had discouraged, the enterprising business man. They preached the divine duty of labor. "At the day of doom," said John Bunyan, "men shall be judged according to their fruits. It will not be said then, Did you Believe? But, were you Doers, or Talkers only?" As this preaching became more concrete, to be a doer meant to do work and make money. Baxter in his *Christian Directory* wrote that "if God show you a way in which you may lawfully get more than in another way (without wrong to your soul or to any other), if you refuse this, and choose the less gainful way, you cross one of the ends of your calling, and you refuse to be God's steward." Richard Steele in *The Tradesman's Calling* pointed out that the virtues enjoined on Christians—diligence, moderation, sobriety, and thrift—are the very qualities which are most needed for commercial success. For "godly wisdom . . . comes in and puts due bounds" to his expenses, "and teaches the tradesman to live rather somewhat below than at all above his income."

However edifying such doctrine may have been, it was clearly an abandonment of the right, once so eloquently asserted by the church, that it had the authority to regulate business in the interest of man's spiritual welfare. That right is still sometimes asserted. Sermons are still preached about business ethics; there are programs of Christian socialism and Christian capitalism. Churchmen still interest themselves, often very effectively, to reform some flagrant industrial abuse like the sweating of women and children. But the modern efforts to moralize business and to subordinate profit-seeking to humane ends are radically different from those of the mediaeval church. They are admittedly experimental—that is to say, debatable—since they do not derive their authority from revelation. And they are presented as an appeal to reason, to conscience, to generosity, not as the commandments of God. The Council of Vienna in 1312 declared that any ruler or magistrate who sanctioned usury and compelled debtors to observe usurious contracts would be excommunicated; all laws which sanctioned money-lending at interest were to be repealed within three months. The churches do not speak in that tone of voice to-day.

Thus if an organization like the Federal Council of Churches of Christ is distressed by, let us say, the labor policy of a great corporation, it inquires courteously of the president's secretary whether it would not be possible for him to confer with a delegation about the matter. If the churchmen are granted an interview, which is never altogether certain, they have to argue with the business man on secular grounds. Were they to say that the eight-hour day was the will of God, he would conclude they were cranks, he would surreptitiously press the buzzer under his desk, and in a few moments his secretary would appear summoning him to an important board meeting. They have to argue with him, if they are to obtain a hearing, about the effect on health, efficiency, turnover, and other such matters which are worked up for them by economists. As churchmen they have kindly impulses, but there is no longer a body of doctrine in the churches which enables them to speak with authority.

The emancipation of business from religious control is

perhaps even more threatening to the authority of the churches than the rivalry of sects or the rise of the civil power. Business is a daily occupation; government meets the eye of the ordinary men only now and then. That the main interest in the waking life of most people should be carried on wholly separated from the faith they profess means that the churches have lost one of the great provinces of the human soul. The sponsors of the Broadway Temple in New York City put the matter in a thoroughly modern, even if it was a rather coarse, way when they proclaimed a campaign to sell bonds as "a five percent investment in your Fellow Man's Salvation—Broadway Temple is to be a combination of Church and Skyscraper, Religion and Revenue, Salvation and 5 Percent—and the 5 percent is based on ethical Christian grounds." The five per cent, they hastened to add, was also based on a gilt-edged real-estate mortgage; the salvation, however, was, we may suppose, a speculative profit.

## 2. THE FAMILY

The family is the inner citadel of religious authority and there the churches have taken their most determined stand. Long after they had abandoned politics to Caesar and business to Mammon, they continued to insist upon their authority to fix the ideal of sexual relations. But here, too, the dissolution of their authority has proceeded inexorably. They have lost their exclusive right to preside over marriages. They have not been able to maintain the dogma that marriage is indissoluble. They are not able to prevent the remarriage of divorced persons. Although in many jurisdictions fornication and adultery are still crimes, there is no longer any serious attempt to enforce the statutes. The churches have failed in their insistence that sexual intercourse by married persons is a sin unless it is validated by the willingness to beget a child. Except to the poorest and most ignorant the means of preventing conception are available to all. There is no longer any compulsion to regard the sexual life as within the jurisdiction of the commissioners of the Lord.

Religious teachers knew long ago what modern psychologists have somewhat excitedly rediscovered: that there is a very intimate connection between the sexual life and the religious life. Only men living in a time when religion has lost so much of its inward vitality could be shocked at this simple truth, for the churches, when their inspiration was fresh, have always known it. That is why they have laid such tremendous emphasis upon the religious control of sexual experience, have extolled chastity, have preached continence after marriage except where parenthood was in view, have inveighed against fornication, adultery, divorce, and all unprocreative indulgence, have insisted that marriages be celebrated within the communion, have upheld the parental authority over children. They were not prudish. That is a state of mind which marks the decay of vigorous determination to control the sexual life. The early teachers did not avert their eyes. They did not mince their words. For they knew what they were doing.

Men like St. Paul and St. Augustine knew in the most direct way what sexual desire can do to distract the religious life; how if it is not sternly regulated, and if it is allowed to run wild, it intoxicates the whole personality to the exclusion of spiritual interests. They knew, too, although perhaps not quite so explicitly, that these same passions, if they are repressed and redirected, may come

forth as an ecstasy of religious devotion. They were not reformers. They did not think of progress. They did not suppose that the animal in man could somehow be refined
until it was no longer animal. When Paul spoke of the law
of his members warring against the law of his mind, and
bringing him into captivity to the law of sin, he had made
a realistic observation which any candid person can verify
out of his own experience. There was no vague finical non-
sense about this war of the members against the inward
man seeking delight in the law of God.

If the sexual impulse were not deeply related to the
religious life, the preoccupation of churchmen with it
throughout the ages would be absurd. They have not been
preoccupied in any comparable degree with the other physiological functions of the body. They have concerned themselves somewhat with eating and drinking, for gluttony and
drunkenness can also distract men from religion. But hunger and thirst are minor passions, far more easily satisfied
than lust, and in no way so pervasive and imperious. The
world, the flesh, and the devil may usually be taken to
mean sexual desire. Around it, then, the churches have built
up a ritual, to dominate it lest they be dominated by it.
Tenaciously and with good reason they have fought against
surrendering their authority.

With equally great insight they have kept the closest
possible association with family life especially during the
childhood of the offspring. Here again they anticipated by
many long ages the discoveries of modern psychologists.
They have always known that it is in the earliest years,
before puberty, that tradition is transmitted. Much is
learned after puberty, but in childhood education is more
than mere learning. There education is the growth of the
disposition, the fixing of the prejudices to which all later

experience is cumulative. In childhood men acquire the forms of their seeing, the prototypes of their feeling, the style of their character. There presumably the very pattern of authority itself is implanted by habit, fitted to the model presented by the child's parents. There the assumption is fixed that there are wiser and stronger beings whom, in the nature of things, one must obey. There the need to obey is fixed. There the whole drift of experience is such as to make credible the idea that above the child there is the father, above the father a king and the wise men, above them all a heavenly Father and King.

It is plain that any change which disturbs the constitution of the home will tend profoundly to alter the child's sense of what he may expect the constitution of the universe to be. There are many disturbing changes of which none is more important surely than the emancipation of women. The God of popular religion has usually been an elderly male. There have been some female divinities worshipped in different parts of the world as there have been matriarchal societies. But by and large the imagination of men has conceived God as a father. They have magnified to a cosmic scale what they had seen at home. It was the male who created the child. It was his seed that the mother cherished in her womb. It was the male who provided for the needs of the family, even if the woman did the hard work. It was the male who fended off enemies. It was the male who laid down the law. It was the name of the male parent which was preserved and passed on from generation to generation. Everything conspired to fix the belief that the true order of life was a hierarchy with a man at the apex.

This general notion becomes less and less credible as women assert themselves. The child of the modern household is soon made to see that there are at least two persons who can give him orders, and that they do not always give him the same ones. This does not educate him to believe that there is one certain guide to conduct in the universe. There are likely to be two guides to conduct in his universe, as women insist that they are independent personalities with minds of their own. This insistence, moreover, tends rather to disarrange the notion that the father is the creator of the child. An observant youngster, especially in these days of frank talk about sex, soon becomes aware of the fact that the role of the male in procreation is a relatively minor one. But most disturbing of all is the very modern household in which the woman earns her own living. For here the child is deprived of the opportunity, which is so conducive to belief in authority, of seeing daily that even his mother is dependent upon a greater person for the good things in life.

Although women, by and large, are by no means able to earn as much money as men, the fact which counts is that they can earn enough to support themselves. They may not actually support themselves. But the knowledge that they could, as it becomes an accepted idea in society, has revolutionary consequences. In former times the woman was dependent upon her husband for bed, board, shelter, and clothing. Her whole existence was determined by her mating; her sexual experience was an integral part of her livelihood and her social position. But once it had become established that a woman could live without a husband, the intimate connection between her sex and her career began to dissolve.

The invention of dependable methods of preventing conception has carried this dissolution much further. Birth control has separated the sexual act from the whole series of social consequences which were once probable if not inevitable. For with the discovery that children need be born only when they are wanted, the sexual experience has become increasingly a personal and private affair. It was once an institutional affair—for the woman. For the man, from time immemorial, there have been two sorts of sexual experience—one which had no public consequences, and one which entailed the responsibilities of a family. The effect of the modern changes, particularly of woman's economic independence and of birth control, is to equalize the freedom and the obligations of men and women.

That the sexual life has become separated from parenthood and that therefore it is no longer subject to external regulation, is evident. While the desires of men and women for each other were links in a chain which included the family and the household and children, authority, and by that token religious authority, could hope to fix the sexual ideal. When the chain broke, and love had no consequences which were not too subtle for the outsider to measure, the ideal of love was fixed not by the church in the name of God, but by prudence, convention, the prevailing rules of hygiene, by taste, circumstances, and personal sensibility.

## 3. ART

### (a) THE DISAPPEARANCE OF RELIGIOUS PAINTING

To walk through a museum of Western European art is to behold a peculiarly vivid record of how the great themes of popular religion have ceased to inspire the imagination of modern men. One can visualize there the whole story of the dissolution of the ancestral order and of our present bewilderment. One can see how toward the close of the Fifteenth Century the great themes illustrating the reign of a heavenly king and of the drama of man's salvation had ceased to be naively believed; how at the close of the next century which witnessed the Reformation and the Counter-Reformation, the beginnings of modern science, the growth of cities, and the rise of capitalism, religious painting ceased to be the concern of the best painters; and finally how in the last hundred years painters have illustrated by feverish experimentation the modern man's effort to find an adequate substitute for the organizing principle of the religion which he has lost.

It has been said by way of explanation that painters must sell their work, and they must, therefore, paint what the rich and powerful will buy. Thus it is pointed out that in the Middle Ages they worked under the patronage of the Church; in the Renaissance their patrons were paganized princes and popes, and artists made pictures which, even when the theme was religious, were no longer Christian in spirit. Later in the north of Europe the bourgeoisie acquired money and station, and the Dutch painters did their portraits, and made faithful representations of their kitchens and their parlors. A little later French painters at the Court of Versailles made pictures for courtiers, and in our time John Sargent painted the wives of millionaires. To say all this is to say that the ruling classes in the modern world are no longer interested in pictures which illustrate or are inspired by the religion they profess.

This attempt at an explanation in terms of supply and demand may or may not be sound for the ordinary run of painters. It leaves out of account, however, those very painters who are the most significant and interesting. It leaves out of account the painters who, by heroic refusal to supply the existing market, deserve universal respect, and in many cases have won an ultimate public vindication. These men do not fit into the theory of supply and demand, for they endured poverty and derision in order to paint what they most wanted to paint. They are not of the tribe, which Mr. Walter Pach calls Ananias, who betray the truth that is in them. But for that truth they did not draw upon the themes nor the sense of life which almost all of them must have been taught when they were children. They did not paint religious pictures. They painted landscapes, streets, interiors, still life, heads, persons, nudes. Whatever else they perceived and tried to express, they did not see their objects in the perspective of human destiny and divine government. There is no reason, then, to say that religious painting, even in the broadest sense of the term, has disappeared because there is no effective demand for it. Obviously it has disappeared because the will to produce it has disappeared.

### (b) THE LOSS OF A HERITAGE

In setting the religious tradition aside as something with which they are not concerned when they are at work, artists are merely behaving like modern men. It is plain that the religious tradition has become progressively less relevant to anyone who as painter or sculptor is engaged in making images. This is a direct result of that increasing sophistication of religious thought which was signalized in Europe by the iconoclasm of the Protestant reformers and the puritanism of the Catholic Counter-Reformation. Before the acids of modernity had begun to dissolve the organic reality of the ancient faith, there was no difficulty about picturing God the Father as a patriarch and the Virgin Mary as a young blonde Tuscan mother. There was no disposition to disbelieve, and so the imagination was at once nourished by a great heritage of ideas and yet free to elaborate it. But when the authority of the old beliefs was challenged, a great literature of controversy and definition was let loose upon the world. And from the point of view of the artist the chief effect of this effort to argue and to state exactly, to defend and to rebut, was to substitute concepts for pictorial ideas. When the nature of God became a matter of definition, it was obviously crude and illiterate to represent him as a benign old man. Thus the more the theologians refined the dogmas of their religion the more impossible they made it for painters to express its significance. No painter who ever lived could make a picture which expressed the religion of the Rev. Harry Emerson Fosdick. There is nothing there which the visual imagination can use.

Painters have, therefore, a rather better reason than most men for having turned their backs upon the religious tradition. They can say with a clear conscience that the contemporary churches have removed from that tradition those very qualities which once made it an inexhaustible source of artistic inspiration. They need only point to modern religious writing in their own support: at its best it has the qualities of an impassioned argument and more often it is intolerably flat and vague because in our intellectual climate skepticism dissolves the concreteness of the imagery and leaves behind sonorous adjectives and opaque nouns.

The full effects of this separation of the artist from the ancient traditions of Christendom have been felt only in the last two or three generations. It is no doubt true that the modern disbelief had its beginnings many generations ago, perhaps in the Fifteenth Century, but the momentum of the ancient faith was so great that it took a long time, even after corrosive doubt had started, before its influence came to an end. The artists of the Seventeenth and Eighteenth Centuries may not have been devout, but they lived in a society in which the forms of the old order, the hierarchy of classes, the sense of authority, and the general fund of ideas about human destiny, still had vast prestige. But in the Nineteenth Century that old order was almost completely dissolved and the prestige of its ideas destroyed. The artist of the last two or three generations has confronted the world without any accepted understanding of human life. He has had to improvise his own understanding of life. That is a new thing in the experience of artists.

(c) THE ARTIST FORMERLY

In 787 the Second Council of Nicaea laid down the rule which for nearly five hundred years was binding upon the artists of Christendom:

> The substance of religious scenes is not left to the initiative of the artists: it derives from the principles laid down by the Catholic Church and religious tradition. . . . His art alone belongs to the painter, its organization and arrangement belong to the clergy.

This was a reasonable rule, since the Church and not the individual was held to be the guardian of those sacred truths upon which depended the salvation of souls and the safety of society. The notion had occurred to nobody that the artist was divinely inspired and knew more than the doctors of the church. Therefore, the artist was given careful specifications as to what he was to represent.

Thus when the Church of St. Urban of Troyes decided to order a set of tapestries illustrating the story of St. Valerian and of his wife, St. Cecilia, a learned priest was deputed to draw up the contract for the artist. In it he wrote among other specifications that: "there shall be portrayed a place and a tabernacle in the manner of a beautiful room, in which there shall be St. Cecilia, humbly on her knees with her hands joined, praying to God. And beside her shall be Valerian expressing great admiration and watching an angel which, being above their heads, should be holding two crowns made of lilies and of roses, which he will be placing the one on the head of St. Cecilia and the other on the head of Valerian, her husband. . . ."

The rest, one might suppose, was left to the artist's imagination. But it was not. Having been given his subject matter and his theme, he was bound further by strict conventions as to how sacred subjects were to be depicted. Jesus on the Cross had to be shown with his mother on the right and St. John on the left. The centurion pierced his left side. His nimbus contained a cross, as the mark of divinity, whereas the saints had the nimbus without a cross. Only God, the angels, Jesus Christ, and the Apostles could be represented with bare feet; it was heretical to depict the Virgin or the Saints with bare feet. The purpose of these conventions was to help the spectator identify the figures in the picture. Thus St. Peter was given a short beard and a tonsure; St. Paul was bald and had a long beard. It is possible that these conventions, which were immensely intricate, were actually codified in manuals which were passed on from master to apprentice in the workshops.

As a general rule the ecclesiastics who drew up specifications did not invent the themes. Thus the learned
priest who drafted the contract for the tapestry of St. Cecilia drew his material from the encyclopedia of Vincent
de Beauvais. This was a compendium of universal knowledge covering the whole of history from Creation to the
Last Judgment. It was a source book to which any man
could turn in order to find the truth he happened to need.
It contained all of human knowledge and the answer to
all human problems. By the Thirteenth Century there
were a number of these encyclopedias, of which the greatest was the *Summa* of St. Thomas Aquinas. From these
books churchmen took the themes which they employed
their artists to embellish. The artist himself had no concern as to what he would paint, nor even as to how he
would paint it. That was given, and his energies could be
employed without the travail of intellectual invention,
upon the task of expressing a clear conception in well-
established forms.

It must not be supposed, of course, that either doctrines, lore, or symbolism were uniformly standardized and
exactly enforced. In an age of faith, contradictions and
discrepancies are not evident; they are merely variations
on the same theme. Thus, while it may be true that enthu-
siastic mediaevalists like M. Mâle have exaggerated the
order and symmetry of the mediaeval tradition, they are
right, surely, on the main point, which is that the organic
character of the popular religion provided a consensus of
feeling about human destiny which, in conjunction with
the resources of the popular lore, sustained and organized
the imagination of mediaeval artists. Because religious
faith was simple and genuine, it could absorb and master
almost anything. Thus the clergy ruled the artists with a

relatively light hand, and they were not disturbed if, in illuminating the pages of a Book of Hours, the artist adorned the margins with a picture of Bacchus or the love of Pyramus and Thisbe.

It was only when the clergy had been made self-conscious by the controversies which raged around the Reformation that they began in any strict and literally-minded modern sense to enforce the rule laid down at Nicaea in 787. At the Council of Trent in 1563 the great liberty of the artist within the Christian tradition came to an end:

> The Holy Council forbids the placing in a church of any image which calls to mind an erroneous dogma which might mislead the simple-minded. It desires that all impurity be avoided, that provocative qualities be not given to images. In order to insure respect for its decisions, the Holy Council forbids anyone to place or to have placed anywhere, and even in churches which are not open to the public, any unusual image unless the bishop has approved it.

In theory this decree at Trent is not far removed from the decree at Nicaea nearly one thousand years earlier. But in fact it is a whole world removed from it. For the dogmas at Nicaea rested upon naive faith and the dogmas at Trent rested upon definition. The outcome showed the difference, for within a generation Catholic scholars made a critical survey of the lore which mediaeval art had employed, and on grounds of taste, doctrine, and the like, condemned the greater part of it. After that, as M. Mâle says, there might still be artists who were Christians but there was no longer a Christian art.

### (d) THE ARTIST AS PROPHET

Whether the necessity of creating his own tradition is a good or a bad thing for the artist, there can be no doubt that it is a novel thing and a burdensome one. Artists have responded to it by proclaiming one of two theories: they have said that the artist, being a genius, was a prophet; when they did not say that, they said that religion, morality, and philosophy were irrelevant, and that art should be practiced for art's sake. Both theories are obviously attempts to find some personal substitute for those traditions upon which artists in all other ages have been dependent.

The theory of the artist as prophet has this serious defect: there is practically no evidence to support it. Why should there be? What connection is there between the capacity to make beautiful objects and the capacity to discover truth? Surely experience shows that it is something of a marvel when a great artist appears who, like Leonardo or Goethe, is also an original and important thinker. Indeed, it is reasonable to ask whether the analysis and abstraction which thinking involves are not radically different psychological processes from the painter's passionate appreciation of the appearance of things. Certainly to think as physicists think is to strip objects of all their secondary characters, not alone of their emotional significance, but of their color, their texture, their fragrance, and even of their superficial forms. The world as we know it through our senses has completely disappeared before the physicist begins to think about it. And in its place there is a collection of concepts which have no pictorial value whatsoever. These concepts are by definition incapable of being visualized, and when as a concession to human weakness, his own or his pupil's, the scientist constructs a mechanical model to illustrate an idea, this model is at best a crude analogy, and in no real sense the portrait of that idea.

Thus when Shelley made Earth say:

> I spin beneath my pyramid of night,
> Which points into the heavens . . .

he borrowed an image from astronomy. But this image, which is, I think, superb poetry, radically alters the original scientific idea, for it introduces into a realm of purely physical relations the notion of a gigantic spectator with a vastly magnified human eye. There are, no doubt, many other concepts in science which, if poets knew more science, would lend themselves to translation into equally noble images. But these images would not state the scientific truth.

The current belief that artists are prophets is an inheritance from the time when science had no critical method of its own, and poets, being reflective persons, had at least as good a chance as anyone else of stumbling upon truths which were subsequently verified. It is due in some measure also to the human tendency to remember the happy guesses of poets and to forget their unhappy ones, a tendency which has gone far to sustain the reputations of fortune-tellers, oracles, and stockbrokers. But above all, the reputation of the artist as one who must have wisdom is sustained by a rather genial fallacy: he finds expression for the feelings of the spectator, and the spectator rather quickly assumes that the artist has found an explanation for the world.

Yet unless I am greatly mistaken the modern painter has ceased not only to depict any theory of destiny but has ceased to express any important human mood in the presence of destiny. One goes to a museum and comes out feeling that one has beheld an odd assortment of nude bodies, copper kettles, oranges, tomatoes, and zinnias, babies, street corners, apple trees, bathing-beaches, bankers, and fashionable ladies. I do not say that this person or that may not find a picture immensely significant to him. But the general impression for anyone, I think, is of a chaos of anecdotes, perceptions, fantasies, and little commentaries, which may be all very well in their way, but are not sustaining and could readily be dispensed with.

The conclusive answer to the romantic theory of the artist as prophet is a visit to a collection of modern paintings.

(e) ART FOR ART'S SAKE

This brings us to the other theory, which is that art has nothing to do with prophecy, wisdom, and the meaning of life, but has to do only with art. This theory must command an altogether different kind of respect than the sentimental theory of the artist as prophet. This indeed is the theory which most artists now hold. "I am convinced," says Mr. R. H. Wilenski in his book *The Modern Movement in Art,* "that all the most intelligent artists of Western Europe in recent centuries have been tormented by this search for a justification of their work and a criterion of its value; and that almost all such artists have attempted to solve the problem by some consciously-held idea of art; or in other words that in place of art justified by service to a religion they have sought to evolve an art justified by service to an idea of art itself."

The instinct of artists in this matter is, I think, much sounder than the rationalizations which they have constructed. As working artists they do not think of themselves as seers, philosophers, or moralists. They do not wish to be judged as thinkers, but as painters, and they are justifiably impatient with the Philistines who are interested primarily in the subject matter and its human significance. The painter knows quite well that in the broadly human sense he has no special qualifications as story-teller or wise man. What he is driving at, therefore, in his expression of contempt for the subject matter of art is the wish that he might again be in the position of the mediaeval artist who did not have to concern himself *as artist* with the significance of his themes. The intuition behind the theory of art for art's sake is the artist's wish to be free of a responsibility which he has never before had put upon him. The peculiar circumstances of modernity have thrust upon him, much against his will and regardless of his aptitudes, the intolerably heavy burden of doing for himself what in other ages was done for him by tradition and authority.

The philosophy which he has invented is an attempt to prove that no philosophy is necessary. Carried to its conclusion, this theory eventuates in the belief that painting must become an arrangement of forms and colors which have no human connotation whatsoever for the artist or the spectator. These arrangements represent nothing in the real world. They signify nothing. They are an esthetic artifice in the same sense that the more esoteric geometries are logical artifices. This much can at least be said of them: they are a consistent effort to practice the arts in a world where there is no human tradition upon which the representative arts can draw.

This absolute estheticism is not, however, art without philosophy. Some sort of philosophy is implied in all human activity. The artist who says that it is delightful above all other things to realize the pure form of objects, regardless of whether this object is a saint, a lovely woman, or a dish of fruit, has made a very important statement about life. He has said that the ordinary meanings which men attach to objects are of no consequence, that their order of moral values is ultimately a delusion, that all facts are equally good and equally bad, and that to contemplate anything, it does not matter what, under the aspect of its esthetic form, is to realize all that the artist can give.

This, too, is a philosophy and a very radical philosophy at that. It is in fact just the philosophy which men were bound to construct for themselves in an age when the traditional theory of the purpose of life had lost its meaning for them. For they are saying that experience has no meaning beyond that which each man can find in the intense realization of each passing moment. He must fail, they would feel, if he attempts to connect these passing moments into a coherent story of his whole experience, let alone the whole experience of the human race. For experience has no underlying significance, man himself has no station in the universe, and the universe has no plan which is more than a drift of circumstances, illuminated here and there by flashes of self-consciousness.

### (f)  THE BURDEN OF ORIGINALITY

As a matter of fact this doctrine is merely the esthetic version of the rather crude mechanistic materialism which our grandfathers thought was the final conclusion of science. The connection is made evident in the famous Conclusions to The Renaissance which Walter Pater wrote in 1868, and then omitted from the second edition because "it might possibly mislead some of those young men into whose hands it might fall." In this essay there was the startling, though it is now hackneyed, assertion that "to burn always with this hard, gem-like flame, to maintain this ecstasy, is success in life," and that "of this wisdom, the poetic passion, the desire of beauty, the love of art for art's sake, has most; for art comes to you professing frankly to give nothing but the highest quality to your moments as they pass, and simply for those moments' sake." What is never quoted, and is apparently forgotten, is the reasoning by which Pater arrived at the conclusion that momentary ecstasy is the end and aim of life. It is, if we turn back a few pages, that scientific analysis has reduced everything to a mere swarm of whirling atoms, upon which consciousness discerns impressions that are "unstable, flickering, inconsistent." It was out of this misunderstanding of the nature of scientific concepts that Pater developed his theory of art for the moment's sake.

I dwell upon this only in order to show that what appeared to be an estheticism divorced from all human concern was really a somewhat casual by-product of a fashionable misunderstanding at the time Pater was writing. We should find that to-day equally far-reaching conclusions are arrived at by half-understood popularizations of Bergson or Freud. I venture to believe that any theory of art is inevitably implicated in some philosophy of life, and that the only question is whether the artist is conscious or unconscious of the theory he is acting upon. For unless the artist deals with purely logical essences, provided he observes and perceives anything in the outer world, no matter how he represents it or symbolizes it or comments upon it, there must be implicit in it some attitude toward the meaning of existence. If his conclusion is that human ex-

istence has no meaning, that, too, is an attitude toward
the meaning of existence. The mediaeval artist worked on
much less tangled premises. He painted pictures which illustrated the great hopes and fears of Christendom. But
he did not himself attempt to formulate those hopes and
fears. He accepted them more or less ready-made, understanding them and believing in them because, as a child
of his age, they were his hopes and fears. But because they
existed and were there for him to work upon, he could put
his whole energy into realizing them passionately. The modern artist would like to have the same freedom from preoccupation, but he cannot have it. He has first to decide
what it is that he shall passionately realize.

In effect the mediaeval artist was reproducing a story
that had often been told before. But the modern artist has
to undergo a whole preliminary labor of inventing, creating, formulating, for which there was almost no counterpart
in the life of a mediaeval artist. The modern artist has to
be original. That is to say, he has to seize experience, pick
it over, and drag from it his theme. It is a very exhausting
task, as anyone can testify who has tried it.

That surely is why we hear so much of the storm and
stress in the soul of a modern artist. The craftsman does
not go through agonies over the choice of words, images,
and rhythms. The agony of the modern artist lies in the
effort to give birth to the idea, to bring some intuition of
order out of the chaos of experience, to create the idea with
which his art can deal. We assume, quite falsely I think,
that this act of 'creation' is an inherent part of the artist's
task. But if we refrain from using words loosely, and reserve
the word creation to mean the finding of the original intuition and idea, then creation is plainly not a necessary part
of the artist's equipment. Creation is an obligation which

the artist has had thrust upon him as a result of the dissolution of the great accepted themes. He is compelled to be creative because his world is chaotic.

This labor of creation has no connection with his gifts as a painter. There is no more reason why a painter should be able to extemporize a satisfactory interpretation of life than that he should be able to govern a city or write a treatise on chemistry. Giotto surely was as profoundly original a painter as the world is likely to see; it has been said of him by Mr. Berenson, who has full title to speak, that he had "a thoroughgoing sense for the significant in the visible world." But with all his genius, what would have been Giotto's plight if, in addition to exercising his sense of the significant, he had had to create for himself all his standards of significance? For Giotto those standards existed in the Catholic Christianity of the Thirteenth Century, and it was by the measure of these standards, within the framework of a great accepted tradition, that he followed his own personal sense of the significant. But the modern artist, though he had Giotto's gifts, would not have Giotto's freedom to use them. A very large part of his energies, consciously or unconsciously, would have to be spent in devising some sort of substitute for the traditional view of life which Giotto took for granted. For there is no longer an accepted view of life organized in stories which all men know and understand.

There is instead a profusion of creeds and philosophies, fads and intellectual experiments among which the modern painter, like every other modern man, finds himself trying to choose a philosophy of life. Everybody is somewhat dithered by these choices: the business of being a Shavian one year, a Nietzschean the next, a Bergsonian the third, then of being a patriot for the duration of the war, and after that a Freudian, is not conducive to the serene exercise of a painter's talents. For these various philosophies which the artist picks up here and there, or by which he is oftener than not picked up and carried along, are immensely in dispute. They are not clear. They are rather personal and somewhat accidental visions of the world. They are essentially unpictorial because they originate in science and are incomplete, abstracted reachings for the meaning of things. As a result the art in which they are implicit is often uninteresting, and usually unintelligible, to those who do not happen to belong to the same cult.

The painter can hardly expect to invent for himself a view of life which will bring order out of the chaos of modernity. Yet he is compelled to try, for he is engaged in setting down a vision of the world, and every vision of the world implies some sort of philosophy. The effects of the modern emancipation are more clearly evident in the history of painting during the last hundred years than in almost any other activity, because in the galleries hang in frames the successive attempts of men, who are deeply immersed in the modern scene, to set down their statements about life. Mr. Wilenski, who is an astute and well-informed critic, has estimated that during the last hundred years in Paris a new movement in painting has been inaugurated every ten years. That would correspond fairly accurately to the birth and death of new philosophies in the advanced and most emancipated circles.

What was happening to painting is precisely what has happened to all the other separated activities of men. Each activity has its own ideal, indeed a succession of ideals, for with the dissolution of the supreme ideal of service to God, there is no ideal which unites them all, and sets them in order. Each ideal is supreme within a sphere of its own.

There is no point of reference outside which can determine the relative value of competing ideals. The modern man desires health, he desires money, he desires power, beauty, love, truth, but which he shall desire the most since he cannot pursue them all to their logical conclusions, he no longer has any means of deciding. His impulses are no longer parts of one attitude toward life; his ideals are no longer in a hierarchy under one lordly ideal. They have become differentiated. They are free and they are incommensurable.

The religious synthesis has dissolved. The modern man no longer holds a belief about the universe which sustains a pervasive emotion about his destiny; he no longer believes genuinely in any idea which organizes his interests within the framework of a cosmic order.

# VII The Drama of Destiny

## 1. THE SOUL IN THE MODERN WORLD

The effect of modernity, then, is to specialize and thus to intensify our separated activities. Once all things were phases of a single destiny: the church, the state, the family, the school were means to the same end; the rights and duties of the individual in society, the rules of morality, the themes of art, and the teachings of science were all of them ways of revealing, of celebrating, of applying the laws laid down in the divine constitution of the universe. In the modern world institutions are more or less independent, each serving its own proximate purpose, and our culture is really a collection of separate interests each sovereign within its own realm. We do not put shrines in our workshops, and we think it unseemly to talk business in the vestibule of a church. We dislike politics in the pulpit and preaching from politicians. We do not look upon our scholars as priests or upon our priests as learned men. We do not expect science to sustain theology, nor religion to dominate art. On the contrary we insist with much fervor on the separation of church and state, of religion and science, of politics and historical research, of morality and art, of business and love.

This separation of activities has its counterpart in a separation of selves; the life of a modern man is not so much the history of a single soul; it is rather a play of many characters within a single body.

That may be why the modern autobiographical novel usually runs to two volumes; the author requires more space to explain how his various personalities came to be what they were at each little crisis of adolescence and of middle age than St. Augustine, St. Thomas à Kempis, and St. Francis put together needed in order to describe their whole destiny in this world and the next. No doubt we are rather long-winded and tiresome about the complexities of our souls. But from the knowledge that we are complex there is no escape.

The modern man is unable any longer to think of himself as a single personality approaching an everlasting judgment. He is one man to-day and another to-morrow, one person here and another there. He does not feel he knows himself. He is sure that no one else knows him at all. His motives are intricate, and not wholly what they seem. He is moved by impulses which he feels but cannot describe. There are dark depths in his nature which no one has ever explored. There are splendors which are unreleased. He has become greatly interested in his moods. The precise nuances of his likes and dislikes have become very important. There is no telling just what he is or what he may become, but there is a certain breathless interest in having one of his selves watch and comment upon the mischief and the frustrations of his other selves. The problems of his character have become dissociated from any feeling that they involve his immortal destiny. They have become dissociated from the feeling that they deeply matter. From the feeling that they are deeply his own. From the feeling that there is any personality to own them. There they are: his inferiority complex and mine, your sadistic impulse and Tom Jones's, Anna's father fixation, and little Willie's pyromania.

The thoroughly modern man has really ceased to believe that there is an immortal essence presiding like a king over his appetites. The word 'soul' has become a figure of speech, which he uses loosely, sometimes to mean his tenderer aspirations, sometimes to mean the whole collection of his impulses, sometimes, when he is in a hurry, to mean nothing at all. It is certainly not the fashion any longer to think of the soul as a little lord ruling the turbulent rabble of his carnal passions; the constitutional form in popular psychology to-day is republican. Each impulse may invoke the Bill of Rights, and have its way if the others will let it. As Bertrand Russell has put it: "A single desire is no better and no worse, considered in isolation, than any other; but a group of desires is better than another group if all of the first group can be satisfied, while in the second group some are inconsistent with others," but since, unhappily as is usually the case, desires are extremely inconsistent, the uttermost that the modern man can say is that the victory must go to the strongest desires. Morality thus becomes a traffic code designed to keep as many desires as possible moving together without too many violent collisions. When men insist that morality is more than that, they are quickly denounced, in general correctly, as Meddlesome Matties, as enemies of human liberty, or as schemers trying to get the better of their fellow men. Morality, conceived as a discipline to fit men for heaven, is resented; morality, conceived as a discipline for happiness, is understood by very few. The objective moral certitudes have dissolved, and in the liberal philosophy there is nothing to take their place.

## 2. THE GREAT SCENARIO

The modern world is like a stage on which a stupendous play has just been presented. Many who were in the audience are still spellbound, and as they pass out into the street, the scenario of the drama still seems to them the very clue and plan of life. In the prologue the earth was without form and void, and darkness was upon the face of the deep. Then at the command of God the sun, the moon, the stars, the earth, its plants and its animals, then man, and after him woman, were created. And in the epilogue the blessed were living in the New Jerusalem, a city of pure gold like clear glass, with walls laid on foundations of precious stones. Between the darkness that preceded creation and the glory of this heavenly city which had no need of the sun, a plot was unfolded which constitutes the history of mankind. In the beginning man was perfect. But the devil tempted him to eat the forbidden fruit, and as a punishment God banished him from paradise, and laid upon him and his descendants the curse of labor and of death.

But in meting out this punishment, God in his mercy promised ultimately to redeem the children of Adam. From among them he chose one tribe who were to be the custodians of this promise. And then in due time he sent his Son, born of a Virgin, to teach the gospel of salvation, and to expiate the sin of Adam upon a cross. Those who believed in this gospel and followed its commandments, would at the final day of reckoning enter into the heavenly Jerusalem; the rest would be consigned to the devil and his everlasting torments.

Into this marvelous story the whole of human history and of human knowledge could be fitted, and only in accordance with it could they be understood. This was the key to existence, the answer to doubt, the solace for pain, and the guarantee of happiness. But to many who were in the audience it is now evident that they have seen a play, a magnificent play, one of the most sublime ever created by the human imagination, but nevertheless a play, and not a literal account of human destiny. They know it was a play. They have lingered long enough to see the scene-shifters at work. The painted drop is half rolled up; some of the turrets of the celestial city can still be seen, and part of the choir of angels. But behind them, plainly visible, are the struts and gears which held in place what under a gentler light looked like the boundaries of the universe. They are only human fears and human hopes, and bits of antique science and half-forgotten history, and symbols here and there of experiences through which some in each generation pass.

Conceivably men might once again imagine another drama which was as great as the epic of the Christian Bible. But like *Paradise Lost* or *Faust,* it would remain a work of the imagination. While the intellectual climate in which we live is what it is, while we continue to be as conscious as we are of how our own minds work, we could not again accept naively such a gorgeous fable of our destiny. Yet only five hundred years ago the whole of Christendom believed that this story was literally and objectively true. God was not another name for the evolutionary process, or for the sum total of the laws of nature, or for a compendium of all noble things, as he is in modernist accounts of him; he was the ruler of the universe, an omnipotent, magical King, who felt, who thought, who remembered and issued his commands. And because there was such a God, whose plan was clearly revealed in all its essentials, human life had a definite meaning, morality had a certain foundation, men felt themselves to be living within the framework of a universe which they called divine because it corresponded with their deepest desires.

If we ask ourselves why it is impossible for us to sum up the meaning of existence in a great personal drama, we have to begin by remembering that every great story of this kind must assume that the universe is governed by forces which are essentially of the same order as the promptings of the human heart. Otherwise it would not greatly interest us. A story, however plausible, about beings who had no human qualities, a plot which unfolded itself as utterly indifferent to our own personal fate, would not serve as a substitute for the Christian epic. This is the trouble with the so-called religion of creative evolution: even if it is true, which is far from certain, it is so profoundly indifferent to our individual fate, that it leaves most men cold. For there are very few who are so mystical as to be able to sink themselves wholly in the hidden purposes of an unconscious natural force. This, too, as the Catholic Church has always insisted, is the trouble with pantheistic religion, for if everything is divine, then nothing is peculiarly divine, and all the distinctions of good and evil are meaningless.

The story must not only assume that human ideals inspire the whole creation, but it must contain guarantees that this is so. There must be no doubt about it. Science must confirm the moral assumptions; the highest and most certain available knowledge must clinch the conviction that the story unfolded is the secret of life.

## 3. EARMARKS OF TRUTH

Religious teachers who were close to the people have always understood that they must perform wonders if they were to make their God convincing and their own title to speak for him valid. The writer of Exodus, for example, was quite clear in his mind about this:

> And Moses answered and said, But, behold, they will not believe me, nor hearken unto my voice: for they will say, The Lord hath not appeared unto thee.
>
> And the Lord said unto him, What is that in thine hand? And he said, A rod.
>
> And he said, Cast it on the ground. And he cast it on the ground, and it became a serpent; and Moses fled from before it.
>
> And the Lord said unto Moses, Put forth thine hand, and take it by the tail. And he put forth his hand, and caught it, and it became a rod in his hand:
>
> That they may believe that the Lord God of their fathers, the God of Abraham, the God of Isaac, and the God of Jacob, hath appeared unto thee.

Even in the wildest flights of his fancy the common man is almost always primarily interested in the prosaic consequences. If he believes in fairies he is not likely to imagine them as spirits inhabiting a world apart, but as little people who do things which affect his own affairs. The common man is an unconscious pragmatist: he believes because he is satisfied that his beliefs change the course of events. He would not be inspired to worship a god who merely contemplates the universe, or a god who created it once, and then rested, while its destiny unfolds itself inexorably. To the plain people religion is not disinterested speculation but a very practical matter. It is concerned with their well-being in this world and in an equally concrete world hereafter. They have wanted to know the will of God because they had to know it if they were to put themselves right with the king of creation.

Those who professed to know God's will had to demonstrate that they knew it. This was the function of miracles. They were tangible evidence that the religious teacher had a true commission. "Then those men, when they had seen the miracle (of the loaves and the fishes) that Jesus did, said, This is of a truth that prophet that should come into the world." When Jesus raised the dead man at the gate of the city of Nain, "there came a fear on all: and they glorified God, saying, That a great prophet is risen up among us; and, That God hath visited his people." The most authoritative Catholic theologians teach that miracles "are not wrought to show the internal truth of the doctrines, but only to give *manifest* reasons why we should accept the doctrines." They are "essentially an appeal to knowledge," demonstrations, one might almost say divine experiments, by which men are enabled to know the glory and the providence of God.

The Catholic apologists maintain that God can be known by the exercise of reason, but the miracle helps, as it were, to clinch the conviction. The persistent attachment of the Catholic Church to miracles is significant. It has a longer unbroken experience with human nature than any other institution in the western world. It has adapted itself to many circumstances, and under the profession of an unalterable creed it has abandoned and then added much. But it has never ceased to insist upon the need of a physical manifestation of the divine power. For with an unerring instinct for realities, Catholic churchmen have understood that there is a residuum of prosaic matter-of-factness, of a need to touch and to see, which verbal proofs can never quite satisfy. They have resolutely responded to that need.

They have not preached God merely by praising him; they have brought God near to men by revealing him to the senses, as one who is great enough and good enough and sufficiently interested in them to heal the sick and to make the floods recede.

But to-day scientists are ever so much superior to churchmen at this kind of demonstration. The miracles which are recounted from the pulpit were, after all, few and far between. There are even theologians who teach that miracles ceased with the death of the Apostles. But the miracles of science seem to be inexhaustible. It is not surprising, then, that men of science should have acquired much of the intellectual authority which churchmen once exercised. Scientists do not, of course, speak of their discoveries as miracles. But to the common man they have much the same character as miracles. They are wonderful, they are inexplicable, they are manifestations of a great power over the forces of nature.

It cannot be said, I think, that the people at large, even the moderately educated minority, understand the difference between scientific method and revelation, or that they have decided upon reflection to trust science. There is at least as much mystery in science for the common man as there ever was in religion; in a sense there is more mystery, for the logic of science is still altogether beyond his understanding, whereas the logic of revelation is the logic of his own feelings. But if men at large do not understand the method of science, they can appreciate some of its more tangible results. And these results are so impressive that scientific men are often embarrassed by the unbounded popular expectations which they have so unintentionally aroused.

Their authority in the realm of knowledge has become virtually irresistible. And so when scientists teach one theory and the Bible another, the scientists invariably carry the greater conviction.

## 4. ON RECONCILING RELIGION AND SCIENCE

The conflicts between scientists and churchmen are sometimes ascribed to a misunderstanding on both sides. But when we examine the proposals for peace, it is plain, I think, that they are in effect proposals for a truce. There is, for example, the suggestion first put out, I believe, in the Seventeenth Century that God made the universe like a clock, and that having started it running he will let it alone till it runs down. By this ingenious metaphor, which can be neither proved nor disproved, it was possible to reconcile for a time the scientific notion of natural law with the older notion of God as creator and as judge. The religious conception was held to be true for the beginning of the world and for the end, the scientific conception was true in between. Later, when the theatre of the difficulty was transferred from physics and astronomy to biology and history, a variation was propounded. God, it was said, created the world and governs it; the way he creates and governs is the way described by scientists as 'evolution.'

Attempts at reconciliations like these are based on a theory that it is feasible somewhere in the field of knowledge to draw a line and say that on one side the methods of science shall prevail, on the other the methods of traditional religion. It is acknowledged that where experiment and observation are possible, the field belongs to the scientists; but it is argued that there is a vast field of great interest to mankind which is beyond the reach of practical scientific inquiry, and that here, touching questions like the ultimate destiny of man, the purpose of life, and immortality, the older method of revelation, inspired and verified by intuition, is still reliable.

In any truce of this sort there is bound to be aggression from both sides. For it is a working policy rather than an inwardly accepted conviction. Scientists cannot really believe that there are fields of possible knowledge which they can never enter. They are bound to enter all fields and to explore everything. And even if they fail, they cannot believe that other scientists must always fail. Their essays, moreover, create disturbance and doubt which orthodox churchmen are forced to resent. For in any division of authority, there must be some ultimate authority to settle questions of jurisdiction. Shall scientists determine what belongs to science, or shall churchmen? The question is insoluble as long as both claim that they have the right to expound the nature of existence.

And so while the policy of toleration may be temporarily workable, it is inherently unstable. Therefore, among men who are at once devoted to the method of science and sensitive to the human need of religion, the hope has arisen that something better can be worked out than a purely diplomatic division of the mind into spheres of influence. Mr. Whitehead, for example, in his book called *Science and the Modern World,* argues "there are wider truths and finer perspectives within which a reconciliation of a deeper religion and a more subtle science will be found." He illustrates what he means in this fashion. Galileo said the earth moves and the sun is fixed; the Inquisition said the earth is fixed and the sun moves; the Newtonian astronomers said that both the sun and the earth move. "But now we say that any one of these three statements is equally true, provided you have fixed your sense of 'rest' and 'mo-

tion' in the way required by the statement adopted. At the
date of Galileo's controversy with the Inquisition, Galileo's
way of stating the facts was beyond question the fruitful
procedure for the sake of scientific research. But at that
time the concepts of relative motion were in nobody's
mind; so that the statements were made in ignorance of
the qualifications required for the more perfect truth. . . .
All sides had got hold of important truths. . . . But with
the knowledge of those times, the truths appeared to be
inconsistent."

This is reconciliation through a higher synthesis. But
I cannot help feeling that the scientist has here produced
the synthesis, and that the churchmen have merely provided one of the ideas which are to be synthesized. Mr.
Whitehead argues in effect that a subtler science would confirm many ideas that were once taken on faith. But he holds
unswervingly to the belief of the scientist that his method
contains the criterion of truth. In his illustration the reconciliation between Galileo, the Inquisition, and the Newtonian physicists is reached if all three parties accept "the
modern concept of relative motion." But the modern concept of relative motion was reached by scientific thought,
and not by apostolic revelation. To Mr. Whitehead, therefore, the ultimate arbiter is science, and what he means by
reconciliation is a scientific view of the universe sufficiently
wide and sufficiently subtle to justify many of the important, but hitherto unverified, claims of traditional religion.
Mr. Whitehead, it happens, is an Englishman as well as a
great logician, and it is difficult to resist the suspicion that
he conceives the church of the future as enjoying the digni-
ties of an Indian Maharajah, with a resident scientist behind the altar.

A reconciliation of this kind may soften the conflict for

a while. But it cannot for long disguise the fact that it is based on a denial of the premises of faith. If the method of science has the last word, then revelation is reduced from a means of arriving at absolute certainty to a flash of insight which can be trusted if and when it is verified by science. Under such terms of peace, the religious experiences of mankind become merely one of the instruments of knowledge, like the microscope and the binomial theorem, usable now and then, but subject to correction, and provisional. They no longer yield complete, ultimate, invincible truths. They yield an hypothesis. But the religious life of most men has not, until this day at least, been founded upon hypotheses which, when accurately stated, included a coefficient of probable error.

## 5. GOSPELS OF SCIENCE

Because its prestige is so great, science has been acclaimed as a new revelation. Cults have attached themselves to scientific hypotheses as fortune-tellers to a circus. A whole series of pseudo-religions have been hastily constructed upon such dogmas as the laws of nature, mechanism, Darwinian evolution, Lamarckian evolution, and psychoanalysis. Each of these cults has had its own Decalogue of Science founded at last, it was said, upon certain knowledge.

These cults are an attempt to fit the working theories of science to the ordinary man's desire for personal salvation. They do violence to the integrity of scientific thought and they cannot satisfy the layman's need to believe. For the essence of the scientific method is a determination to investigate phenomena without conceding anything to naive human prejudices. Therefore, genuine men of science shrink from the attempts of poets, prophets, and popular lecturers to translate the current scientific theory into the broad and passionate dogmas of popular faith. As a matter of common honesty they know that no theory has the kind of absolute verity which popular faith would attribute to it. As a matter of prudence they fear these popular cults, knowing quite well that freedom of inquiry is endangered when men become passionately loyal to an idea, and stake their personal pride and hope of happiness upon its vindication. In the light of human experience, men of science have learned what happens when investigators are not free to discard any theory without breaking some dear old lady's heart. Their theories are not the kind of revelation which the old lady is seeking, and their beliefs are relative and provisional to a degree which must seem utterly alien and bewildering to her.

Here, for example, is the conclusion of some lectures by one of the greatest living astronomers. I have italicized the words which the dear old lady would not be likely to hear in a sermon:

> I have dealt mainly with two salient points—the problem of the source of a star's energy, and the change of mass which must occur if there is any evolution of faint stars from bright stars. I have shown how these *appear* to meet in the *hypothesis* of the annihilation of matter. I *do not hold this as a secure conclusion.* I *hesitate even to advocate it as probable,* because there are many details which seem to me to throw *considerable doubt* on it, and I have formed a strong impression that there must be *some essential point which has not yet been grasped.* I *simply* tell it you as the *clue* which at the moment we are *trying* to follow

up—*not knowing whether it is false scent or true.* I should have liked to have closed these lectures by leading up to some great climax. But perhaps it is more in accordance with the true conditions of scientific progress that they should *fizzle out* with a glimpse of the *obscurity* which marks the frontiers of present knowledge. I do not apologize for the *lameness* of the conclusion, *for it is not a conclusion. I wish I could feel confident that it is even a beginning.*

This great climax, to which Dr. Eddington was unable to lead up, is what the layman is looking for. We know quite well what the nature of that great climax would be: it would be a statement of fact which related the destiny of each individual to the destiny of the universe. That is the kind of truth which is found in revelation. It is the kind of truth which men would like to find in science. But is the kind of truth which science does not afford. The difficulty is deeper than the provisional character of scientific hypothesis; it is not due merely to the inability of the scientist to say that his conclusion is absolutely secure. The layman in search of a dogma upon which to organize his destiny might be willing to grant that the conclusions of science to-day are as yet provisional. What he tends to misunderstand is that even if the conclusions were guaranteed by all investigators now and for all time to come, those conclusions would still fail to provide him with a conception of the world of which the great climax was a prophecy of the fate of creation in terms of his hopes and fears.

The radical novelty of modern science lies precisely in the rejection of the belief, which is at the heart of all popular religion, that the forces which move the stars and atoms are contingent upon the preferences of the human heart. The science of Aristotle and of the Schoolmen, on the other hand, was a truly popular science. It was in its inspiration the instinctive science of the unscientific man. "They read into the cause and goal of the universe," as Dr. Randall has said, "that which alone justifies it for man, its service of the good." They provided a conception of the universe which was available for the religious needs of ordinary men, and in the *Divine Comedy* we can see the supreme example of what science must be like if it is to satisfy the human need to believe. The purpose of the whole poem, said Dante himself, "is to remove those who are living in this life from the state of wretchedness, and to lead them to the state of blessedness." Mediaeval science, which follows the logic of human desire, was such that Dante could without violence either to its substance or its spirit say at the summit of Paradise:

> To the high fantasy here power failed; but already my desire and will were rolled—even as a wheel that moveth equally—by the Love that moves the sun and the other stars.

This is the great climax which men instinctively expect: the ability to say with perfect assurance that when the truth is fully evident it will be seen that their desire and will are rolled by the love that moves the sun and the other stars. They hope not only to find the will of God in the universe but to know that his will is fundamentally like their own. Only if they could believe that on the basis of scientific investigation would they really feel that science had 'explained' the world.

Explanation, in this sense, cannot come from modern

science because it is not in this sense that modern science attempts to explain the universe. It is wholly misleading to say, for example, that the scientific picture of the world is mechanical. All that can properly be said is that many scientists have found it satisfying to think about the universe as if it were built on a mechanical model. "If I can make a mechanical model," said Lord Kelvin, "I can understand it. As long as I cannot make a mechanical model all the way through, I cannot understand it." But what does the scientist mean by "understanding it"? He means, says Professor Bridgman, that he has "reduced a situation to elements with which we are so familiar that we accept them as a matter of course, so that our curiosity rests." Modern men are familiar with machines. They can take them apart and put them together, so that even though we should all be a little flustered if we had to tell just what we mean by a machine, our curiosity tends to be satisfied if we hear that the phenomenon, say, of electricity or of human behavior, is like a machine.

The place at which curiosity rests is not a fixed point called 'the truth.' The unscientific man, like the Schoolmen of the Middle Ages, really means by the truth an explanation of the universe in terms of human desire. What modern science means by the truth has been stated most clearly perhaps by the late Charles S. Peirce when he said that "the opinion which is fated to be ultimately agreed to by all those who investigate, is what we mean by the truth, and the object represented in this opinion is the real." When we say that something has been 'explained' by science, we really mean only that our own curiosity is satisfied. Another man, whose mind was more critical, who commanded a greater field of experience, might not be satisfied at all. Thus "the savage is satisfied by explaining

the thunderstorm as the capricious act of an angry God.
. . . (But) even if the physicist believed in the existence of
the angry god, he would not be satisfied with this explanation of the thunderstorm because he is not so well ac-
quainted with angry gods as to be able to predict when
anger is followed by a storm. He would have to know why
the god had become angry, and why making a thunderstorm eased his ire.'' But even carrying the explanation to
this point would not be carrying it to its limit. For there is
no formal limit. The next scientist might wish to know
what a god was and what anger is. And when he had been
told what their elements are, the next man might be dis-
satisfied until he had found the elements of these elements.

The man who says that the world is a machine has
really advanced no further than to say that he is so well
satisfied with this analogy that he is through with searching any further. That is his business, as long as he does not
insist that he has reached a clear and ultimate picture of
the universe. For obviously he has not. A machine is something in which the parts push and pull each other. But why
are they pushing and pulling, and how do *they* work? Do
they push and pull because of the action of the electrons in
their orbits within the atoms? If that is true, then how does
an electron work? Is it, too, a machine? Or is it something
quite different from a machine? Shall we attempt to explain
machines electrically, or shall we attempt to explain electricity mechanically?

It becomes plain, therefore, that scientific explanation
is altogether unlike the explanations to which the common
man is accustomed. It does not yield a certain picture of
anything which can be taken naively as a representation of
reality. And therefore the philosophies which have grown
up about science, like mechanism or creative evolution, are

in no way guaranteed by science as the account of creation in Genesis is guaranteed by the authority of Scripture. They are nothing but provisional dramatizations which are soon dissolved by the progress of science itself.

That is why nothing is so dead as the scientific religion of yesterday. It is far more completely dead than any revealed religion, because the revealed religion, whatever may be the defects of its cosmology or its history, has some human experience at its core which we can recognize and to which we may respond. But a religion like scientific materialism has nothing in it, except the pretension that it is a true account of the world. Once that pretension is exploded, it is wholly valueless as a religion. It has become a collection of discarded concepts.

## 6. THE DEEPER CONFLICT

It follows from the very nature of scientific explanation, then, that it cannot give men such a clue to a plan of existence as they find in popular religion. For that plan must suppose that existence is explained in terms of human destiny. Now conceivably existence might again be explained, as it was in the Middle Ages, as the drama of human destiny. It does not seem probable to us; yet we cannot say that it is impossible. But even if science worked out such an explanation, it would still be radically different from the explanations which popular religion employs.

For if it were honestly stated, it would be necessary to say first, that it is tentative, and subject to disproof by further experiment; second, that it is relative, in that the same facts seen from some other point and with some other purpose in mind could be explained quite differently; third, that it is not a picture of the world, as God would see it, and as all men must see it, but that it is simply one among many possible creations of the mind into which most of the data of experience can be fitted. When the scientist had finished setting down his qualifications, the essence of the matter as a simple, devout man sees it, would have evaporated. Certainty, as the devout desire it, would be gone; verity, as they understand it, would be gone; objectivity, as they imagine it, would be gone. What would remain would be a highly abstracted, logical fiction, suited to disinterested inquiry, but utterly unsuited to be the vehicle of his salvation.

The difficulty of reconciling popular religion with science is far deeper than that of reconciling Genesis with Darwin, or any statement of fact in the Bible with any discovery by scientists. It is the difficulty of reconciling the human desire for a certain kind of universe with a method of explaining the world which is absolutely neutral in its intention. One can by twisting language sufficiently 'reconcile' Genesis with 'evolution.' But what no one can do is to guarantee that science will not destroy the doctrine of evolution the day after it has been triumphantly proved that Genesis is compatible with the theory of evolution. As a matter of fact, just that has happened. The Darwinian theory, which theologians are busily accepting, is so greatly modified already by science that some of it is almost as obsolete as the Babylonian myth in Genesis. The reconciliation which theologians are attempting is an impossible one, because one of the factors which has to be reconciled— namely, the scientific theory, changes so rapidly that the layman is never sure at any one moment what the theory is which he has to reconcile with religious dogma.

Yet the purpose of these attempts at reconciliation is

evident enough. It is to find a solid foundation for human ideals in the facts of existence. Authority based on revelation once provided that foundation. It gave an account of how the world began, of how it is governed, and of how it will end, which made pain and joy, hope and fear, desire and the denial of desire the central motives in the cosmic drama. This account no longer satisfies our curiosity as to the nature of things; the authority which certifies it no longer commands our complete allegiance. The prestige, which once adhered to those who spoke by revelation, has passed to scientists. But science, though it is the most reliable method of knowledge we now possess, does not provide an account of the world in which human destiny is the central theme. Therefore, science, though it has displaced revelation, is not a substitute for it. It yields a radically different kind of knowledge. It explains the facts. But it does not pretend to justify the ways of God to man. It enables us to realize some of our hopes. But it offers no guarantees that they can be fulfilled.

## 7. THEOCRACY AND HUMANISM

There is a revolution here in the realm of the spirit. We may describe it briefly by saying that whereas men once felt they were living under the eye of an all-powerful spectator, to-day they are watched only by their neighbors and their own consciences. A few, perhaps, act as if posterity were aware of them; the great number feel themselves accountable only to their own consciences or to the opinion of the society in which they live. Once men believed that they would be judged at the throne of God. They believed that he saw not only their deeds but their motives; there was no hole deep enough into which a man could crawl to hide himself from the sight of God; there was no mood, however fleeting, which escaped his notice.

The moral problem for each man, therefore, was to make his will conform to the will of God. There were differ- ences of opinion as to how this could be done. There were differing conceptions of the nature of God, and of what he most desired. But there was no difference of opinion on the main point that it was imperative to obey him. Whether they thought they could serve God best by burnt offerings or a contrite heart, by slaying the infidel or by loving their neighbors, by vows of poverty or by the magnificence of their altars, they never doubted that the chief duty of man, and his ultimate chance of happiness, was to discover and then to cultivate a right relationship to a supreme being.

This was the major premise upon which all human choices hinged. There followed from it certain necessary conclusions. In determining what was a right relationship to God, the test of rightness lay in a revelation of the puta- tive experience of God and not in the actual experience of His creatures. It was God alone, therefore, who really un- derstood the reasons for righteousness and its nature. "The procedure of Divine Justice," said Calvin, "is too high to be scanned by human measure or comprehended by the feebleness of human intellect." That was good which man understood was good in the eyes of God, regardless of how it seemed to men.

Thus the distinction between good and evil, including not only all rules of personal conduct but the whole arrange- ment of rights and duties in society, were laws established not by the consent of the governed, but by a king in heaven. They were his commandments. By obedience men could obtain happiness. But they obtained it not because virtue is the cause of happiness but because God rewarded with happiness those who obeyed his commandments. Men did not really know why God preferred certain kinds of conduct; they merely professed to know what kind of conduct he preferred. They could not really ask themselves what the difference was between good and evil. That was a secret locked in the nature of a being whose choices were ultimately inscrutable. The only question was what he willed. Even Job had to be content without fathoming his reasons.

The moral commandments based upon divine authority were, in the nature of things, rather broad generalizations. Obviously there could not be special revelation as to the unique aspects of each human difficulty. The divine law, like our ordinary human law, was addressed to typical rather than to individual cases. Nevertheless, for much the greater part of recorded history men have accepted such law without questioning its validity. They could not have done so if the rules of morality had not, at least in some rough way, worked. It is not difficult to see why they worked. They were broad rules of conduct imposed upon people living close to the soil, upon people, therefore, whose ways of living changed little in the course of generations. The same situations were so nearly and so often repeated that a typical solution would on the whole be satisfactory.

These typical solutions, such as we find in the Mosaic law or the code of Hammurabi, were no doubt the deposits of custom. They had, therefore, become perfected in practice, and were solidly based upon human experience. In the society in which they originated, there was nothing arbitrary or alien about them. When, therefore, the lawgiver carried these immemorial usages up with him on to Sinai, and brought them down again graven on tablets of stone, the rationality of the revelation was self-evident. It appeared to be arbitrary only when a radical change in the way of life dissolved the premises and the usages upon which the authoritative code was established.

That dissolution has proceeded to great lengths within the centuries which we call modern. The crisis was reached, it seems, during the Eighteenth Century, and in the teaching of Immanuel Kant it was made manifest to the educated classes of the western world. Kant argued in the *Critique of Pure Reason* that the existence of God cannot be demonstrated. He then insisted that without belief in God, freedom, and immortality, there was no valid and true morality. So he insisted that God must exist to justify morality. This highly sophisticated doctrine marks the end of simple theism in modern thought. For Kant's proof of the existence of God was nothing but a plea that God ought to exist, and the whole temper of the modern intellect is to deny that what ought to be true necessarily is true.

Insofar as men have now lost their belief in a heavenly king, they have to find some other ground for their moral choices than the revelation of his will. It follows necessarily that they must find the tests of righteousness wholly within human experience. The difference between good and evil must be a difference which men themselves recognize and understand. Happiness cannot be the reward of virtue; it must be the intelligible consequence of it. It follows, too, that virtue cannot be commanded; it must be willed out of personal conviction and desire. Such a morality may properly be called humanism, for it is centered not in superhuman but in human nature. When men can no longer be theists, they must, if they are civilized, become humanists. They must live by the premise that whatever is righteous is inherently desirable because experience will demonstrate its desirability. They must live, therefore, in the belief that the duty of man is not to make his will conform to the will of God but to the surest knowledge of the conditions of human happiness.

It is evident that a morality of humanism presents far greater difficulties than a morality premised on theism. For one thing, it is put immediately to a much severer test. When Kant, for example, argued that theism was necessary to morality, his chief reason was that since the good man is often defeated on earth, he must be permitted to believe in a superhuman power which is "able to connect happiness and morality in exact harmony with each other." Humanism is not provided with such reserves of moral credit; it cannot claim all eternity in which its promises may be fulfilled. Unless its wisdom in any sphere of life is demonstrated within a reasonable time in actual experience, there is nothing to commend it.

A morality of humanism labors under even greater difficulties. It appears in a complex and changing society; it is an attitude toward life to which rational men necessarily turn whenever their circumstances have rendered a theistic view incredible. It is just because the simpler rules no longer work that the subtler choices of humanism present themselves. These choices have to be made under conditions, like those which prevail in modern urban societies, where the extreme complexity of rapidly changing human relations makes it very difficult to foresee all the consequences of any moral decision. The men who must make their decisions are skeptical by habit and unsettled amidst the novelties of their surroundings.

The teachers of a theistic morality, when the audience is devout, have only to fortify the impression that the rules of conduct are certified by God the invisible King. The ethical problem for the common man is to recognize the well-known credentials of his teachers. In practice he has merely to decide whether the priest, the prince, and the elders, are what they claim to be. When he has done that, there are no radical questions to be asked. But the teachers of humanism have no credentials. Their teaching is not certified. They have to prove their case by the test of mundane experience. They speak with no authority, which can be scrutinized once and for all, and then forever accepted. They can proclaim no rule of conduct with certainty, for they have no inherent personal authority and they cannot be altogether sure they are right. They cannot command. They cannot truly exhort. They can only inquire, infer, and persuade. They have only human insight to guide them and those to whom they speak must in the end themselves accept the full responsibility for the consequences of any advice they choose to accept.

Yet with all its difficulties, it is to a morality of humanism that men must turn when the ancient order of things dissolves. When they find that they no longer believe seriously and deeply that they are governed from heaven, there is anarchy in their souls until by conscious effort they find ways of governing themselves.

Part Two

# THE
# FOUNDATIONS
# OF
# HUMANISM

*The stone which the builders rejected,*
*The same is become the head of the corner.*

LUKE XX, 17.

# Introduction

The upshot of the discussion to this point is that modernity destroys the disposition to believe that behind the visible world of physical objects and human institutions there is a supernatural kingdom from which ultimately all laws, all judgments, all rewards, all punishments, and all compensations are derived. To those who believe that this kingdom exists the modern spirit is nothing less than treason to God.

The popular religion rests on the belief that the kingdom is an objective fact, as certain, as definite, and as real, in spite of its invisibility, as the British Empire; it holds that this faith is justified by overwhelming evidence supplied by revelation, unimpeachable testimony, and incontrovertible signs. To the modern spirit, on the other hand, the belief in this kingdom must necessarily seem a grandiose fiction projected by human needs and desires. The humanistic view is that the popular faith does not prove the existence of its objects, but only the presence of a desire that such objects should exist. The popular religion, in short, rests on a theory which, if true, is an extension of physics and of history; the humanistic view rests on human psychology and an interpretation of human experience.

It follows, then, that in exploring the modern problem it is necessary consciously and clearly to make a choice between these diametrically opposite points of view. The choice is fundamental and exclusive, and it determines all the conclusions which follow. For obviously to one who believes that the world is a theocracy, the problem is how to bring the strayed and rebellious masses of mankind back to their obedience, how to restore the lost provinces of God the invisible King. But to one who takes the humanistic view the problem is how mankind, deprived of the great fictions, is to come to terms with the needs which created those fictions.

In this book I take the humanistic view because, in the kind of world I happen to live in, I can do no other.

# VIII Golden
## Memories

It will be granted, I suppose, that there would be no need for certainty about the plan and government of the universe if, as a matter of course, all our desires were regularly fulfilled. In a world where no man desired what he could not have, there would be no need to regulate human conduct and therefore no need for morality. In a world where each man could have what he desired, there would be no need for consolation and for reassuring guarantees that justice, mercy, and love will ultimately prevail. In a world where there was perfect adjustment between human desires and their environment, there would be no problem of evil: we should not know the meaning of sin, sorrow, crime, fear, frustration, pain, and emptiness. We do not live in such a well-ordered world. But we can imagine it by making either of two assumptions: that we have ceased to desire anything which causes evil, or that omnipotence fulfills all our desires. The first of these assumptions leads to the Nirvana of the Buddhists, where all craving has ceased and there is perfect peace. The second leads to the heaven of all popular religions, to some paradise like that of Mohammed perhaps where, as Mr. Santayana says, men may "sit in well-watered gardens, clad in green silks, drinking delicious sherbets, and transfixed by the gazelle-like glance of some young girl, all innocence and fire."

Among educated men it has always been difficult to imagine a heaven of fulfilled desires. For since no two persons have exactly the same desires, one man's imagination of heaven may not suit another man's. In general, the attempts which have been made to picture the Christian heaven reflect the temperaments of highly contemplative spirits, and it is customary nowadays to say that this heaven would be a most uninteresting place. No doubt it would be to those who are not contemplative. But the objectors have missed the main point, which is that no one is supposed to pass through the pearly gates who is not suited to dwell in Paradise. That is what St. Peter is there for, to see that the unfit do not enter; the other places, Purgatory and the Inferno, are available to those spirits who could not be happy in Heaven. There are, by definition, no uncongenial spirits in Heaven. There were once, but Satan and his followers were thrown out headlong, and they now live in places which are suited to their temperaments. A devout man may quite properly, therefore, advise those who do not think they would enjoy Heaven to go to Hell.

The attempt to imagine a heaven is an attempt to conceive a world in which the disorders of human desire no longer exist. Now it is in their prayers that men have sought to come to terms with their disorders, and their prayers reveal most concretely how much the hunger for certainty and for help is a hunger for the fulfillment of desire. For prayer, says Father Wynne, is "the expression of our desires to God whether for ourselves or for others." In the higher reaches of religion "the expression is not intended to instruct or direct God what to do, but to appeal to His goodness for the things we need; and the appeal is necessary, not because He is ignorant of our needs or sentiments, but to give definite form to our desires, to concentrate our whole attention on what we have to recommend to Him, to help us appreciate our close personal relation with Him." But in order to know what to pray for, we need grace, that is to say, God Himself must teach us what to ask Him for. We can be sure that we should pray for salvation, but in particular we need guidance from God "to know the special means that will most help us in any particular need." But besides the spiritual objects of prayer "we are to ask also for temporal things, our daily bread and all that it implies, health, strength, and other worldly or temporal goods . . ."; we are to pray also for escape from evils, "the penalty of our sins, the dangers of temptation, and every manner of physical or spiritual affliction."

There has, however, always been a logical difficulty about offering petitions to an all-wise and all-powerful Providence. Thus in the *Dialogue of Dives and Pauper,* which was published in 1493, the question is put: "Why pray we to God with oure mouth sithe he knowyth alle oure thoughte, all our desire, al our wyl and what us nedeth?" To this question the only answer which was not evasive came from the mystics who led a life of contemplation. Prayer, they said, is not mere petition; it is communion with God. It is not because prayer gives a man what he wants, but because it "ones the soul to God," that it is rational and necessary. This, too, is the conception of prayer held by a liberal pastor like Dr. Fosdick who looks with scorn upon "clamorous petition to an anthropomorphic God" and says that "true prayer . . . is to assimilate

. . . (the) spirit which is God (that) . . . surrounds our lives." The same idea, stated in somewhat more precise language, is set down by Mr. Santayana when he says that "in rational prayer the soul may be said to accomplish three things important to its welfare: it withdraws within itself and defines its good, it accommodates itself to destiny, and it grows like the ideal which it conceives."

But, of course, this is not the way the common man through the ages has conceived prayer. In fact he must have prayed before he had any clear conception of what a prayer is or of whom it is addressed to. Thus we are told that in Arcadia the girls invoked Hera by the title of "Hera the Girl," the married women prayed to "Hera the Married One," and the widows prayed to "Hera the Widow." Sometimes the prayer is a spontaneous expression of sorrow or of delight, a lyrical cry which has no ulterior purpose and is addressed to no one. Sometimes prayer is a magical formula which compels the deity to listen and to obey. The subject is both complicated and obscure. But this much at least is clear: along with elements which can be described only as spontaneous and lyrical, with traces of magic, and at times with a purely disinterested desire to commune with God, simple people have looked upon prayer as "an instrument for applying God's illimitable power to daily life."

Popular discussion of prayer has often been extremely practical: "How can prayer be made most efficient? Is it by ordinary Masses or by other offices? Is it by the elaboration or the multiplication of services?" Lady Alice West who died in 1395 ordered 4400 Masses "in the most haste that it may be do, withynne xiiii nyght next after my deces." Thomas Walwayn who died in 1415 left orders for 10,000 Masses "with oute pompe whyche may not profyt myn soule." John Plot, however, wished his Masses said "with solempne seruise that ys for to sayn wyth Belle Ryngyng." There was debate as to whether prayers were most effective if said in Rome or in the Holy Land . . . by certain priests rather than by others . . . by the friars rather than by the priests . . . whether there were more potent prayers than the *Pater* . . . whether prayers should be addressed to the Father, the Son, or to St. Mary . . . whether St. Mary could be approached best through her mother, St. Anne. . . .

It is not necessary to dogmatize by saying that prayer is magic, or soliloquy, or communion, or petition for this and that, in order to see that it is the expression of a human need. The quality of the need varies. It may be anything from a desire for rain to a desire for friendship with unseen spirits, but always it illustrates the saying that "all men stand in need of God."

If we ask ourselves what we mean by 'need,' we must answer, I suppose, that the resources of our own natures and the power we are able to exercise over events are insufficient to satisfy the cravings of our natures. We must eat, but we cannot be sure that drought will not destroy the crops. We are beset by enemies, and we are not sure we can conquer them. We are threatened by earthquake, storm, and disease against which we cannot wholly protect ourselves. We become deeply attached to other persons. But they must die and we must die, and we cannot stay the doom. In brief, we find ourselves in a world in which our hopes are defeated.

Somehow we are so constituted that we demand the impossible. There is in us somewhere an intimation that we ought not to be defeated. But where did this intimation come from? How is it that we are not born satisfied with our mortality, content with our fate? Why is it that the normal fate of man seems to us abnormal? What is there in the back of our heads which keeps telling us that life as we find it is not what it ought to be?

The biologist might answer, I suppose, that this craving for a different kind of world is simply our own consciousness of that blind push of natural forces which create the variations on which natural selection works to produce the survival of the fittest. Nature, he might say, is wholly indifferent to the outcries of the individual; this vast process of which each of us is so insignificant a part keeps going because there is in all the parts a superabundant urging to go on. There is no human economy in it and no human order. Man, for example, has far more sexual desire than is needed for the rational propagation of the species. But there is no rational plan in nature. It works here, and everywhere, on the principle that by having too much there will surely be enough; the seeds which do not germinate, the seedlings which perish, the desires which are left over, are no concern of nature's. For nature has no concern. There is no concern except that which we ourselves feel, and that is a mere flicker on the stream of time, and will soon go out.

While there is no way of gainsaying that this explanation is true, it is true only if we look at life from the particular point of view which the biologist adopts. If, however, we look inwardly upon ourselves, instead of surveying our species from the outside, we find, I think, that this sense that the world ought not to be what it is seems to originate in a kind of dim memory that it once was what we feel it ought to be. Indeed, so vivid is this memory that for ages men took it to be an account of historical events; in absolute good faith they constituted for themselves the picture of a Golden Age which existed before evil came into the world. Hope was, therefore, a kind of memory; the ideal was to achieve something which had been lost. The memory of an age of innocence has haunted the whole of mankind. It has been a light behind their present experience which cast shadows upon it, and made it seem insubstantial and not inevitable. Before this life, there had been another which was happier. And so they reasoned that what once was possible must somehow be possible again. Having once known the good, it was unbelievable that evil should be final.

Even after criticism has dissolved the beautiful legends in which it was embodied, this memory of a Golden Age persists. It persists as an intimation of our own inward experience, and like an uneasy spirit it intrudes itself upon our most realistic efforts to accept the world as we find it. For it takes many shapes, which sometimes deceive us, appearing then not as the memory of a happiness we have lost, but as the anticipation of utopia to come.

It is an intimation that man is entitled to live in the land of heart's desire. It is a deep conviction that happiness is possible, and all inquiry into the foundations of morals turns ultimately upon whether man can achieve this happiness by pursuing his desires, or whether he must first learn to desire the kind of happiness which is possible.

# IX The Insight of Humanism

## 1. THE TWO APPROACHES TO LIFE

The land of heart's desire is a place in which no man desires what he cannot have and each man can have what he desires. There have been great differences of opinion among men as to how they could best enter this happy land.

If they thought their natural impulses were by way of being lecherous, greedy, and cruel, they have accepted some form of the classical and Christian doctrine that man must subdue his naive impulses, and by reason, grace, or renunciation, transform his will. If they thought that man was naturally innocent and good, they have accepted some one of the many variants of liberalism, and concerned themselves not with the reform of desire but with the provision of opportunities for its fulfilment.

There are differences of emphasis among liberals, but they all accept the same premise, which is that if only external circumstances are favorable the internal life of man will adjust itself successfully. So completely does this theory of human nature dominate the field of contemporary thought that modern men are rarely reminded, and then only by those whom it is the fashion to ignore, that they are challenging the testimony not merely of their maiden aunts, but of all the greatest teachers of wisdom. Yet if the modern man is an optimist on the subject of his impulses, the reason is to be found less in his own self-confidence than in his distrust of men and in his intoxication over things.

Owing to the dissolution of the ancestral order he has learned to distrust those who exercise authority. Owing to the progress of science he has acquired an unbounded confidence in his capacity to create desirable objects. He is so rebellious and so constructive that he has still to ask himself whether the free and naive pursuit of desirable objects can really produce a desirable world. Yet in all the books of wisdom that is the question which confronts him. There it is written in many languages and in the idiom of many different cultures that if man is to find happiness, he must reconstruct not merely his world, but, first of all, himself.

Is this wisdom dead and done with, or has it a bearing upon the deep uneasiness of the modern man? The answer depends upon what we must conceive to be the nature of man.

## 2. FREEDOM AND RESTRAINT

It is significant that fashions in human nature are continually changing. There are, as it were, two extremes: at the one is the belief that our naive passions are evil, at the other that they are good, and between these two poles, the prevailing opinion oscillates. One might suppose that somewhere, perhaps near the center, there would be a point which was the truth, and that on that point men would reach an agreement. But experience shows that there is no agreement, and that there is no known point where the two views are perfectly balanced. The fact is that the prevailing view is invariably a rebound from the excesses of the other, and one can understand it only by knowing what it is a reaction from.

It is impossible, for example, to do justice to Rousseau and the romantics without understanding the dead classicism, the conventionalities, and the tyrannies of the Eighteenth Century. It is equally impossible to do justice to the Eighteenth Century without understanding the licentiousness of the High Renaissance and the political disorders resulting from the Reformation. These in their turn become intelligible only when we have understood the later consequences of the mediaeval view of life. No particular view endures. When human nature is wholly distrusted and severely repressed, sooner or later it asserts itself and bursts its bonds; and when it is naively trusted, it produces so much disorder and corruption that men once again idealize order and restraint.

We happen to be living in an age when there is a severe reaction against the distrust and repression practiced by those whom it is customary to describe as Puritans. It is, in fact, a reaction against a degenerate form of Puritanism which manifested itself as a disposition to be prim, prudish, and pedantic. For latter-day Puritanism had become a rather second-rate notion that less obvious things are more noble than grosser ones and that spirituality is the pursuit of rarefied sensations. It had embraced the idea that a man had advanced in the realm of the spirit in proportion to his concern with abstractions, and cults of grimly spiritual persons devoted themselves to the worship of sonorous gen-

eralities. All this associated itself with a rather prepos-
terous idealism which insisted that maidens should be wan
and easily frightened, that draperies and decorations should
conceal the essential forms of objects, and that the good
life had something to do with expurgated speech, with pale
colors, and shadows and silhouettes, with the thin music
of harps and soprano voices, with fig leaves and a general
conspiracy to tell lies to children, with philosophies that
denied the reality of evil, and with all manner of affectation
and self-deception.

Yet in these many attempts to grow wings and take off
from the things that are of the earth earthy, it is impossible not to recognize a resemblance, somewhat in the nature
of a caricature, to the teaching of the sages. There is no
doubt that in one form or another, Socrates and Buddha,
Jesus and St. Paul, Plotinus and Spinoza, taught that the
good life is impossible without asceticism, that without renunciation of many of the ordinary appetites, no man can
really live well. Prejudice against the human body and a
tendency to be disgusted with its habits, a contempt for
the ordinary concerns of daily experience is to be found in
all of them, and it is not surprising that men, living in an
age of moral confusion like that associated with the name
of the good Queen Victoria, should have come to believe
that if only they covered up their passions they had conquered them. It was a rather ludicrous mistake as the sat-
irists of the anti-Victorian era have so copiously pointed
out. But at least there was a dim recognition in this cult
of the genteel that the good life does involve some kind of
conquest of the carnal passions.

That conception of the good life has become so repulsive to the present generation that it is almost incapable
of understanding and appreciating the original insight of

which the works of Dr. Bowdler and Mrs. Grundy are a caricature. Yet it is a fact, and a most arresting one, that in all the great religions, and in all the great moral philosophies from Aristotle to Bernard Shaw, it is taught that one of the conditions of happiness is to renounce some of the satisfactions which men normally crave. This tradition as to what constitutes the wisdom of life is supported by testimony from so many independent sources that it cannot be dismissed lightly. With minor variations it is a common theme in the teaching of an Athenian aristocrat like Plato, an Indian nobleman like Buddha, and a humble Jew like Spinoza; in fact, wherever men have thought at all carefully about the problem of evil and of what constitutes a good life, they have concluded that an essential element in any human philosophy is renunciation. They cannot all have been so foolish as Anthony Comstock. They must have had some insight into experience which led them to that conclusion.

If asceticism in all its forms were as stupid and cruel as it is now the fashion to think it is, then the traditions of saintliness and of heroism are monstrously misleading. For in the legends of heroes, of sages, of explorers, inventors and discoverers, of pioneers and patriots, there is almost invariably this same underlying theme of sacrifice and unworldliness. They are poor. They live dangerously. By ordinary standards they are extremely uncomfortable. They give up ease, property, pleasure, pride, place, and power to attain things which are transcendent and rare. They live for ends which seem to yield them no profit, and they are ready to die, if need be, for that which the dead can no longer enjoy. And yet, though there is nothing in our current morality to justify their unworldliness, we continue to admire them greatly.

In saying all this I am not trying to clinch an argument by appealing to great names. There is much in the teaching of all the spiritual leaders of the past which is wholly obsolete to-day, and there is no compulsive authority in any part of their teaching. They may have been as mistaken in their insight into the human soul as they usually were in their notions of physics and history. To say, then, that there is an ascetic element in all the great philosophies of the past is not proof that there must be one in modern philosophy. But it creates a presumption, I think, which cannot be ignored, for we must remember that the least perishable part of the literature and thought of the past is that which deals with human nature. Scientific method and historical scholarship have enormously increased our competence in the whole field of physics and history. But for an understanding of human nature we are still very largely dependent, as they were, upon introspection, general observation, and intuition. There has been no revolutionary advance here since the Hellenic philosophers. That is why Aristotle's ethics is still as fresh for anyone who accustoms himself to the idiom as Nietzsche, or Freud, or Bertrand Russell, whereas Aristotle's physics, his biology, or his zoology is of interest only to antiquarians.

It is, then, as an insight into human nature, and not as a rule authoritatively imposed or highly sanctioned by the prestige of great men, that I propose now to inquire what meaning there is for us in the fact that men in the past have so persistently associated the good life with some form of ascetic discipline and renunciation. The modern world, as it has emancipated itself from its ancestral regime, has assumed almost as a matter of course that the human passions, if thoroughly liberated from all tyrannies and distortions, would by their fulfilment achieve happiness.

All those who teach asceticism deny this major premise of modernity, and the result is that the prevailing philosophy is at odds on the most fundamental of all issues with the wisdom of the past.

## 3. THE ASCETIC PRINCIPLE

The average man to-day, when he hears the word asceticism, is likely to think of St. Simeon Stylites who sat on top of a pillar, of hermits living in caves, of hair-shirts, of long fasts, chastity, strange vigils, and even of tattooing, self-mutilation, and flagellation. Or if he does not think of such examples, which the modern man regards as pathological and for the psychiatrist to explain, the word asceticism may connote some such attitude of mind as Herbert Asbury has recorded in the biography of his kinsman, Bishop Asbury, the founder of American Methodism, of whom a friend, who knew him well, wrote: "I never saw him indulge in even innocent pleasantry. His was the solemnity of an apostle; it was so interwoven with his conduct that he could not put off the gravity of the bishop either in the parlour or the dining-room. He was a rigid enemy to ease; hence the pleasures of study and the charms of recreation he alike sacrificed to the more sublime work of saving souls. . . . He knew nothing about pleasing the flesh at the expense of duty; flesh and blood were enemies with whom he never took counsel."

If asceticism meant only this sort of thing, it might be interesting only as a curiosity. But apart from the asceticism of primitive peoples and of the pathological, there is a sane and civilized asceticism which presents a quite different face. There is, for example, the argument of Socrates in the *Phaedo* that the body is a nuisance to a philosopher in search of truth. It is, he says, "a source of endless trouble to us by reason of the mere requirement of food; and is liable also to diseases which overtake and impede us in the search after true being: it fills us full of loves, and lusts, and fears, and fancies of all kinds, and endless foolery, and in fact, as men say, takes away from us the power of thinking at all. Whence come wars, and fightings, and factions? Whence but from the body and the lusts of the body? Wars are occasioned by the love of money, and money has to be acquired for the sake and in the service of the body; and by reason of all these impediments we have no time to give to philosophy; and, last and worst of all, even if we are at leisure and betake ourselves to some speculation, the body is always breaking in upon us, causing us turmoil and confusion in our inquiries, and so amazing us that we are prevented from seeing the truth."

Plato, in pursuing the argument in this particular dialogue, concludes that because the body is such a nuisance the only pure philosopher is a dead one. It is, perhaps, a logical conclusion. But in other places, particularly in the *Republic,* Plato described a system of education which he thought would produce philosophers: the neophytes were put through a stern discipline of hard living and gymnastics and learning, were compelled to live in tents, to own nothing which they could call their own, and to cut themselves off from all family ties.

When the description of this regime provokes Adeimantus to remark that "you are not making the men of this class particularly happy," Socrates is made to reply that while it is not his object to make any class particularly happy, yet it would not surprise him if in the given circumstances even this class were very happy. When we look further for his meaning, we find it to be that the guardians are trained by their ascetic discipline to abandon all private aims and to find their happiness in an appreciation of a perfectly ordered commonwealth. If we understand this we shall, I believe, understand what civilized asceticism means. We shall have come back to the original meaning of the word itself, which is derived from the Greek ἀσχέω, "I practice," and "embodies a metaphor taken from the ancient wrestling place or palaestra, where victory rewarded those who had best trained their bodies." An ascetic in the original meaning of the term is an athlete; and it was in this spirit that the early Christians trained themselves deliberately as "athletes of Christ" to bear without flinching the tortures of their martyrdom.

When asceticism is irrational, it is a form of totemism or fetich worship and derives from a belief that certain things are tabu or that evil spirits can be placated by human suffering. Or without any coherent belief whatsoever asceticism may be merely a perversion arising out of that ambivalence of the human passions which often makes pain, inflicted on others or self-inflicted, an exquisite pleasure. But when asceticism is rational, it is a discipline of the mind and body to fit men for the service of an ideal. Its purpose is to harden and to purify, to suppress contrary passions, and thus to intensify the passion for the ideal. "I chastise my body," said St. Paul, "and bring it into subjection." The Church, especially in the earlier centuries, was compelled to fight continually against irrational asceticism, and as late as the Middle Ages, the Inquisition pursued sects which regarded marriage as the "greater adultery" and practiced self-emasculation. The rational view was the view of St. Jerome: "Be on your guard when you begin to mortify your body by abstinence and fasting, lest you imagine yourself to be perfect and a saint; for perfection does not consist in this virtue. It is only a help; a disposition; a means, though a fitting one, for the attainment of true perfection.''

Now when St. Paul said that he had to bring his body into subjection, when Aristotle defined the barbarians' ideal as "the living as one likes," when Plato made Socrates say that the soul is infected by the body, when Buddha preached the extinction of all craving, when Spinoza wrote that because we rejoice in virtue we are able to control our lusts, they accepted a view of human nature which is quite diametrically opposed to one which has had wide currency in our civilization since the Renaissance.

This contrary view was undoubtedly provoked by the evils which came from the attempt to put the ascetic principle extensively into practice. Rabelais is by all odds the most convincing of the moderns who revolted, for Rabelais not only talked about the natural man but actually knew him and delighted in him. Thus when Villers writes to Madame de Staël that in her work "primitive, incorruptible, naive, passionate nature" is "in conflict with the barriers and shackles of conventional life," we feel, I think, that neither Villers nor the lady would really have cared very much for primitive nature in all its naivete. The natural man that they were talking about lived in Arcady and his passions were as violent as those of a lapdog; throughout the romantic movement, with rare exceptions, the talk about passion and impulse and instinct has this air of unreality and of neurotic confusion. There is not in it, as there is in Rabelais, for example, an honest gusto for the passions that are to be liberated from the restraints imposed by that "rabble of squint-minded fellows, dissembling and counterfeit saints, demure lookers, hypocrites, pretended zealots, tough friars, buskin-monks, and other such sects of men, who disguise themselves like masquers to deceive the world."

Rabelais advised his readers that if they desired to become good Pantagruelists, "that is to say, to live in peace, joy, health, making yourself always merry—never trust those men that always peep out through a little hole." And in establishing the Abbey of Theleme, Gargantua furnished it magnificently and barred the gates against bigots, hypocrites, dissemblers, attorneys, barristers, usurers, drunkards, and cannibals; he invited in all noble blades and brisk and handsome people, faithful expounders of the Scripture, and lovely ladies, proper, fair, and mirthful. "Their life," he says, "was spent not in laws, statutes, or rules, but at their own free will and pleasure. They rose from bed when they thought good, drank, ate, worked, slept, when the desire came to them. None did awaken them, none constrained them either to drink or eat, nor to do any other thing: for so had Gargantua established it. The Rule of their order had but one clause: *Do What Thou Wilt.*"

But there was a catch in this rule. Not only had drunkards and cannibals been excluded in the first place, but Rabelais assures us that those who were admitted, because they were "free, well born, well educated, and accustomed to good company, have by nature an instinct and spur which prompts them to virtuous acts and withdraws them from vice. This they call honor." And in another passage Rabelais limits the propensities of the natural man even more radically when he speaks of "a certain gaiety of spirit *cured* in contempt of chance and fortune."

There is always a catch in any doctrine of the natural goodness of man. For mere passive obedience to impulse as it comes and goes, without effort to check it or direct it, ends in something like Alfred de Musset's Rolla, of whom it was said:

> It was not Rolla who ruled his life,
> It was his passions; he let them go
> As a drowsy shepherd watches the water flow.

So even Dora Russell at the crisis of her assault upon the Christian tradition advises us to "live by instinct *and* intelligence," which must mean, if it means anything, that intelligence is to be in some respects the master as well as the servant of instinct. That this is what Mrs. Russell means is abundantly plain by her fury at capitalists, imperialists, conservatives, and churchmen, whose instincts lead them to do things of which she does not approve. For like her distinguished husband she trusts those impulses which are creative and beneficent, and distrusts those which are possessive and destructive. That is to say, like every other moralist, she trusts those parts of human nature which she trusts.

## 4. OSCILLATION BETWEEN TWO PRINCIPLES

These cycles of action and reaction are disastrous to the establishment of a stable humanism. A theocratic culture depends upon an assured view of the way in which God governs the universe, and as long as that view suits the typical needs of a society made stable by custom, the theocratic culture is stable. But humanism arises in complex and changing societies, and if it is to have any power to make life coherent and orderly, it must hold an assured view of how man can govern himself. If he oscillates aimlessly between the belief that he must distrust his impulses and the belief that he may naively obey them, it is impossible for him to fix any point of reference for the development of his moral code, his educational plans, his human relationships, his politics, and his personal ideals.

It is not hard to see, I think, why he oscillates in this fashion between trust and distrust. He cannot obey every impulse, for he has conflicting impulses within himself. There are also his neighbors with their impulses. They cannot all be satisfied, for the very simple reason that the sum of their demands far outruns the available supply of satisfactions. There is not room enough, there are not objects enough in the world to fulfill all human desires. Desires are, for all practical purposes, unlimited and insatiable, and therefore any ethics which does not recognize the necessity of putting restraint upon naive desire is inherently absurd. On the other hand, it is impossible to distrust every impulse, for the only conclusion then is to commit suicide. Buddha did, to be sure, teach that craving was the source of all misery, and that it must be wholly extinguished. But it is evident from an examination of what he actually advised his disciples to renounce, that while they were to be poor, chaste, unworldly, and incurious about the nature of things, they were to be rewarded with the highest of all satisfactions, and were to be "like the broad earth, unvexed; like the pillar of the city gate, unmoved; like a pellucid lake, unruffled." For Nirvana meant, as Rhys Davids says, the extinction of a sinful, grasping condition of mind.

Confronted by two opposed views of human nature, neither of which can be taken unreservedly, moralists have had to pick and choose, deciding how much or how little they would trust the different impulses. But there is no measure by which they could decide how much of an impulse is virtuous, how much more is intemperate, and how much more than that is utterly sinful. The attempts to regulate the sexual impulse illustrate the difficulty. Shall the moralist call the complete absence of all conscious sexual desire virtue? Then he disobeys the commandment to be fruitful and multiply and replenish the earth. Shall he then limit virtuous desire to that which is felt for a lawful mate? That implies that man and woman must mate with the first person for whom they feel any sexual desire. But this cannot always be arranged. The first person may be otherwise engaged. It becomes necessary then to permit a certain amount of promiscuous, though unfulfilled, sexual desire in the process of sexual selection. And then having somehow gotten past that difficulty, and with two persons safely mated, a whole new series of problems arise out of the question of how far sexual satisfaction depends for its virtue upon its being the successful means to, or more subtly still, the intended means to, procreation. I shall not pursue the matter further. The attempt to measure the degree in which impulse is to be permitted to express itself is obviously full of difficulties.

The moral problem remains utterly insoluble as long as men regard it as an attempt to separate their good impulses from their bad ones, and to decide how much their good impulses are to be encouraged. Morality, if it is not fixed by custom and authority, becomes a mere matter of taste determined by the idiosyncrasies of the moralist.

## 5. THE GOLDEN MEAN AND ITS DIFFICULTIES

Aristotle faced this fundamental difficulty of humanism in the *Ethics*. He had expounded the theory that happiness is due to virtue, and that virtue is a mean between two extremes. There must, he said, be neither defect nor excess of any quality. We must, in brief, go so far but no further in obedience to our impulses. Thus between rashness and cowardice the mean is courage; between prodigality and niggardliness it is liberality; between incontinence and total abstinence it is temperateness; between ostentation and meanness it is magnificence; between empty boasting and little-mindedness it is magnanimity; between flattery and moroseness it is friendliness; between bashfulness and impudence it is modesty; between arrogance and false modesty, it is truthfulness.

So runs the Aristotelian catalogue, and probably no code ever described so well the ideal of a gentleman. But having laid down his general precepts, Aristotle, unlike most moralists, faced the difficulty of applying them. He recognized that it is one thing to accept the theory of a golden mean, and quite another to know where that mean lies. "For in each case it is difficult to find the mean . . . thus it is easy, and in every man's power to be angry, and to give and spend money; but to determine the person to whom, and the quantity, and the time, and the motive, and the manner, is no longer in every man's power, nor is it easy; therefore excellence is rare, and praiseworthy and honorable." For while the mean between excess and defect is excellent, "it is easy to miss a mark, but difficult to hit it."

If we look at the matter more closely in order to find out why moral codes are, as Aristotle says, so hit and miss, we must, I think, come to the conclusion that there is an undetected fallacy in most moral thinking which renders moral insight abortive. It is that fallacy which I now propose to examine.

A moral code like Aristotle's, which we may fairly regard as the rational prototype of all humanistic codes, consists of an inventory of good and bad appetites and of good and bad satisfactions. All conventional moralizing, which does not rest on the sheer fiat of public opinion, custom, or God, assumes the existence of some such inventory of permissible desires and permissible fulfilments. But what does the making of such inventories mean? It means that good and evil are believed to be objective qualities of the natural world like weight, dimension, and motion, that certain desires are inherently good, certain others are inherently bad, and that the same is true of the different objects of desire. But this is nothing but what is known as the pathetic fallacy. For surely each desire and each object as such, taken separately without relation to anything else, is as innocent and as neutral as the forces that move the planets.

The categories of good and evil would not apply if there were no sentient being to experience good and evil. In such a world no object would be any better or any worse than any other object; nobody talks about good and bad electrons. All electrons are morally alike because no sentient being can tell them apart. Nor would the categories of good and evil apply to a world in which each impulse was in a vacuum of its own. In such a world all our impulses would be like our digestive tracts on a day when we do not know we have a stomach. If our impulses did not impinge upon each other and upon objects there would be no problem of good and evil. Therefore the quality of good and evil lies not in impulses as such, nor in objects as such, but in the relationship between impulses and objects. Therefore the making of inventories is fundamentally misleading.

There is another fallacy which is closely associated

with this one. We make lists of our impulses. A standard list which is much used comprises the following: flight, repulsion, curiosity, pugnacity, self-abasement, self-assertion, parental, reproductive, gregarious, acquisitive, constructive. Whether this is a good list or not is neither here nor there. Through the ages men have been making such lists in the fond belief that they were analyzing the human character. No doubt these terms describe something; we all recognize that these words are the names of impulses that move us. But if we consider them further, we must also recognize that these impulses do not move all persons the same way, nor any one person the same way at all times in his life and under all circumstances.

It is hardly necessary, I am sure, to labor the point very much. There is the instinct to be curious: it disposes one man to measure the diameter of Betelgeuse when he is forty years old; when he was a child it disposed him to find out whether he could hang up a cat by its tail; that curious child's companion in the experiment on the cat was disposed, when he grew up, to take much trouble in finding out how much income tax his neighbor paid and whether his employer was faithful to his wife. The parental instinct of one man is to launch his child on the world as an independent human being; in another man the instinct manifests itself as a determination to have children who will depend upon him and cater to him all his days long. So when we make lists of our impulses we really do not know enough about them to pass judgment. For desires are complex, and their greatest complexity lies in the fact that they change.

The objects of desire are no less complex. Take, for example, a jade goddess. To a Chinese coolie it is an object with mysterious powers, a part of the mechanism which governs the universe. But the jade goddess is now in a

Fifth Avenue shop window, and a policeman on his beat sees it. It is a green stone figure to him. The dealer inside knows that it is rare and is worth a thousand dollars. The collector could enjoy it immensely if he possessed it. The connoisseur finds intricate pleasure in it as a work of art and an elaborate interest in it as a memento of a whole culture. The objects of desire, then, are not simple things. We help to create them. We say that this man desires that woman. But what, in fact, does he desire? A few moments of ecstasy from her body, something which a thousand women could give him equally well, or an intimate union with so much of her whole being that for that very reason she is unique to him? The quality of his passion and the character of his mistress will depend in a very large degree on how much of her being he takes into account. It depends also, I hasten to add, on how much there is to take into account.

At any moment in our lives we desire only those objects which we are then capable of desiring and in the way we are then capable of desiring them. But our desires do not remain fixed from the cradle to the grave. They change. And as they change the desirability of objects about us changes too. It is impossible, then, to make lists of good and evil desires and of good and evil objects. For good and evil are qualities in the relationship between variable desires and variable objects of desire.

The attempt to construct moral codes on the basis of an inventory is an attempt to understand something which is always in process of change by treating it as a still life and taking snapshots of it. That is what moralists have almost always attempted to do. They have tried to capture the essence of a changing thing in a collection of fixed concepts. It cannot be done. The reality of human nature is bound to elude us if we look only at a momentary cross-section of it. To understand it, therefore, for the purposes of moralizing, we have to revise our intellectual apparatus, and learn to look upon each moment of behavior not as the manifestation of certain fixed elements in human nature, but as a stage in the evolution of human nature. We grow up, mature, and decline; being endowed with memory and the capacity to form habits, our conduct is cumulative. We drag our past along with us and it pushes us on. We do not make a new approach to each new experience. We approach new experiences with the expectations and habits developed by previous experience, and under the impact of novelty these expectations and habits become modified.

## 6. THE MATRIX OF HUMANISM

The conception of human nature as developing behavior is, of course, accepted by all modern psychologists. If they study the child they are bound to consider him as potentially an adult. If they study the adult they are bound to regard him as originally a child. Abnormal psychology makes sense only insofar as it can be understood as an abnormal development of the personality, regardless of whether that abnormality is traceable to prenatal variations, to organic disease, or to functional disturbance. Folk psychology, whether or not one accepts the interesting but speculative hypothesis that there is a parallel between the development of the individual and the development of the race, is another mode of investigating the evolution of behavior. The concept of development is thoroughly established in psychology as the major clue to the understanding of human nature.

The moralist, since he is concerned with human nature, is compelled to employ this concept. But he employs it somewhat differently than the scientist. Being a moralist, he is interested in understanding the principles of behavior in order that he may understand the principles of right behavior. The psychologist, as such, is interested in the development of behavior, regardless of whether that development leads to misery or to happiness. He studies the various processes no matter where they lead. For in science the concept of development implies no judgment as to whether there is a good or a bad development. The development of an idiot and of a genius are on the same footing, and are theoretically of equal interest. But to the moralist the study of development is focussed on the effort to discover those processes of development which can be made to produce right relationships between the individual and his environment, and by a right relationship he is bound to mean one in which there is an harmonious adjustment between desires and the objects of desire. How often, and how nearly, it is possible for human beings to approximate such perfection is an unanswerable question. The proof of that pudding lies in the eating of it, and it is not the function of the moralist under humanism to guarantee the outcome. His function is to point out as clearly as it is possible to do so the path which presumably leads toward the good life.

In describing that path he is bound to depend upon the best available insight into the processes by which good and bad adjustments are made. In the present state of our knowledge this means that he must rely to a very large degree upon his own intuitions, commonsense, and sense of life. Great progress has been made in scientific psychology within the last generation, enough progress, I think, to supplement in important ways our own unanalyzed and intuitive wisdom about life. But it would be idle to suppose that the science of psychology is in a stage where it can be used as a substitute for experienced and penetrating imaginative insight. We can be confident that on the whole a good meteorologist can tell us more about the weather than even the most weather-wise old sea captain. But we cannot have that kind of confidence in even the best of psychologists. Indeed, an acquaintance with psychologists will, I think, compel anyone to admit that, if they are good psychologists, they are almost certain to possess a gift of insight which is unaccounted for by their technical apparatus. Doubtless it is true that in all the sciences the difference between a good scientist and a poor one comes down at last, after all the technical and theoretical procedure has been learned, to some sort of residual flair for the realities of that subject. But in the study of human nature that residual flair, which seems to be composed of intuition, commonsense, and unconsciously deposited experience, plays a much greater role than it does in the more advanced sciences.

The uses of psychology to the moralist are, therefore, in confirming and correcting, in broadening and organizing, his insight into human nature. He is confronted, of course, with a great deal of confusion. There is, to begin with, no agreed terminology, and therefore it is often almost impossible to know whether two psychologists using the same word mean the same thing. Anyone who has stumbled about amidst words like instinct, impulse, consciousness, the unconscious, will know how confusing it all is. Psychologists are still using a literary language in which the connotations of words tend to overwhelm their precise signification. To make the confusion greater there is the elaborate system-making, the headstrong generalizing, and the fierce dogmatism which have produced the psychological sects. But all of this is characteristic of a young science, and if that is borne in mind, there is nothing disconcerting about it. The Eighteenth Century in dealing with the Newtonian physics, and the Nineteenth in dealing with the Darwinian biology, went through a hullabaloo similar to that which we are now going through in connection with behaviorism, psychoanalysis, and the so-called *gestalt-theorie*. Our only concern here is to ask whether underneath all the controversy there is not some trustworthy common ground on which the moralist can stand.

I have already said that there was common ground in the concept of development. We can go further than that, however, and say, I think, that with the help of psychology we are in position now to construct reliable and useful pictures, which confirm and correct our own intuitive understanding, of the infantile and of the mature approach to experience. We can, as it were, fix these two poles and regard the history of each soul as the history of its progress from infantilism to maturity. We are by no means able as yet to describe all the phases of development between these two poles; we know that progress is often temporarily interrupted, often completely arrested, and sometimes turned into a rout. But insofar as we are able to realize clearly what a fully matured character is like, the word progress has a meaning because we know what we mean by the goal of moral effort. That goal is maturity. If we knew all the stages in the development to maturity, and how to control them, we should have an adequate science of education, we could deal successfully with functional disorders, we should have a very great mastery of the art of life. For the problems of education are at bottom problems in how to lead the child from one stage of development to another until at last he becomes an harmonious and autonomous personality; the functional disorders of the character are problems in the fixations and repressions on the path to maturity; the art of living is to pass gracefully from youth to old age, and, at last, as Montaigne said, to learn to die.

It is this progress which we have to understand and imaginatively to conceive. For in conceiving it we conceive the matrix of humanism. In this conception is to be found, I believe, the substitute for that conception of divine government which gives shape and form to the theocratic culture. To replace the conception of man as the subject of a heavenly king, which dominates the whole ancestral order of life, humanism takes as its dominant pattern the progress of the individual from helpless infancy to self-governing maturity.

## 7. THE CAREER OF THE SOUL

If our scientific knowledge of human nature were adequate, we could achieve in the humanistic culture that which all theologies have tried to achieve: we could found our morality on tested truths. They would be truths about the development of human nature, and not, as in the popular religions, truth of physics and of history. But our knowledge of human nature is inadequate, and therefore, like the teachers of popular religion, we have in place of exact knowledge to invent imaginative fictions in the hope that the progress of science will confirm and correct, but will not utterly contradict, our hypotheses. We can claim no more than this: for our understanding of human nature we are compelled to use our insight and the best available psychological science of our age, exactly as Dante, for his understanding of the divine constitution of the universe, had to use the accepted astronomy of his day. If our psychology turns out to be wrong, the only difference will be that we shall have to discard an hypothesis whereas our forefathers had to discard a revealed dogma.

The sketch which I am about to make of the progress from infancy to maturity is to be taken, then, not as tested scientific truth, but as an imaginative construction. It will be, if you like, a modern fable which symbolizes rather than describes, as the primitive legends of the sun god symbolized, rather than described, the observed facts. Because it is an imaginative construction, the same meaning might be expressed in other ways and with many variations of detail. But though the fiction itself is of no consequence, the meaning it conveys is of the highest consequence, and it is confirmed, as I shall attempt to show, not only by ordinary insight but by the deepest wisdom of the greatest teachers.

Freud, in a famous paper, has described the passage from infancy to maturity as a transition from the dominion of momentary pleasure and pain to the dominion of reality. This theory is not peculiar to psychoanalysis in any of its several schools, and it does not depend upon the controverted points of doctrine. It is, in fact, more or less of a commonplace in psychological thought. I am employing it here because a distinguished colleague of Freud's, Dr. S. Ferenczi of Budapest, has made an attempt to indicate the chief stages in the development between these two poles of experience. It is a most useful bit of speculation, and while I believe it could be duplicated in terms either of behaviorism or of the *gestalt-theorie,* I do not happen to have come across any portrait of the idea which is as vivid as Dr. Ferenczi's.

The first stage of human development, says Ferenczi, takes place in the womb where the embryo lives as a parasite of the mother's body. An outer world exists for it only in a very restricted degree; all it needs for protection, warmth, and nourishment is assured by the mother. Because everything is there which is necessary for the satisfaction of the instincts, Ferenczi calls this the Period of Unconditional Omnipotence.

It is, therefore, rather disagreeable and perhaps terrifying to be born, for with the detachment from the mother and the "rude disturbance of the wish-less tranquillity he had enjoyed in the womb," the trouble of living begins, and evokes feelings which might perhaps be described as a longing to recover the perfect pre-natal adjustment. Nurses instinctively recognize this longing, says Ferenczi, and as soon as the infant expresses his discomfort by struggling and crying, they deliberately create a situation which resembles as closely as possible the one he has just left. They lay him down by the warm body of the mother, or wrap him up in soft, warm coverings, shield his eyes from the light and his ears from noise. The illusion is more or less complete, for, of course, the infant is unaware of the activities of the nurse. For all he knows "his wishes are realized simply by imagining the satisfaction of them." Ferenczi calls this the Period of Magical-Hallucinatory Omnipotence.

But this period does not last very long, since the nurse is unable to anticipate every desire that the growing infant feels. "The hallucinatory representation of the wish-fulfilment soon proves inadequate to bring about any longer a real wish-fulfilment." So the infant has to give signals, and the more complicated his wishes become the more signals he has to give. He begins to use a gesture-language, and if there is a willing nurse always at hand without too many newfangled notions, the child gets what he wants for the mere trouble of expressing his wants. Ferenczi calls this the Period of Omnipotence by the Help of Magic Gestures.

But as time goes on and as the number of his wants increases these gestures lose some of their magic. The number of the conditions increase to which he has to submit. "The outstretched hand must often be drawn back empty. . . . Indeed, an invincible hostile power may forcibly oppose itself to this gesture and compel the hand to resume its former position." At this point his sense of reality begins; the sense, that is to say, of something outside himself which does not submit to his wishes. "Till now the 'all-powerful' being has been able to feel himself one with the world that obliged him and followed his every nod, but gradually there appears a painful discordance in his experiences." Because all experiences are no longer incorporated in the ego, Ferenczi calls this the Projection Phase.

But though the child has now begun to discern the existence of reality, his sense of that reality is still quite imperfect. At first, perhaps, he regards this outer world, though it opposes his wishes, as having qualities like his own. Ferenczi calls this the Animistic Period. The child then begins to talk and to substitute for gestures actual statements of what he desires. Provided he lives in a household bent on fulfilling his wants as soon as possible, he retains to a very great degree the illusion that his wishes are sovereign. Ferenczi calls this the Period of Magic Thoughts and Magic Words.

Finally, if he matures successfully, he passes into the last period where he is no longer under the domination of the pleasure-principle: the feeling of omnipotence gives way to the full appreciation of the force of circumstances.

Now unfortunately neither Freud nor Ferenczi, nor, so far as I know, any other psychoanalyst, devotes much attention to this last phase of maturity in which the sense of reality has become perfected. They are preoccupied with pathology; that is to say, with the problems which arise out of a failure to attain this last stage in which the adult makes a complete adjustment with his world because his wishes are matured to accept the conditions which reality imposes.

Yet it is this last stage which plainly constitutes the goal of moral effort, for here alone the adult once again recovers that harmony between himself and his environment which he lost in that period of infancy when he first discovered that his wishes were no longer sovereign. It is the memory of that earliest harmony which he carries with him all his days. This is his memory of a golden age, his intimation, as Wordsworth says, of immortality. But insofar as he expects by an infantile philosophy to recover that heaven which lay about him in his infancy, he is doomed to disappointment. In the womb, and for a few years of his childhood, happiness was the gratification of his naive desires. His family arranged the world to suit his wishes. But as he grows up, and begins to be an independent personality, this providence ministering to his wishes disappears. He can then no longer hope that the world will be adjusted to his wishes, and he is compelled by a long and difficult process of learning and training to adjust his wishes to the world. If he succeeds he is mature. If he is mature, he is once again harmonious with the nature of things. He has virtue. And he is happy.

The process of maturing consists then of a revision of his desires in the light of an understanding of reality. When he is completely infantile there is nothing in the world but his wishes. Therefore, he does not need and does not have an understanding of the outer world. It exists for him merely as gratification or denial. But as he begins to learn that the universe is not composed of his wishes, he begins to see his wishes in a context and in perspective. He begins to acquire a sense of space and to learn how much there is beyond his reach, until at last he realizes how small a figure he is on this earth, and how small a part of the universe is the solar system of which ours is one of the smaller planets. He has learned a lot from the days when he put out his hand and reached for the moon. He begins, also, to acquire a sense of time and to realize that the moment in which he feels the intense desire to seize something is an instant in a lifetime, an infinitesimal point in the history of the race. He acquires a sense of birth and decay and death, a knowledge that that which he craves, his craving itself, and he himself who feels that craving, did not have this craving yesterday and will no longer have it to-morrow. He acquires a sense of cause and effect, a knowledge, that is to say, that the sequences of events are not to be interrupted by his preferences. He begins to discern the existence of other beings besides himself, and to understand that they too have their preferences and their wishes, that these wishes are often contrary to his own, and that there is not room enough in the world, nor are there things enough, to gratify all the wishes of everybody.

Thus to learn the lessons of experience is to undergo a transvaluation of the values we bring with us from the womb and to transmute our naive impulses. The breakdown of the infantile adjustment in which providential powers ministered to every wish compels us either to flee from reality or to understand it. And by understanding it we create new objects of desire. For when we know a good deal about a thing, know how it originated, how it is likely to behave, what it is made of, and what is its place amidst other things, we are dealing with something quite different from the simple object naively apprehended.

The understanding creates a new environment. The more subtle and discriminating, the more informed and sympathetic the understanding is, the more complex and yet ordered do the things about us become. To most of us, as Mr. Santayana once said, music is a pleasant noise which produces a drowsy revery relieved by nervous thrills. But the trained musician hears what we do not hear at all; he hears the form, the structure, the pattern, and the significance of an ideal world. A naturalist out of doors perceives a whole universe of related life which the rest of us do not even see. A world which is ordinarily unseen has become visible through the understanding. When the mind has fetched it out of the flux of dumb sensations, defined it and fixed it, this unseen world becomes more real than the dumb sensations it supplants. When the understanding is at work, it is as if circumstance had ceased to mutter strange sounds and had begun to speak our language. When experience is understood, it is no longer what it is wholly to the infant, very largely to youth, and in great measure to most men, a succession of desirable objects at which they instinctively grasp, interspersed with undesirable ones from which they instinctively shrink. If objects are seen in their context, in the light of their origin and destiny, with sympathy for their own logic and their own purposes, they become interesting in themselves, and are no longer blind stimuli to pleasant and unpleasant sensations.

For when our desires come into contact with the world created by the understanding, their character is altered. They are confronted by a much more complex stimulus which evokes a much more complex response. Instead of the naive and imperious lust of our infantile natures which is to seize, to have and to hold, our lusts are offset by other lusts and a balance between them is set up. That is to say, they are made rational by the ordered variety with which the understanding confronts them. We learn that there are more things in heaven and earth than we dreamed of in our immature philosophy, that there are many choices and that none is absolute, that beyond the mountains, as the Chinese say, there are people also. The obviously pleasant or unpleasant thus becomes less obviously what we felt it was before our knowledge of it became complicated by anticipation and memory. The immediately desirable seems not quite so desirable and the undesirable less intolerable. Delight is perhaps not so intense nor pain so poignant as youth and the romantics would have them. They are absorbed into a larger experience in which the rewards are a sustained and more even enjoyment, and serenity in the presence of inescapable evil. In place of a world, where like children we are ministered to by a solicitous mother, the understanding introduces us into a world where delight is reserved for those who can appreciate the meaning and purpose of things outside ourselves, and can make these meanings and purposes their own.

## 8. THE PASSAGE INTO MATURITY

The critical phase of human experience, then, is the passage from childhood to maturity; the critical question is whether childish habits and expectations are to persist or to be transformed. We grow older. But it is by no means certain that we shall grow up. The human character is a complicated thing, and its elements do not necessarily march in step.

It is possible to be a sage in some things and a child in others, to be at once precocious and retarded, to be shrewd and foolish, serene and irritable. For some parts of our personalities may well be more mature than others; not infrequently we participate in the enterprises of an adult with the mood and manners of a child.

The successful passage into maturity depends, therefore, on a breaking-up and reconstruction of those habits which were appropriate only to our earliest experience.

In a certain larger sense this is the essence of education. For unless a man has acquired the character of an adult, he is a lost soul no matter how good his technical equipment. The world unhappily contains many such lost souls. They are often in high places, men trained to manipulate the machinery of civilization, but utterly incapable of handling their own purposes in any civilized fashion. For their purposes are merely the relics of an infancy when their wishes were law, and they knew neither necessity nor change.

When a childish disposition is carried over into an adult environment the result is a radically false valuation of that environment. The symptoms are fairly evident. They may appear as a disposition to feel that everything which happens to a man has an intentional relation to himself; life becomes a kind of conspiracy to make him happy or to make him miserable. In either case it is thought to be deeply concerned with his destiny. The childish pattern appears also as a deep sense that life owes him something, that somehow it is the duty of the universe to look after him, and to listen sharply when he speaks to it. The notion that the universe is full of purposes utterly unknown to him, utterly indifferent to him, is as outrageous to one who is imperfectly matured as would be the conduct of a mother who forgot to give a hungry child its lunch. The childish pattern appears also as a disposition to believe that he may reach out for anything in sight and take it, and that having gotten it nobody must ever under any circumstances take it away. Death and decay are, therefore, almost an insult, a kind of mischief in the nature of things, which ought not to be there, and would not be there, if everything only behaved as good little boys believe it should. There is indeed authority for the belief that we are all being punished for the naughtiness of our first grandmother; that work and trouble and death would not really be there to plague us but for her unhappy transgression; that by rights we ought to live in paradise and have everything we want for ever and ever.

Here, too, is the source of that common complaint of the world-weary that they are tired of their pleasures. They have what they yearned for; yet having it they are depressed at finding that they do not care. Their inability to enjoy what they can have is the obverse of the desire to possess the unattainable: both are due to carrying over the expectations of youth into adult life. They find themselves in a world unlike the world of their youth; they themselves are no longer youths. But they retain the criteria of youth, and with them measure the world and their own deserts.

Here, too, is the origin of the apparent paradox that as men grow older they grow wiser but sadder. It is not a paradox at all if we remember that this wisdom which makes them sadder is, after all, an incomplete wisdom. They have grown wiser as to the character of the world, wiser too about their own powers, but they remain naive as to what they may expect of the world and themselves. The expectations which they formed in their youth persist as deeply ingrained habits to worry them in their maturity. They are only partially matured; they have become only partially wise. They have acquired skill and information, but the parts of them which are adult are embedded in other parts of their natures which are childish. For men do not necessarily mature altogether and in unison; they learn to do this and that more easily than they learn what to like and what to reject. Intelligence is often more completely educated than desire; our outward behavior has an appearance of being grown up which our inner vanities and hopes, our dim but powerful cravings, often belie. In a word, we learn the arts and the sciences long before we learn philosophy.

If we ask ourselves what is this wisdom which experience forces upon us, the answer must be that we discover the world is not constituted as we had supposed it to be. It is not that we learn more about its physical elements, or its geography, or the variety of its inhabitants, or the ways in which human society is governed. Knowledge of this sort can be taught to a child without in any fundamental way disturbing his childishness. In fact, all of us are aware that we once knew a great many things which we have since forgotten. The essential discovery of maturity has little if anything to do with information about the names, the locations, and the sequences of facts; it is the acquiring of a different sense of life, a different kind of intuition about the nature of things.

A boy can take you into the open at night and show you the stars; he might tell you no end of things about them, conceivably all that an astronomer could teach. But until and unless he feels the vast indifference of the universe to his own fate, and has placed himself in the perspective of cold and illimitable space, he has not looked maturely at the heavens. Until he has felt this, and unless he can endure this, he remains a child, and in his childishness he will resent the heavens when they are not accommodating. He will demand sunshine when he wishes to play, and rain when the ground is dry, and he will look upon storms as anger directed at him, and the thunder as a personal threat.

The discovery that our wishes have little or no authority in the world brings with it experience of the necessity that is in the nature of things. The lesson of this experience is one from which we shrink and to which few ever wholly accommodate themselves. The world of the child is a kind of enchanted island. The labor that went into procuring his food, his clothes, his toys, is wholly invisible at first. His earliest expectations are, therefore, that somehow the Lord will provide. Only gradually does the truth come home to him how much effort it costs to satisfy his wants. It takes even longer for him to understand that not only does he not get what he wants by asking for it but he cannot be sure to get what he wants by working for it. It is not easy to accept the knowledge that desire, that prayer, that effort can be and often are frustrated, that in the nature of things there is much fumbling, trial and error, deadlock and defeat.

The sense of evil is acquired late; by many persons it is never acquired at all. Children suffer, and childhood is by no means so unreservedly happy as some make it out to be. But childish suffering is not inherently tragic. It is not stamped with the irrevocability which the adult feels to be part of the essence of evil. Evil for the child is something which can be explained away, made up for, done away with. Pretentious philosophies have been built on this fancy purporting somehow to absorb the evil of the world in an all-embracing goodness, as a child's tears are dried by its mother's kisses. The discovery that there is evil which is as genuine as goodness, that there is ugliness and violence which are no less real than joy and love, is one of those discoveries that the adult is forced somehow to accept in his valuation of experience.

And then there is the knowledge, which only experience can give, that everything changes and that everything comes to an end. It is possible to tell a child about mortality, but to realize it he must live long enough to experience it. This knowledge does not come from words; it comes in feeling, in the feeling that he himself is older, in the death of kin and friends, in seeing well-known objects wear out, in discarding old things, in awakening to the sense that there is a whole new generation in the world which looks upon him as old. There is an intimation of immortality in our youth because we have not yet had experience of mortality. The persons and the things which surround us seem eternal because we have known them too briefly to realize that they change. We have seen neither their beginning nor their end.

In the last analysis we have no right to say that the world of youth is an illusion. For the child it is a true picture of the world in that it corresponds to, and is justified in, his experience. If he did not have to grow older, it would be quite sufficient because nothing in his experience would contradict it. Our sense of life as we mature is quite different, but there is no reason to think that it has any absolute finality. Perhaps if we lived several hundred years we should acquire a wholly different sense of life, compared with which all our adult philosophy would seem quite callow.

The child's sense of life can be called an illusion only if it is carried over into manhood, for then it ceases to fit his experience and to be justified by events. The habits

formed in a childish environment become progressively unworkable and contradictory as the youth is thrust out from
the protection of his family into an adult environment.
Then the infantile conviction that his wants will somehow
be met collides with the fact that he must provide for himself. The world begins to seem out of joint. The child's
notion that things are to be had for the asking becomes a
vast confusion in which words are treated as laws, and
rhetoric as action. The childish belief that each of us is the
center of an adoring and solicitous universe becomes the
source of endless disappointments because we cannot reconcile what we feel is due us with what we must resign ourselves to. The sense of the unreality of evil, which our
earliest experience seemed to justify, becomes a deep pref-
erence for not knowing the truth, an habitual desire to
think of the world as we should prefer it to be; out of this
rebellion against truth, out of this determination that the
facts shall conform to our wishes, are born all manner of
bigotry and uncharitableness. The child's sense that things
do not end, that they are there forever, becomes, once it
is carried over into maturity, a vain and anxious effort to
possess things forever. The incapacity to realize that the
objects of desire will last only a little while makes us put an
extravagant value upon them, and to care for them, not as
they are and for what they can actually give us, but for
what we foolishly insist they ought to be and ought always
to give us.

The child's philosophy rests upon the assumption that
the world outside is in gear with his own appetites. For
this reason an adult with a childish character will ascribe
an authority to his appetites which may easily land him
in fanaticism or frustration, in a crazy indulgence or a
miserable starvation. And to the environment he will as-

cribe a willingness to conform to him, a capacity to be owned by him, which land him in all sorts of delusions of grandeur. Only the extreme cases are in the asylums. The world is full of semi-adult persons who secretly nurse the notion that they are, or that by rights they ought to be, Don Juan, Croesus, Napoleon, or the Messiah.

They have brought with them the notion that they are still as intimately attached to nature and to society as the child is to its household. The adult has to break this attachment to persons and things. His world does not permit him to remain fused with it, but compels him to stand away from things. For things no longer obey his wishes. And therefore he cannot let his wishes become too deeply involved in things. He can no longer count on possessing whatever he may happen to want. And therefore he must learn to want what he can possess. He can no longer hold forever the things at which he grasps; for they change, and slip away. And therefore he must learn to hold on to things which do not slip away and change, to hold on to things not by grasping them, but by understanding them and by remembering them. Then he is wholly an adult. Then he has conquered mortality in the only way mortal men can conquer it. For he has ceased to expect anything of the world which it cannot give, and he has learned to love it under the only aspect in which it is eternal.

## 9. THE FUNCTION OF HIGH RELIGION

In the light of this conception of maturity as the ultimate phase in the development of the human personality, we are, I think, in a position to understand the riddle which we set ourselves at the beginning of this chapter. I asked what significance there was for us in the fact that men have so persistently associated the good life with some form of ascetic discipline and renunciation. The answer is that asceticism is an effort to overcome immaturity. When men do not outgrow their childish desires, they seek to repress them. The ascetic discipline, if it is successful, is a form of education; if it is unsuccessful, it is an agonized conflict due to an imperfect education or an incapacity to grow up. By the same token, moral regulations imposed on others, insofar as they are at all rational, and not methods of exploitation or expressions of jealousy, are attempts to curb the social disorders which result from the activities of grown-up children.

It follows that asceticisms and moralities are at best means to an end; they are more or less inadequate substitutes for the educational process and the natural growth of wisdom. They are often confused with virtue, but they are not virtue. For virtue is the quality of mature desire, and when desire is mature the tortures of renunciations and of prohibitions have ceased to be necessary. "Blessedness," says Spinoza, "is not the reward of virtue, but virtue itself; nor should we rejoice in it for that we restrain our lusts, but, on the contrary, because we rejoice therein we can restrain our lusts." The mature character may be attained by growth and experience and insight, or by ascetic discipline, or by that process of being reborn which is called conversion; when it is attained, the moral problem of whether to yield to impulse or to check it, and how much to check it and how much to yield, has disappeared. A mature desire is innocent. This, I think, is the final teaching of the great sages. "To him who has finished the Path, and passed beyond sorrow, who has freed himself on all sides, and thrown

away every fetter, there is no more fever of grief," says a
Buddhist writer.

> The Master said,
> "At fifteen I had my mind bent on learning.
> "At thirty, I stood firm.
> "At forty, I had no doubts.
> "At fifty, I knew the decrees of Heaven.
> "At sixty, my ear was an obedient organ for
>   the reception of truth.
> "At seventy, I could follow what my heart de-
>   sired, without transgressing what was right."

To be able, as Confucius indicates, to follow what the
heart desires without coming into collision with the stubborn facts of life is the privilege of the utterly innocent and
of the utterly wise. It is the privilege of the infant and of
the sage who stand at the two poles of experience; of the
infant because the world ministers to his heart's desire and
of the sage because he has learned what to desire. Perhaps
this is what Jesus meant when he told his followers that
they must become like little children.

If this is what he meant, and if this is what Buddha,
Confucius, and Spinoza meant, then we have here the clue
to the function of high religion in human affairs. I venture,
at least, to suggest that the function of high religion is to
reveal to men the quality of mature experience, that high religion is a prophecy and an anticipation of what life is like
when desire is in perfect harmony with reality. It announces
the discovery that men can enter into the realm of the spirit
when they have outgrown all childishness.

# X    High
Religion
and the
Modern
World

## 1. POPULAR RELIGION AND THE GREAT TEACHERS

In popular thought it is taken for granted that to be religious is to accept in some form or other the theocratic view that God governs the universe. If that assumption is correct then the orthodox who inveigh against the godlessness of contemporary thought and the militant atheists who rejoice in this godlessness are both right when they insist that religion is disappearing. Insofar as religion is identical with a belief in theocracy, it has indeed lost much of its reality for modern men.

There is little doubt, I think, that popular religion has been always and everywhere theocratic in principle. If, then, we are to define as religion that which the overwhelming majority of mankind have cherished, it would be necessary to concede at once that the dissolution of the belief in a supernatural government of human affairs is a dissolution of religion itself. But if that is conceded, then it is necessary to concede also that many whom the world recognizes as its greatest religious teachers were not themselves religious men. For it could be demonstrated, I think, that in the central intuition of Aristotle, of the author of the Fourth Gospel, of Buddha, of Spinoza, to name only originating minds, the theocratic principle is irrelevant. No one of these teachers held the belief, which is at the heart of theocratic religion, that the relationship between God and man is somehow analogous with that of a king to his subjects, that the relationship is in any sense a transaction between personalities involving, however subtly, a quid pro quo, that God's will and the human will are interacting forces.

In place of the popular conception of religion as a matter of commandments and obedience, reward and punishment, in a word, as a form of government, these great teachers placed their emphasis upon the conversion, the education, and the discipline of the human will. Such beliefs as they had about God were not in the nature of oaths of allegiance to a superior; their concern was not to placate the will of God but to alter the will of man. This alteration of the human will they conceived as good not because God commands it, but because it is intrinsically good for man, because by the test of experience it yields happiness, serenity, whole-heartedness. Belief is not, as it is in popular religion, an act which by creating a claim upon divinity insures man's salvation; the force of belief, as Mr. Whitehead has put it, is in "cleansing the inward parts." Thus religion becomes "the art and the theory of the internal life of man, so far as it depends on the man himself and on what is permanent in the nature of things."

The difference between religion conceived as the art and theory of the internal life of man and religion conceived as cosmic government is the great difference between the religion of these great sages and the religion of the multitude. Though in matters of this kind the distinction is not always absolutely clear in every case, on the whole it cannot be disputed, I believe, that the difference is real and of fundamental importance. If we observe popular religions as they are administered by ecclesiastical establishments, it is overwhelmingly plain that their main appeal rests upon the belief that through their offices the devout are able to obtain eternal salvation, and even earthly favors, from an invisible king. But if we observe truly, I think, we shall see also that side by side with the popular religion, sometimes in open conflict with it, sometimes in outward conformity with it, there is generally to be found in cultivated communities a minority to whom religion is primarily a reconditioning of their own souls. They may be mystics like Eckhart, they may be platonists like Origen or Dean Inge, they may be protestants like St. Augustine and Luther in certain phases of their thought, they may be humanists like Erasmus and Montaigne; as of Confucius, it may be said of them that "the subjects on which the Master did not talk were: extraordinary things, feats of strength, disorder, and spiritual beings." They may be inside the churches or outside them, but in intention, in the inner meaning of their religion, they are wholly at variance with the popular creeds. For in one form or another they reject the idea of attaining salvation by placating God; in one form or another they regard salvation as a condition of the soul which is reached only by some kind of self-discipline.

It must be obvious that religion, conceived in this way, "as the art and theory of the internal life of man," is not dissolved by what I have been calling the acids of modernity. It is the popular religion which is dissolved. But just because this vast dissolution is destroying the disposition to believe in a theocratic government of the universe, just because men no longer find it wholly credible that their affairs are subject to the ordinances of a heavenly king, just because they no longer vividly believe in an invisible power which regulates their lives, judges them, and sustains them, their only hope of salvation lies in a religion which provides an internal discipline.

The real effect of modernity upon religion, therefore, is to make the religion which was once the possession of an aristocracy of the spirit the only possible kind of religion for all modern men.

## 2. THE ARISTOCRATIC PRINCIPLE

To those who want salvation cheap, and most men do, there is very little comfort to be had out of the great teachers. Spinoza might have been speaking for all of them when he said:

> If the way which I have pointed out . . . seems exceedingly hard, it may nevertheless be discovered. Needs must it be hard, since it is so seldom found. How would it be possible, if salvation were ready to our hand, and could without great labor be found, that it should be by almost all men neglected? But all things excellent are as difficult as they are rare.

But why, we may ask, is salvation by almost all men neglected? The answer is that they do not desire that which they have never learned to desire. "One cannot," as Voltaire said, "desire that which one does not know." Can a man love good wine when he has drunk nothing but ginger beer? Did we have naturally and instinctively a taste for that which constitutes the happiness of the saved, we should already be saved, and their happiness would be ours. We lack the taste, which is, I suppose, another way of saying what the theologians meant when they spoke of original sin. To be saved, in the sense which the sages had in mind, is by conversion, education, and self-discipline to have achieved a certain quality and harmony of the passions. Then the good life is possible. But although men have often heard this said, and have read about it, unless in some measure they already desire it, the whole teaching remains mere words and abstractions which are high, cold, and remote. As long as they feel that the way to happiness is through a will other than their own, and that somehow events can in this fashion be made to yield to their unregenerate wishes, in this world or another, the wisdom of the sages will not touch their hearts, and the way which is pointed out will be neglected.

Wisdom will seem inhuman. In a sense it is inhuman, for it is so uncommon. Those who have it speak a strange language, of which the words perhaps have a familiar sound, but the meaning is too high and abstract; their delights are strange delights, and unfathomable, like a passion which we have never known. And if we encounter them in their lives or in their writings, they seem to us a mixture of grandeur and queerness. For they are at once more deeply at home in the world than the transients who make up most of mankind; yet, because of the quality of their passions, they are not wholly of the world as the worldling understands it. But unless the worldling is entirely without the capacity to transcend himself, he is bound in such an encounter to catch a glimpse now and then of an experience where there is a serenity he himself has never known, a peace that passes his understanding, an ecstasy exquisite and without regret, and happiness so clarified that it seems like brilliant and kindly light.

Yet no teacher has ever appeared in the world who

was wise enough to know how to teach his wisdom to all mankind. In fact, the great teachers have attempted nothing so utopian. They were quite well aware how difficult for most men is wisdom, and they have confessed frankly that the perfect life was for a select few. It is arguable, in fact, that the very idea of teaching the highest wisdom to all men is the recent notion of a humanitarian and romantically democratic age, and that it is quite foreign to the thought of the greatest teachers. Gautama Buddha, for example, abolished caste within the religious order which he founded, and declared that the path to Nirvana was open to the lowest outcast as well as to the proudest Brahman. But it was necessary to enter the order and submit to its stringent discipline. It is obvious that Buddha never believed that very many could or would do that. Jesus, whom we are accustomed to think of as wholly catholic in his sympathies, spoke the bitter words: "Give not what is holy to the dogs and cast not your pearls before swine." In Mohammedanism that which is mystical is esoteric: "all those emotions are meant only for a small number of chosen ones . . . even some of the noblest minds in Islam restrict true religious life to an aristocracy, and accept the ignorance of the multitude as an irremediable evil."

There is an aristocratic principle in all the religions which have attained wide acceptance. It is significant that Jesus was content to leave the governance of the mass of men to Caesar, and that he created no organization during his lifetime beyond the appointment of the Apostles. It is significant, because it shows how much more he was concerned with the few who could be saved than with arranging the affairs of the mass of mankind. Plato, who was a more systematic teacher than either Jesus or Buddha, did work out an elaborate social order which took account not only of the philosophers, but of all the citizens of the state.

But in that very attempt he rested upon the premise that most men will not attain the good life, and that for them it is necessary to institute the laws. "The worthy disciples of philosophy will be but a small remnant," he said, ". . . the guardian . . . must be required to take the longer circuit, and toil at learning as well as at gymnastics, or he will never reach the highest knowledge of all which is his proper calling."

Perhaps because they looked upon the attempts as hopeless, perhaps because they did not know how to go about it, perhaps because they were so wise, the greatest teachers have never offered their full wisdom to the multitude. Like Mr. Valiant-for-truth in *The Pilgrim's Progress* they said: "My sword I give to him that shall succeed me in my pilgrimage, and my courage and skill to him that can get it."

## 3. THE PECULIARITY OF THE MODERN SITUATION

But because the teaching of the sages was incomprehensible, the multitude, impressed but also bewildered, ignored them as teachers and worshipped them as gods. In their wisdom the people were not interested, but in the legends of their power, which rumor created, there was something understandable. And thus, the religions which have been organized around the names of great spiritual teachers have been popular in proportion, one might almost say, to the degree in which the original insight into the necessity for conversion and self-discipline has been reduced to a system of commands and promises which the common man can understand.

For popular religion is suited to the capacities of the unconverted. The adherents of a popular religion necessarily include an enormous number of people who are too young, or too feeble, too dull or too violent, too unstable or too incurious, to have any comprehension whatsoever of anything but the simplest scheme of rewards and punishments. An organized religion cannot neglect them if it has any pretensions to being universal. The great ecclesiastical establishments have often sheltered spiritual lives, and drawn new vitality from them. But fundamentally the great churches are secular institutions; they are governments preoccupied inevitably with the regulation of the unregenerate appetites of mankind. In their scriptures there is to be found the teaching that true salvation depends upon internal reform of desire. But since this reform is so very difficult, in practice the churches have devoted themselves not so much to making real conversions, as to governing the dispositions of the unconverted multitude.

They are immensely engaged by the task of administering their moral codes, persuading their congregations with promises, and threatening them with punishments if they do not keep their childish lusts within bounds. The fact that they use rewards and punishments, and appeal even to Caesar, is evidence enough that they are dealing with the unconverted. The fact that they invoke authority is in itself evidence that they are speaking to the naive. The fact that they pretend to have certain knowledge about the constitution of the universe is evidence that they are interested in those who are not wise enough to understand the limitations of knowledge. For to the few who are converted, goodness is pleasant, and needs no sanctions. It needs no authority, for it has been verified by experience. But when men have to be coerced into goodness, it is plain that they do not care for it.

Now although the great teachers saw clearly enough

the difference between the popular religion and their own insight, they were under no great compulsion to try and overcome it. They accepted the fact that the true religion was esoteric and for the few. They saw that it demanded the re-education of desire, but they had no systematic and tested knowledge of how new habits can be formed. Invincible as was their insight into the principle of happiness, they were compelled to depend upon introspection, and to generalize from a limited observation. They understood that the good life was in some degree an acquired disposition; they were aware that it is not easily or naively acquired.

For those who somehow had the disposition, the teachers instituted stern disciplines which were really primitive experiments in the re-education of desire. But there was no very urgent practical need which impelled them to search for ways of making disciplines more widely available. Those who submitted to them were in general individuals who were already out of the ordinary. The mass of mankind lived solidly within the framework of custom and the psychological compulsions of theocracy. There was no pressing reason, as there is to-day, now that this ancestral order is dissolved, why anyone should seek to formulate a mode of life by which ordinary men, thrown upon their own resources, can find their way without supernatural rules, commands, punishments, and compensations. In the past there were a few men here and there who had somehow, for reasons which we do not understand, outgrown the ancestral society in which they lived. But the society itself remained. It sheltered them. And it ruled the many.

The peculiarity of our modern situation is that multitudes, instead of a few, are compelled to make radical and original adjustments. These multitudes, though they have lost the ancient certainties, have not outgrown the needs to which they ministered. They need to believe, but they cannot. They need to be commanded, but they cannot find a commander. They need support, and there is none. Their situation is adult, but their dispositions are not. The religion of the spirit would suit their needs, but it would seem to be beyond their powers.

## 4. THE STONE WHICH THE BUILDERS REJECTED

The way of life which I have called high religion has in all ages seemed so unapproachably high that it has been reserved for a voluntary aristocracy of the spirit. It has, in fact, been looked upon not only as a kind of splendid idiosyncrasy of a few men here and there, but as incompatible, in essence, with the practical conditions under which life is lived. It is for these reasons, no doubt, that the practice of high religion has almost invariably been associated either with a solitary asceticism or with a specially organized life in monastic establishments. High religion has been regarded as something separate from the main concerns of mankind.

It is not difficult to see why this was so if we realize that the insight into the value of disinterestedness, which is the core of high religion, was not a sudden discovery nor a complete one, anywhere or any time. Like all other things associated with evolutionary man, this insight must have had very crude beginnings; it would be possible to show, I think, that there have been many tentative and partial perceptions of it which, under the clarifying power of men of genius, have at times become coherent. When we remember that we are dealing with an insight into the qualities of a matured personality, there is no reason to suppose that the full significance of this insight has ever been completely exhausted. It seems far more likely that the sages demonstrated the existence of the realm of the spirit, but that it still remains to be thoroughly explored.

If that is true then the attempt to live by these partial insights must necessarily have presented inordinate practical difficulties. Pythagoras, for example, seems to have grasped the idea that the disinterested study of mathematics and music was cleansing to the passions and also that in order to be disinterested it was necessary to have purity of mind. So when he established his society in Southern Italy he evidently attempted to combine the serious pursuit of science with an ascetic discipline. But the pursuit of science was too much for the mass of the faithful who assumed that "to follow Pythagoras meant to go barefoot and to abstain from animal flesh and beans." And this in turn was too much for the dignity of the learned who proceeded to dissociate themselves from the disciplinary aspect of the Pythagorean teaching. It is a fair conclusion, I think, that the breakdown of this early experiment must have been due fundamentally to the fact that Pythagoras could not have known any well-tested method of equipping his followers to appreciate science or anything besides a crude asceticism as a means of moral discipline. If this is true, then the reason for the failure lay in the fact that though the original insight was marvelously good, it was not implemented with the necessary technical knowledge for applying it. Only a few, we may suppose, who were already by the accidents of nature and nurture suited to the Pythagorean ideal, can ever have successfully applied it.

In the Christian pursuit of the higher religious life the practical difficulties presented themselves in a different way. In its beginning Christianity was a sect of obscure men and women who were out of touch with the intellectual interests of the Roman world. They were persecuted aliens both in Palestine and elsewhere, and they came to the conclusion that the Roman Empire and all its concerns was the Kingdom of Satan. This, together with the widespread belief in the Second Coming of Christ, dissociated the Christian life at the outset from the life of the world. Later on, when Christianity became the official religion of the Empire, and the Church a great secular institution which concerned itself with government and property and diplomacy and war, those who wished to live as nearly as possible according to the original meaning of the Gospels were quite evidently compelled to withdraw and live a separated life. "If any man love the world, the love of the Father is not in him. For all that is in the world, the lust of the flesh, and the lust of the eyes, and the pride of life, is not of the Father, but is of the world. And the world passeth away, and the lust thereof: but he that doeth the will of God abideth forever."

Although for some centuries the monasteries were the centers of what learning there was, the impression left by monasticism on mankind seems to have been that the highest type of religious life is not disinterested in human affairs, but uninterested; that it requires not merely the renunciation of worldly desires, but of the world itself. The insight was imperfect, and therefore as an example to mankind the practice was abortive and confusing. Yet only an uncomprehending person can fail to see that the vows of poverty, chastity, and obedience proceeded from a profound, if partial, understanding of human nature and its most perfect harmony. Plainly all manner of disorder both in society and in the individual result from greed, uncontrollable sexual desire, arrogance, and imperiousness. That was so plain to the early Christians, and on the other hand it was so little plain how those powerful passions could be civilized, that the monastics in effect gave up and attempted to excise them entirely from their natures. In this they did not succeed.

Had they known any way of curing the fever of human passion except by attempting to excise it, the insight of high religion would have had some practicable meaning for those who did not withdraw from the world. But no way was known, and therefore the practice of high religion had to mean separation from human society and violence to human nature. But why was there no other way known of overcoming the chaos of the passions? Was it because there is no other way? If that were so then the world is as hopeless as the early Christians thought it was; indeed it is more hopeless because it does not show any signs, as they believed, of coming to an end. Was it because the early Christian Fathers were not wise enough to discover a way? It is always a good rule, I think, to discard any idea based on the premise that the best minds of another age were congenitally inferior to our own. My conviction is that necessity is the mother of discovery and invention, and that the reason why the insight of high religion and the methods of practicing it were so imperfectly developed is that there was no practical necessity for developing them.

The mass of men lived in an ancestral order which was regulated by custom and authority, and made endurable by usage and compensatory consolations. The organic quality of that society into which they fitted took care of their passions; those who had outgrown such a society, or were so constituted that they did not fit it, were the exceptions. From them came the insight of high religion; for them a separated life was a possible solution of their personal problems. There was nothing in the nature of things to compel men to work out a way of life, I won't say for all men, but at least for many men, by which they could govern their own natures. Behind any such effort there would almost certainly have to be an urgent need. For the inertia of the human race is immense.

It is my thesis that because the acids of modernity have dissolved the adjustments of the ancestral order, there exists to-day, on a scale never before experienced by mankind and of an urgency without a parallel, the need for that philosophy of life of which the insight of high religion is a prophecy. For it is immature and unregenerate desire which creates the disorders and the frustrations that confound us. The preoccupation of the popular religion has been to find a way of governing these disorders and of compensating for their frustrations. The preoccupation of high religion is with the regeneration of the passions that create the disorders and the frustrations. Insofar as modernity has dissolved the power of the popular religion to govern and to compensate, the need for a high religion which regenerates becomes imperative, and what was once a kind of spiritual luxury of the few has, under modern conditions, become an urgent necessity of the many. The insight of high religion which has hitherto indicated a kind of bypath into rare experiences is now a trail which the leaders of mankind are compelled to take.

There is implied in this a radical displacement in the field of morals. The main interest of the practical moralist in the past has been to interpret, administer, and enforce a moral code. He knew what was right. The populace acknowledged that he knew what was right. His task was to persuade and compel them to do what was right. There was a tacit assumption, which was quite correct, that very often the populace and even the moralist himself would much rather have done what was wrong. Very often they did it. Then they were punished in this world or in the next. But to-day the moralist finds himself in a different position. He is no longer absolutely sure that he knows what is right. The populace, even if it respects him, is disinclined to believe that a thing is right simply because he says it is. The populace continues very frequently to prefer what was once regarded as wrong. It no longer knows whether it is right or wrong, and of course it gives itself the benefit of the doubt. The result is that there no longer exists a moral code which the moralist can interpret, administer, and enforce. The effect of that is moral anarchy within and without. Since there is no principle under modern conditions which authorizes the re-establishment of a moral code, the moralist, unless he revises his premises, becomes entirely ineffectual. To revise his premises can, under the circumstances, mean only one thing: that he occupies himself with the problem of how to encourage that growth into maturity, that outgrowing of naive desire, that cultivation of disinterestedness, which render passion innocent and an authoritative morality unnecessary.

The novelty of all this lies in the fact that the guardians of morality among the people are compelled at last to take seriously what the teachers of wisdom have taught. The insight of high religion may be said, then, to be a discovery in the field of human experience comparable with those prophetic conceptions in the natural sciences which, after being looked upon for long periods as a curiosity, are at last, because circumstances are ripe, seen to be the clue to otherwise insoluble perplexities. The concept of evolution was discovered by sheer insight innumerable times before the time of Darwin. Not much came of it until the rapid evolution of human affairs after the industrial revolution had somehow brought this neglected insight into focus with men's interests. There are many conceptions in the science of the Greeks which are true intimations of what modern physicists have found. But an insight of this sort comes into its own only when circumstances conspire to make it inevitably appropriate. It is my contention that in the field of morals circumstances are producing a somewhat analogous condition: that the insight of the sages into the value of disinterestedness has become the clue to otherwise insoluble perplexities.

Part Three

# THE
# GENIUS
# OF
# MODERNITY

*Where is the way where light dwelleth?*

JOB 38:19.

# XI The Cure of Souls

## 1. THE PROBLEM OF EVIL

The greatest of all perplexities in theology has been to reconcile the infinite goodness of God with his omnipotence. Nothing puts a greater strain upon the faith of the common man than the existence of utterly irrational suffering in the universe, and the problem which tormented Job still troubles every devout and thoughtful man who beholds the monstrous injustices of nature. If there were no pain in the world except that which was felt by responsible beings who had knowingly transgressed some law of conduct, there would, of course, be no problem of evil. Pain would be nothing but a rational punishment. But the pain which is suffered by those who according to all human standards are innocent, by children and by animals, for example, cannot be fitted into any rational theory of reward and punishment. It never has been. The classic attempts to solve the problem of evil invariably falsify the premises. This falsification may for a time satisfy the inquirer, but it does not settle the problem. That is why the problem is forever presenting itself again.

The solutions which have been proposed neglect one

or the other of the attributes of God: tacitly or otherwise
either his infinite power or his infinite love is denied. In the
Old Testament, at least in the older parts of it, the power
of God is exalted at the expense of his goodness. For it is
simply impossible by any human standard and within any
intelligible meaning of the words to regard Yahveh as
wholly good. His cruelty is notorious and his capricious-
ness is that of an Oriental despot. It is admitted, I believe,
by all but the most literally-minded of the fundamentalists that there are innumerable incidents in the Old Testament which have to be expurgated if the Bible is to be used
as a source book of conduct for impressionable children.
Now for the ancient Hebrews who conceived God in their
fashion, the problem of evil did not exist because it had not
occurred to them that a ruler should be just and good as
well as great and powerful.

As men came to believe that God must be just, beneficent, and loving, the problem soon presented itself. And
in the Book of Job, which is supposed to date from the
Fifth or Fourth Century B.C., we have a poignant effort
to solve it. Job's conclusion is that the goodness of Jehovah
is among the "things too wonderful for me." He accepts the
judgments of God, and acknowledges their goodness by at-
tributing to God a kind of goodness which is unlike the
human conception of goodness. He holds fast to the premise that God is omnipotent—"I know that thou canst do
all things"—and the other premise that God is beneficent
he redefines. Job's mind was satisfied, and it is reported
that he prospered greatly thereafter. What had really happened was that Job gave up the attempt to prove that God
was like Job, that the world was as Job wished it to be, and
so piously and with his mind at rest he made the best of
things, and went about his affairs.

In Job the solution is reached by claiming that what seems evil to us would really be recognized as goodness if our minds were not so limited. To the naive this is no solution at all, for it depends upon using the word 'good' in two senses; actually it was a perfect solution, for Job had resigned himself to the fact that God and the universe in which he was manifest are not controlled by human desires. Those who refused to accept this solution involved themselves in intricate theorizing. Some of them argued that evil is an illusion. This theory has been widely held, though it is rather difficult to see how, if evil is an illusion, good is not also an illusion. The one seems as vividly real as the other. It has also been argued by some that evil is not important. This, of course, does not solve the theoretical problem. In fact it ignores the problem and is really a piece of advice as to how men ought to conduct themselves in the presence of God. Many have argued, also, that evil exists in the world to test human character, that by bearing it and conquering it men prove their worth. There is a core of truth in this observation as there is in the theory that many things are not so bad as they seem. But it does not explain why a good and all-powerful Deity chose to make men go through a school of suffering to achieve goodness, when he might have created them good in the first place.

These theoretical difficulties have furnished the material for endless debate. I shall not pursue the matter in all its intricacies, but I venture to point out that what is attempted in all these solutions is ultimately to make plain why the ruler of the universe does not order things as we should order them if we had his power. Once we confess, as Job finally did, that the plan of the universe is not what we naively wish it would be, there is no problem of evil. For the whole difficulty arises because of our desire to impute to the universe itself, or to the god who rules it, purposes like our own; failing to find them, we are disappointed, and are plunged into elaborate and interminable debate.

The final insight of Job, though it seems to be consistent with the orthodox popular religion, is really wholly inconsistent with the inwardness of popular religion. The God of the Book of Job does not minister to human desires, and the story of Job is really the story of a man's renunciation of the belief in such a God. It is the story of how a man learned to accept life maturely. The God whose ways Job finally acknowledges is no longer a projection of Job's desires. He is like the God of Spinoza who cannot be cajoled into returning the love of his worshipper. He is, in short, the God of an impersonal reality.

Whether God is conceived as a creator of that reality, who administers it inexorably, or whether he is identified with reality and is conceived as the sum total of its laws, or whether, as in the language of modern science, the name of God is not employed at all, is a matter of metaphysical taste. The great divide lies between those who think their wishes are of more than human significance and those who do not. For these latter the problem of evil does not arise out of the difficulty of reconciling the existence of evil with their assumptions. They do not assume that reality must conform to human desire. The problem for them is wholly practical. It is the problem of how to remove evil and of how to bear the evil which cannot be removed.

Thus from the attempt to explain the ways of God in the world as it now is, nature and human nature being what they are, the center of interest is shifted to an attempt to discover ways of equipping man to conquer evil. This displacement has in fact taken place in the modern world. In their actual practice men do not try to account for evil in order that they may accept it; they do not deny evil in order that they may not have to account for it; they explain it in order that they may deal with it.


## 2. SUPERSTITION AND SELF-CONSCIOUSNESS

This change of attitude toward evil is not, as at first perhaps it may seem, merely a new way of talking about the same thing. It alters radically the nature of evil itself. For evil is not a quality of things as such. It is a quality of our relation to them. A dissonance in music is unpleasant only to a musical ear. Pain is an evil only if someone suffers, and there are those to whom pain is pleasure and most men's evil their good. For things are neutral and evil is a certain way of experiencing them.

To realize this is to destroy the awfulness of evil. I use the word 'awful' in its exact sense, and I mean that in abandoning the notion that evil has to be reconciled with a theory of how the world is governed, we rob it of universal significance. We deflate it. The psychological consequences are enormous, for a very great part of all human suffering lies not in the pain itself, but in the anxiety contributed by the meaning which we attach to it. Lucretius understood this quite well, and in his superb argument against the fear of death he reasoned that death has no terror because nothing can be terrible to those who no longer exist. Before we were born, he says, "we felt no distress when the Poeni from all sides came together to do battle. . . . For he whom evil is to befall, must in his own person exist at the very time it comes, if the misery and suffering are haply to have any place at all." St. Thomas defines superstition as the vice of excess in religion, and in this sense of the word it may be said that the effect of the modern approach is to take evils out of the context of superstition.

They cease to be signs and portents symbolizing the whole of human destiny and become specific and distinguishable situations which have to be dealt with. The effect of this is not only to limit drastically the meaning, and therefore the dreadfulness, of any evil, but to substitute for a general sense of evil an analytical estimate of particular evils. They are then seen to be of long duration and of short, preventable, curable, or inevitable. As long as all evils are believed somehow to fit into a divine, if mysterious, plan, the effort to eradicate them must seem on the whole futile, and even impious. The history of medical progress offers innumerable instances of how men have resisted the introduction of sanitary measures because they dreaded to interfere with the providence of God. It is still felt, I believe, in many quarters, even in medical circles, that to mitigate the labor pains in childbirth is to blaspheme against the commandment that in pain children shall be brought forth. An aura of dread surrounds evil as long as evil situations remain entangled with a theory of divine government.

The realization that evil exists only because we feel it to be painful helps us not only to dissociate it from this aura of dread but to dissociate ourselves from our own feelings about it. This is a momentous achievement in the inner life of man. To be able to observe our own feelings as if they were objective facts, to detach ourselves from our own fears, hates, and lusts, to examine them, name them, identify them, understand their origin, and finally to judge them, is somehow to rob them of their imperiousness. They are no longer the same feelings. They no longer dominate the whole field of consciousness. They seem no longer to command the whole energy of our being. By becoming conscious of them we in some fashion or other destroy their concentration and diffuse their energy into other channels. We cease to be possessed by one passion; contrary passions retain their vitality, and an equilibrium tends to establish itself.

Just what the psychological mechanism of all this is I do not pretend to say. It is something to which psychologists are giving increasing attention. But since Hellenic times the phenomenon which I have been describing has been well known. It was undoubtedly what the Sophists meant by the injunction: know thyself. It was in large measure to achieve control through detachment that Socrates elaborated his dialectic, for the Socratic dialectic is an instrument for making men self-conscious, and therefore the masters of their motives. Spinoza grasped this principle with great clarity. "An emotion," he says, "which is a passion ceases to be a passion as soon as we form a clear and distinct idea of it." He goes on to say that "insofar as the mind understands all things as necessary, it has more power over the emotions, or is less passive to them."

The more recent discoveries in the field of psychoanalysis are an elaboration of this principle. They are based on the discovery of Freud and Breuer at the close of the last century that a catharsis of emotion is often obtained if the patient can be made to recall, and thus to relive by describing it, the emotional situation which troubles him. The release of the psychic poison is known technically as an abreaction. Where the new psychology supplements the insights of the Sophists, of Socrates, and Spinoza, is in the demonstration that there are powerful passions affecting our lives of which it is impossible by ordinary effort of memory "to form a clear and distinct idea." They are said to be unconscious, or more accurately, I suppose, they are out of the reach of the normal consciousness. Freud and his school have invented an elaborate technic by which the analyst is able frequently to help the patient thread his way back through a chain of associations to the buried passion and fetch it into consciousness.

The special technic of psychoanalysis can be tested only by scientific experience. The therapeutic claims made by psychoanalysts, and their theories of the functional disorders, lie outside the realm of this discussion. But the essential principle is not a technical matter. Anyone can confirm it out of his own experience. It has been discovered and rediscovered by shrewd observers of human nature for at least two thousand years. To become detached from one's passions and to understand them consciously is to render them disinterested. A disinterested mind is harmonious with itself and with reality.

This is the principle by which a humanistic culture becomes bearable. If the principle of a theocratic culture is dependence, obedience, conformity in the presence of a superhuman power which administers reality, the principle of humanism is detachment, understanding, and disinterestedness in the presence of reality itself.

## 3. VIRTUE

It can be shown, I think, that those qualities which civilized men, regardless of their theologies and their allegiances, have agreed to call virtues, have disinterestedness as their inner principle. I am not talking now about the eccentric virtues which at some time or other have been held in great esteem. I am not talking about the virtue of not playing cards, or of not drinking wine, or of not eating beef, or of not eating pork, or of not admitting that women have legs. These little virtues are historical accidents which may or may not once have had a rational origin. I am talking about the central virtues which are esteemed by every civilized people. I am talking about such virtues as courage, honor, faithfulness, veracity, justice, temperance, magnanimity, and love.

They would not be called virtues and held in high esteem if there were no difficulty about them. There are innumerable dispositions which are essential to living that no one takes the trouble to praise. Thus it is not accounted a virtue if a man eats when he is hungry or goes to bed when he is ill. He can be depended upon to take care of his immediate wants. It is only those actions which he cannot be depended upon to do, and yet are highly desirable, that men call virtuous. They recognize that a premium has to be put upon certain qualities if men are to make the effort which is required to transcend their ordinary impulses. The premium consists in describing these desirable and rarer qualities as virtues. For virtue is that kind of conduct which is esteemed by God, or public opinion, or that less immediate part of a man's personality which he calls his conscience.

To transcend the ordinary impulses is, therefore, the common element in all virtue. Courage, for example, is the willingness to face situations from which it would be more or less natural to run away. No one thinks it is courageous to run risks unwittingly. The drunken driver of an automobile, the boy playing with a stick of dynamite, the man drinking water which he does not know is polluted, all take risks as great as those of the most renowned heroes. But the fact that they do not know the risks, and do not, therefore, have to conquer the fear they would feel if they did know them, robs their conduct of all courage. The test is not the uselessness or even the undesirability of their acts. It is useless to go over Niagara Falls in a barrel. But it is brave, assuming the performer to be in his right mind. It is a wicked thing to assassinate a king. But if it is not done from ambush, it is brave, however wicked and however useless.

Because courage consists in transcending normal fears, the highest kind of courage is cold courage; that is to say, courage in which the danger has been fully realized and there is no emotional excitement to conceal the danger. The world instantly recognized this in Colonel Lindbergh's flight to Paris. He flew alone; he was not an impetuous fool, but a man of the utmost sobriety of judgment. He had no companion to keep his courage screwed up; he knew exactly what he was doing, yet apparently he did not realize the rewards which were in store for him. The world understood that here was somebody who was altogether braver than the average sensual man. For Colonel Lindbergh did not merely conquer the Atlantic Ocean; he conquered those things in himself which the rest of us would have found unconquerable.

The cold courage of a man like Noguchi who, though in failing health, went into one of the unhealthiest parts of Africa to study a deadly disease, could come only from a nature which was overwhelmingly interested in objects outside itself. Noguchi must have known exactly how dangerous it was for him to go to Africa, and exactly how horrible was the disease to which he exposed himself. To have gone anyway is really to have cared for science in a way which very few care for anything so remote and impersonal. But even courage like Lindbergh's and Noguchi's is more comprehensible than the kind of courage which anonymous men have displayed. I am thinking of the four soldiers at the Walter Reed Hospital who let themselves be used for the study of yellow fever. They did not even have Lindbergh's interest in performing a great feat or Noguchi's interest in science to buoy them up and carry them past the point where they might have faltered. Their courage was as near to absolute courage as it is possible to imagine, and I who think this cannot even recall their names.

To understand the inwardness of courage would be, I think, to have understood almost all the other important virtues. It is "not only the chiefest virtue and most dignifies the haver," but it embodies the principle of all virtue, which is to transcend the immediacy of desire and to live for ends which are transpersonal. Virtuous action is conduct which responds to situations that are more extensive, more complicated, and take longer to reach their fulfilment, than the situations to which we instinctively respond. An infant knows neither vice nor virtue because it can respond only to what touches it immediately. A man has virtue insofar as he can respond to a larger situation.

He has honor if he holds himself to an ideal of conduct though it is inconvenient, unprofitable, or dangerous to do so. He has veracity if he says and believes what he thinks is true though it would be easier to deceive others or himself. He is just if he acknowledges the interests of all concerned in a transaction and not merely his own apparent interest. He is temperate if, in the presence of temptation, he can still prefer Philip sober to Philip drunk. He is magnanimous if, as Aristotle says, he cares "more for truth than for opinion," speaks and acts openly, will not live at the will of another, except it be a friend, does not recollect injuries, does not care that he should be praised or that others should be blamed, does not complain or ask for help in unavoidable or trifling calamities. For such a man, as the word 'magnanimous' itself implies, is "conversant with great matters."

A man who has these virtues has somehow overcome the inertia of his impulses. Their disposition is to respond to the immediate situation, and not merely to the situation at the moment, but to the most obvious fragment of it, and not only to the most obvious fragment, but to that aspect which promises instant pleasure or pain. To have virtue is to respond to larger situations and to longer stretches of time and without much interest in their immediate result in convenience and pleasure. It is to overcome the impulses of immaturity, to detach one's self from the objects that preoccupy it and from one's own preoccupations. There are many virtues in the catalogues of the moralists, and they have many different names. But they have a common principle, which is detachment from that which is apparently pleasant or unpleasant, and they have a common quality, which is disinterestedness, and they spring from a common source, which is maturity of character.

Few men, if any, possess virtue in all its varieties because few men are wholly matured to the core of their being. We are for the most part like fruit which is partly ripened: there is sourness and sweetness in our natures. This may be due to the casualness of our upbringing; it may be due to unknown congenital causes; it may be due to functional and organic disease, to partial inferiorities of mind and body. But it is due also to the fact that we can give our full attention only to a few phases of our experience. With the equipment at our disposal we are forced to specialize and to neglect very much. Hence the mature scientist with petty ambitions and ignoble timidities. Hence the realistic statesman who is a peevish husband. Hence the man who manages his affairs in masterly fashion and bungles every personal relationship when he is away from his office. Hence the loyal friend who is a crooked politician, the kind father who is a merciless employer, the champion of mankind who is an intolerable companion. If any of these could carry over into all their relationships the qualities which have made them distinguished in some, they would be wholly adult and wholly good. It would not be necessary to imagine the ideal character, for he would already exist.

It is out of these practical virtues that our conception of virtue has been formed. We may be sure that no quality is likely to have become esteemed as a virtue which did not somewhere and sometime produce at least the appearance of happiness. The virtues are grounded in experience; they are not idle suggestions inadvertently adopted because somebody took it into his head one fine day to proclaim a new ideal. There are, to be sure, certain residual and obsolete virtues which no longer correspond to anything in our own experience and now seem utterly arbitrary and capricious. But the cardinal virtues correspond to an experience so long and so nearly universal among men of our civilization, that when they are understood they are seen to contain a deposited wisdom of the race.

## 4. FROM CLUE TO PRACTICE

The wisdom deposited in our moral ideals is heavily obscured at the present time. We continue to use the language of morality, having no other which we can use. But the words are so hackneyed that their meanings are concealed, and it is very hard, especially for young people, to realize that virtue is really good and really relevant. Morality has become so stereotyped, so thin and verbal, so encrusted with pious fraud, it has been so much monopolized by the tender-minded and the sentimental, and made so odious by the outcries of foolish men and sour old women, that our generation has almost forgotten that virtue was not invented in Sunday schools but derives originally from a profound realization of the character of human life.

This sense of unreality is, I believe, due directly to the widespread loss of genuine belief in the premises of popular religion. Virtue is a product of human experience: men acquired their knowledge of the value of courage, honor, temperance, veracity, faithfulness, and love, because these qualities were necessary to their survival and to the attainment of happiness. But this human justification of virtue does not carry conviction to the immature, and would not of itself break up the inertia of their naive impulses. Therefore, virtue which derives from human insight has to be imposed on the immature by authority; what was obtained on Sinai was not the revelation of the moral law but divine authority to teach it.

Now the very thing which made moral wisdom convincing to our ancestors makes it unconvincing to modern men. We do not live in a patriarchal society. We do not live in a world which disposes us to a belief in theocratic government. And therefore insofar as moral wisdom is entangled with the premises of theocracy it is unreal to us. The very thing which gave authority to moral insight for our forefathers obscures moral insight for us. They lived in the kind of world which disposed them to practice virtue if it came to them as a divine commandment. A thoroughly modernized young man to-day distrusts moral wisdom precisely because it is commanded.

It is often said that this distrust is merely an aspect of

the normal rebellion of youth. I do not believe it. This distrust is due to a much more fundamental cause. It is due not to a rebellion against authority but to an unbelief in it. This unbelief is the result of that dissolution of the ancient order out of which modern civilization is emerging, and unless we understand the radical character of this unbelief we shall never understand the moral confusion of this age. We shall fail to see that morals taught with authority are pervaded with a sense of unreality because the sense of authority is no longer real. Men will not feel that wisdom is authentic if they are asked to believe that it derives from something which does not seem authentic.

We may be quite certain, therefore, that we shall not succeed in making the traditional morality convincingly authentic to modern men. The whole tendency of the age is to make it seem less and less authentic. The effort to impose it, nevertheless, merely deepens the confusion by converting the discussion of morals from an examination of experience into a dispute over its metaphysical sanctions. The consequence of this dispute is to drive men, especially the most sensitive and courageous, further away from insight into virtue and deeper and deeper into mere negation and rebellion. What they are actually rebelling against is the theocratic system in which they do not believe. But because that system appears to them to claim a vested interest in morality they empty out the baby with the bath, and lose all sense of the inwardness of deposited wisdom.

For that reason the recovery of moral insight depends upon disentangling virtue from its traditional sanctions and the metaphysical framework which has hitherto supported it. It will be said, I know, that this would rob virtue of its popular prestige. My answer is that in those communities which are deeply under modern influences the loss of belief in these very traditional sanctions and this very metaphysical framework has robbed virtue of its relevance. I should readily grant that for communities and for individuals which are outside the orbit of modernity, it is neither necessary nor desirable to disentangle morality from its ancient associations. It is also impossible to do so, for when the ancestral order is genuinely alive, there is no problem of unbelief. But where the problem exists, when the ancient premises of morality have faded into mere verbal acknowledgments, then these ancient premises obscure vision. They have ceased to be the sanctions of virtue and have become obstructions to moral insight. Only by deliberately thinking their way past these obstructions can modern men recover that innocence of the eye, that fresh, authentic sense of the good in human relations on which a living morality depends.

I have tried in these pages to do that for myself. I am under no illusion as to the present value of the conceptions arrived at. I regard them simply as a probable clue to the understanding of modernity. If the clue is indicative, the more we explore the modern world the more coherence it will give to our understanding of it. A true insight is fruitful; it multiplies insight, until at last it not only illuminates a situation but provides a practical guide to conduct. I believe the insight of high religion into the value of disinterestedness will, if pursued resolutely, untangle the moral confusion of the age and make plain, as it is not now plain, what we are really driving at in our manifold activity, what we are compelled to want, what, rather dimly now, we do want, and how to proceed about achieving it. To say that is to say that I believe in the hypothesis. I do believe in it. I believe that this valuation of human life, which was once the possession of an élite, now conforms to the premises of a whole civilization.

The proof of that must lie in a detailed and searching examination of the facts all about us. If the ideal of human character which is prophesied in high religion is really suitable and necessary in modern civilization, then an examination ought to show that events themselves are pregnant with it. If they are not, then all this is moonshine and cobwebs and castles in the air. Unless circumstance and necessity are behind it, the insight of high religion is still, as it has always been hitherto, a noble eccentricity of the soul. For men will not take it seriously, they will not devote themselves to the discovery and invention of ways of cultivating maturity, detachment, and disinterestedness unless events conspire to drive them to it.

The realization of this ideal is plainly a process of education in the most inclusive sense of that term. But it will not do much good to tell mothers that they should lead their children away from their childishness; an actual mother, even if she understood so abstruse a bit of advice, and did not reject it out of hand as a reflection upon the glory of childhood, would insist upon being told very concretely what this good advice means and how with a bawling infant in the cradle you go about cultivating his capacity to be disinterested. It is not much better to offer the advice to school-teachers; they will wish to know what they must not do that they now do, and what they must do that they leave undone. But the answers of these questions are no more to be had from the original concept than are rules for breeding fine cattle to be had from the theory of evolution and Mendel's law. By the use of the concept, psychologists and educators may, if the concept is correct and if they are properly encouraged, thread their way by dialectic and by experiment to practical knowledge which is actually usable as a method of education and as a personal discipline.

If they are to do that they will have to see quite clearly just how and in what sense the ideal of disinterestedness is inherent and inevitable in the modern world. The remaining chapters of this book are an attempt to do that by demonstrating that in three great phases of human interest, in business, in government, and in sexual relations, the ideal is now implicit and necessary.

# XII The Business of the Great Society

## 1. THE INVENTION OF INVENTION

One of the characteristics of the age we live in is that we are forever trying to explain it. We feel that if we understood it better we should know better how to live in it, and should cease to be aliens who do not know the landmarks of a strange country. There is, however, a school of philosophic historians who argue that this sense of novelty in the modern world is an illusion, and that as a matter of fact mankind has passed before through the same phase of the same inexorable cycle. The boldest of them, like Oswald Spengler, cite chapter and verse to show that there have been several of these great cycles of development from incubation through maturity to decay, and that our western civilization which began about 900 A.D. is now in the phase which corresponds with the century after Pericles in the classical world.

That the analogy is striking no reader of Spengler will deny who can endure Spengler's procrustean determination to make the evidence fit the theory. We can see the growth of towns at the expense of the farms, the rise of capitalism, the growth of international trade and finance, a development of nationalism, of democracy, attempts at the abolition of war through international organization, and with it all a dissolution of the popular religion of the traditional morality, and vast and searching inquiry into the meaning of life. There is little doubt that the speculation of the Greek philosophers seems extraordinarily fresh to us, because they were confronted with a situation in many respects remarkably like our own.

But however nicely such analogies are worked out they are superficial and misleading. There is something radically new in the modern world, something for which there is no parallel in any other civilization. This new thing is usually described as power-driven machinery. Thus Mr. Charles A. Beard says that "what is called Western or modern civilization by way of contrast with the civilization of the Orient or Mediaeval times is at bottom a civilization that rests upon machinery and science as distinguished from one founded on agriculture or handicraft commerce. It is in reality a technological civilization . . . and . . . it threatens to overcome and transform the whole globe." By way of illustrating how deeply machinery affects human life, Mr. Beard says that because they are untouched by this machine civilization "there are more fundamental resemblances between the culture of a peasant in a remote village in Spain and that of a peasant in a remote village in Japan than between the culture of a Christian priest of the upper Pyrenees and that of a Baptist clergyman in a thriving manufacturing town in Illinois."

Mr. H. G. Wells uses much the same argument to show that in spite of the apparent similarities there is an essential difference between our civilization and the later phases of the classical. "The essential difference," he says, "between the amassing of riches, the extinction of small farmers and small business men, and the phase of big finance in the latter centuries of the Roman republic on the one hand, and the very similar concentration of capital in the eighteenth and nineteenth centuries on the other, lies in the profound difference in the character of labor that the mechanical revolution was bringing about. The power of the old world was human power; everything depended ultimately upon the driving power of human muscle, the muscle of ignorant and subjugated men. A little animal muscle, supplied by draft oxen, horse traction, and the like contributed. Where a weight had to be lifted, men lifted it; where a rock had to be quarried, men chipped it out; where a field had to be ploughed, men and oxen ploughed it; the Roman equivalent of the steamship was the galley with its banks of sweating rowers. . . . The Roman civilization was built upon cheap and degraded human beings; modern civilization is being rebuilt upon cheap mechanical power."

These differences are genuine enough, and yet it is doubtful whether Mr. Wells has described the really "new thing in human experience." After all a great deal of cheap man power is still used in conjunction with cheap mechanical power; it is somewhat of an idealization to talk as if the machine had supplanted the drudge. What Mr. Wells has in mind, of course, is that in the Roman world a vast proportion of mankind were doomed to "purely mechanical drudgery" whereas in the modern world there is tangible hope that they will be released from it. They are not yet released from it, however, and their hope of release rests upon the really new element in human experience.

The various mechanical inventions from James Watt's steam engine to the electric dishwasher and vacuum cleaner are not this new element. All these inventions, singly or collectively, though they have revolutionized the manner of human life, are not the ultimate reason why men put such hope in machines. Their hope is not based on the machines we possess. They are obviously a mixed blessing. Their hope is based on the machines that are yet to be made, and they have reason to hope because a really new thing has come into the world. That thing is the invention of invention.

Men have not merely invented the modern machines. There have been machines invented since the earliest days, incalculably important, like the wheel, like sailing ships, like the windmill and the watermill. But in modern times men have invented a method of inventing, they have discovered a method of discovery. Mechanical progress has ceased to be casual and accidental and has become systematic and cumulative. We know, as no other people ever knew before, that we shall make more and more perfect machines. When Mr. Beard says that "the machine civilization differs from all others in that it is highly dynamic, containing within itself the seeds of constant reconstruction," he is, I take it, referring to this supreme discovery which is the art of discovery itself.

## 2. THE CREATIVE PRINCIPLE IN MODERNITY

Although the disposition to scientific thought may be said to have originated in remote antiquity, it was not until the Sixteenth Century of our era that it ceased to appear spasmodically and as if by chance. The Greeks had their schools on the shores of the Aegean, in Sicily, and in Alexandria, and in them some of the conclusions and much of the spirit of scientific inquiry was imaginatively anticipated. But the conscious organized effort to relate "general principles to irreducible and stubborn facts," as Mr. Whitehead puts it, began about three hundred years ago. The first society chiefly devoted to science seems to have been founded by della Porta at Naples in 1560, but it was closed by the ecclesiastical authorities. Forty years later the *Accademia dei Lincei* was founded at Rome with Galileo among its early members. The Royal Society of London was chartered in 1662. The French Academy of Sciences began its meetings in 1666, the Berlin Academy in 1700, the American Philosophical Association was proposed by Benjamin Franklin in 1743 and organized in 1769.

The active pursuit of science is a matter, then, of only a few hundred years. The practical consequences in the form of useful inventions are still more recent. Newcomen's air-and-steam engine dates from 1705, but it was not until 1764 that James Watt produced a practicable steam engine. It was not until the beginning of the Nineteenth Century that invention really got under way and began to transform the structure of civilization. It was not until about 1850 that the importance of invention had impressed itself upon the English people, yet they were the first to experience the effects of the mechanical revolution. They had seen the first railway, the first steamboat, the illumination of towns by gas, and the application of power-driven machinery to manufacture. Professor Bury fixes the Exhibition of London in 1851 as the event which marks the public recognition of the role of science in modern civilization. The Prince Consort who originated the Exhibition said in his opening speech that it was designed "to give us a true test and a living picture of the point of development at which the whole of mankind has arrived in this great task, and a new starting-point from which the nations will be able to direct their further exertions."

But this public recognition was at first rather sentimental and gaping. The full realization of the place of science in modern life came slowly, and only in our generation can it be said that political rulers, captains of industry, and leaders of thought have actually begun to appreciate how central is science in our civilization, and to act upon that realization. In our time governments have begun to take science seriously and to promote research and invention not only in the art of war, but in the interest of trade, agriculture, and public hygiene. Great corporations have established laboratories of their own, not merely for the perfecting of their own processes, but for the promotion of pure research. Money has become available in great quantities for scientific work in the universities, and the educational curriculum down to the lowest grades has begun to be reorganized not only in order to train a minority of the population for research and invention, but to train the great majority to understand and use the machines and the processes which are available.

The motives and the habits of mind which are thus brought into play at the very heart of modern civilization are mature and disinterested. That may not be the primary intention, but it is the inevitable result. No doubt governments encourage research in order to have powerful weapons with which to overawe their neighbors; no doubt industries encourage research because it pays; no doubt scientists and inventors are in some measure moved by the desire for wealth and fame; no doubt the general public approves of science because of the pleasures and conveniences it provides; no doubt there is an intuitive sense in modern communities that the prospects of survival both for nations and for individuals are somehow related to their command of scientific knowledge. But nevertheless, whatever the motives which cause men to endow laboratories, to work patiently in laboratories or to buy the products, the fact remains that inside the laboratory, at the heart of this whole business, the habit of disinterested realism in dealing with the data is the indispensable habit of mind. Unless this habit of mind exists in the actual research, all the endowments and honorary degrees and prize awards will not produce the results desired. This is an original and tremendous fact in human experience: that a whole civilization should be dependent upon technology, that this technology should be dependent upon pure science, and that this pure science should be dependent upon a race of men who consciously refuse, as Mr. Bertrand Russell has said, to regard their "own desires, tastes, and interests as affording a key to the understanding of the world."

When I say that the refusal is conscious I do not mean merely that scientists tell themselves that they must ignore their prejudices. They have developed an elaborate method for detecting and discounting their prejudices. It consists of instruments of precision, an accurate vocabulary, controlled experiment, and the submission not only of their results but of their processes to the judgment of their peers. This method provides a body in which the spirit of disinterestedness can live, and it might be said that modern science, not in its crude consequences but in its inward principle, not, that is to say, as manifested in automobiles, electric refrigerators, and rayon silk, but in the behavior of the men who invent and perfect these things, is the actual realization in a practicable mode of conduct which can be learned and practiced, of the insight of high religion. The scientific discipline is one way in which this insight, hitherto lyrical and personal and apart, is brought down to earth and into direct and decisive contact with the concerns of mankind.

It is no exaggeration to say that pure science is high religion incarnate. No doubt the science we have is not the whole incarnation, but as far as it goes it translates into a usable procedure what in the teaching of the sages has been an esoteric insight. Scientific method can be learned. The learning of it matures the human character. Its value can be demonstrated in concrete results. Its importance in human life is indisputable. But the insight of high religion as such could be appreciated only by those who were already mature; it corresponded to nothing in the experience and the necessities of the ordinary man. It could be talked about but not taught; it could inspire only the few who were somehow already inspired. With the discovery of scientific method the insight has ceased to be an intangible and somewhat formless idea and has become an organized effort which moves mankind more profoundly than anything else in human affairs. Therefore, what was once a personal attitude on the part of a few who were somewhat withdrawn and disregarded has become the central principle in the careers of innumerable, immensely influential, men.

Because the scientific discipline is, in fact, the creative element in that which is distinctively modern, circumstances conspire to enhance its prestige and to extend its acceptance. It is the ultimate source of profit and of power, and therefore it is assured of protection and encouragement by those who rule the modern state. They cannot afford not to cultivate the scientific spirit: the nation which does not cultivate it cannot hold its place among the nations, the corporation which ignores it will be destroyed by its competitors. The training of an ever increasing number of pure scientists, of inventors, and of men who can operate and repair machinery is, therefore, a sheer practical necessity. The scientific discipline has become, as Mr. Graham Wallas would say, an essential part of our social heritage. For the machine technology requires a population which in some measure partakes of the spirit which created it.

Naturally enough, however, the influence of the scientific spirit becomes more and more diluted the further one goes from the work of the men who actually conceive, discover, invent, and perfect the modern machines. From Faraday, Maxwell, and Hertz who did the chief work which made possible the wireless it is a long way to the broker who sells radio stock or the householder with his six-tube set. I have not been supposing that these latter partake in any way of the original spirit which made the radio possible. But it is a fact of enormous consequences, cumulative in its effect upon the education of succeeding generations, that the radio, and all the other contrivances around which modern civilization is constructed, should be possible only by the increasing use of a scientific discipline.

## 3. NAIVE CAPITALISM

The application of science to the daily affairs of men was acclaimed at first with more enthusiasm than understanding. "That early people," said Buffon, speaking of the Babylonians, "was very happy, because it was very scientific." Entranced with the success of the Newtonian physics and by the dazzling effect of inventions, the intellectuals of the Eighteenth Century persuaded themselves that science was a messianic force which would liberate mankind from pain, drudgery, and error. It was believed that science would somewhat mysteriously endow mankind with invincible power over the forces of nature, and that men, if they were released from the bondage of religious custom and belief, could employ the power of science to their own consummate happiness. The mechanical revolution, in short, was inaugurated on the theory that the natural man must be liberated from moral conventions and that nature must be subjugated by mechanical instruments.

There are intelligible historical reasons why our great-grandfathers adopted this view. They found themselves in a world regulated by the customs and beliefs of a landed society. They could not operate their factories successfully in such a society, and they rebelled fiercely against the customs which restricted them. That rebellion was rationalized in the philosophy of *laissez-faire* which meant in essence that machine industry must not be interfered with by landlords and peasants who had feudal rights, nor by governments which protected those rights. On the positive side this rebellion expressed itself in declarations of the rights of man. These declarations were a denial of the vested rights of men under the old landed order and an assertion of the rights of men, particularly the new middle-class men, who proposed to make the most of the new industrial and mechanical order. By the rights of men they meant primarily freedom of contract, freedom of trade, freedom of occupation—those freedoms, that is to say, which made it possible for the new employer to buy and sell, to hire and fire without being accountable to anyone.

The prophet of this new dispensation was Adam Smith. In the *Wealth of Nations* he wrote that

> All systems either of preference or of restraint . . . being thus completely taken away, the obvious and simple system of natural lib-

> erty establishes itself of its own accord. Every
> man, as long as he does not violate the laws of
> justice, is left perfectly free to pursue his own
> interest his own way, and to bring both his in-
> dustry and capital into competition with those
> of any other man, or order of men.

The employing class in the early days of capitalism
honestly believed, and indeed its less enlightened members
still believe to this very day, that somehow the general
welfare will be served by trusting naively to the acquisitive
instincts of the employing capitalist. Thus at the outset
the machine technology was applied under the direction of
men who scorned as sentimental, when they did not regard
as subversive, that disinterestedness which alone makes
possible the machine technology itself. They did not understand science. They merely exploited certain of the inventions which scientists produced. What they believed, insofar
as they had any philosophy, was that there exists a pre-
established harmony in the universe—an "obvious and simple system of natural liberty," in Adam Smith's language,
"which establishes itself of its own accord"—by which if
each man naively pursued his primitive impulse to have
and to hold in competition with other men, peace, prosperity, and happiness would ensue.

They did not ensue. And the social history of the last
seventy-five years has in large measure been concerned with
the birth pains of an industrial philosophy that will really
suit the machine technology and the nature of man. For
the notion that an intricate and delicately poised industrial
mechanism could be operated by uneducated men snatch-
ing competitively at profits was soon exposed as a simple-
minded delusion.

It was discovered that if each banker was permitted
to do what seemed to him immediately most profitable,

the result was a succession of disastrous inflations and deflations of credit; that if natural resources in oil, coal, lumber, and the like were subjected to the competitive principle, the result was a shocking waste of irreplaceable wealth; that if the hiring and firing of labor were carried on under absolute freedom of contract, a whole chain of social evils in the form of child labor, unsuitable labor for women, sweating, unemployment, and the importation of cheap and unassimilable labor resulted; that if business men were left to their own devices the consumer of necessary goods was helpless when he was confronted with industries in which there was an element of monopoly. There is no need here to recount the well-known story of how in every modern community the theory of free competition has in the course of the last generation been modified by legislation, by organized labor, by organized business itself. So little has *laissez-faire* worked under actual experience that all the powers of the government have actually had to be invoked to preserve a certain amount of compulsory "free competition." For the industrial machine, as soon as it passes out of the early phase of rough exploitation in virgin territory, becomes unmanageable by naively competitive and acquisitive men.

## 4. THE CREDO OF OLD-STYLE BUSINESS

It was frequently pointed out by moralists like Ruskin and William Morris, and by churchmen as well, that this "obvious and simple system of natural liberty" by which "every man was left perfectly free to pursue his own interest his own way," was not only contrary to the dogmas of the popular religion but irreconcilable with moral wisdom. The credo of the unregenerate business man was utterly atheistical in its premises, for it displaced the notion that there is any higher will than his own to which the employer is accountable. It was more than atheistical, however; it was, in Aristotle's sense of the word, barbarous in that it implied "the living as one likes" with virtually complete acquiescence in the supremacy of the acquisitive instinct.

There is no reason to suppose that such theoretical comments on the credo of naive capitalism did more than rub off a little of its unction. Capitalism may be, as Mr. Maynard Keynes has said, "absolutely irreligious . . . often, though not always, a mere congeries of possessors and pursuers." Were the credo workable in practice, some way would have been found of anointing it with attractive phrases. The real reason for the gradual abandonment of the credo, proclaimed by Adam Smith and repeated so steadily since his day, is that the credo of naive capitalism is deeply at variance with the real character of modern industry. It rests upon false premises, is therefore contradicted by experience, and has proved to be unworkable.

The system of natural liberty assumes that if each man pursues his own interest his own way, each man will promote his interest. There is an unanalyzed fallacy in this theory which makes it utterly meaningless. It is assumed that each man knows his own interest and can therefore pursue it. But that is precisely what no man is certain to know, and what few men can possibly know if they consult only their own impulses. There is nothing in the natural equipment of man which enables him to know intuitively whether it will be profitable to increase his output or reduce it, to enter a new line of business, to buy or to sell, or to make any of the other thousand and one decisions on which the conduct of business depends. Since he is not born with this wisdom, since he does not automatically absorb it from the air, to pursue his own interest his own way is a fairly certain way to disaster.

The fallacy of the theory of natural liberty is undetected in a bonanza period of industrial development. Where the business man has unexhausted natural resources to draw upon, where there is a surplus of customers competing for his goods, he can with naive and furious energy pursue his own interests his own way and reap enormous profits. There is no real resistance from the outside; there are no stubborn and irreducible facts to which he must adjust himself. He can proceed with an infantile philosophy to achieve success. But this bonanza period when the omnipotence of the capitalist is unthwarted, and his omniscience therefore assumed, soon comes to an end. In advanced communities the mere multiplication of industries produces such a complicated environment that the business man is compelled to substitute considered policies for his intuitions, objective surveys for his guesses, and conferences world without end for his natural liberties.

What has upset the idea of the old-style business man that he knows what's what is that the relevant facts are no longer visible. The owner of a primitive factory might have known all his working men and all his customers; the keeper of a little neighborhood shop may still, to a certain extent, know personally his whole business. But for most men to-day the facts which matter vitally to them are out of sight, beyond their personal control, intricate, subject to more or less unpredictable changes, and even with highly technical reporting and analysis almost unintelligible to the average man.

It is, of course, the machine process itself which has created these complications. Men are forced to buy and sell in markets that for many commodities are world-wide: they do not buy and sell in one market but in many markets, in markets for raw materials, in markets for semi-finished goods, in wholesale and retail markets, in labor markets, in the money market. They employ and are employed in corporate organizations which are owned here, there, and everywhere. They compete not only with their obvious competitors in the same line of business, but with competitors in wholly different lines of business, automobiles with railroads, railroads with ships, cotton goods with silk and silk with artificial silk, pianos with furs and cigarettes with chewing-gum. The modern environment is invisible, complex, without settled plan, subtly and swiftly changing, offering innumerable choices, demanding great knowledge and imaginative effort to comprehend it.

It is not a social order at all as the Greek city state or the feudal society was a social order. It is rather a field for careers, an arena of talents, an ordeal by trial and error, and a risky speculation. No man has an established position in the modern world. There is no system of rights and duties to which he is clearly subject. He moves among these complexities which are shrouded in obscurity, making the best he can out of what little it is possible for him to know.


## 5. OLD-STYLE REFORM AND REVOLUTION

Naive capitalism—that is to say, the theory of each for himself according to such light as he might happen to possess—produced such monstrous evils the world over that an anti-capitalist reaction was the inevitable result. What had happened was that the most intricate and consequential technology which man has ever employed on this planet was given over to the direction of a class of enterprising, acquisitive, uneducated, and undisciplined men. No doubt it could not have been otherwise. The only discipline that was known was the discipline of custom in a society of farmers, hand-workers, and traders. The only education available was one based on the premises of the past. The revolution in human affairs produced by the machine began slowly, and no one could have anticipated its course. It would be absurd, therefore, to complain in retrospect over the fact that no one was prepared for the industrial changes which took place. The only absurdity, and it is still a prevalent one, is to go on supposing that the political philosophy and the "economic laws" which were extemporized to justify the behavior of the first bewildered capitalists have any real bearing upon modern industry.

But it is almost equally absurd to take too seriously the "reforms" and "solutions" which were devised by kindhearted men to alleviate the pains suffered by those who were hurt by the results of this early capitalist control of the machine. These proposals, when they are examined, turn out almost invariably to have been proposals for coercing or for abolishing the then masters of industry. I do not mean to deny the utility of the long series of legislative enactments which began about the middle of the Nineteenth Century and are still being elaborated. The factory acts, the regulatory laws, the measures designed to protect the consumers against fraud were, looked at singly, good, bad, or indifferent. As a whole they were a necessary attempt to police those who had been left free to pursue their own interest their own way. But when it has been said that they were necessary, and that they are still necessary, it is important to realize just what they imply. They imply that the masters of industry are unregenerate and will remain unregenerate. The whole effort to police capitalism assumes that the capitalist can be civilized only by means of the police. The trouble with this theory is that there is no way to make sure that the policemen will themselves be civilized. It presupposes that somehow politicians and office-holders will be wise enough and disinterested enough to make business men do what they would not otherwise do. The fundamental problem, which is to find a way of directing industry wisely, is not solved. It is merely deposited on the doorsteps of the politician.

The revolutionary programs sponsored by the socialists in the half-century before the Great War were based on the notion that it is impossible to police the capitalist employers and that, therefore, they should be abolished. In their place functionaries were to be installed. The theory was that these functionaries, being hired by the state and being deprived of all incentive for personal profit, would administer the industrial machine disinterestedly. The trouble with this theory is in its assumption that the removal of one kind of temptation, namely, the possibility of direct personal pecuniary profit—will make the functionaries mature and disinterested men.

This is nothing but a new variant of the ascetic principle that it is possible to shut off an undesirable impulse by thwarting it. Human nature does not work that way. The mere frustration of an impulse like acquisitiveness produces either some new expression of that impulse or disorders due to its frustration. It produces, that is to say, either corruption or the lethargy, the pedantry, and the officiousness which are the diseases of bureaucracy the world over. The socialists are right, as the early Christians were right, in their profound distrust of the acquisitive instinct as the dominant motive in society. But they are wrong in supposing that by transferring the command of industry from business men to socialist officials they can in any fundamental sense alter the acquisitive instinct. That can be done only by refining the human character through a better understanding of the environment. I do not mean to say that a revolution like the Russian does not sweep away a vast amount of accumulated rubbish. I am talking not about the salutary destruction which may accompany a revolution, but of the problem which confronts the successful revolutionists when they have to carry on the necessary affairs of men.

When that time comes they are bound to find that the administration of industry under socialism no less than under capitalism depends upon the character of the administrators. Corrupt, stupid, grasping functionaries will make at least as big a muddle of socialism as stupid, selfish, and acquisitive employers can make of capitalism. There is no escape from this elementary truth, and all social policies which attempt to ignore it must come to grief. They are essentially utopian. The early doctrine of *laissez-faire* was utopian because it assumed that unregenerate men were destined somehow to muddle their way to a harmonious result. The early socialism was utopian because it assumed that these same unregenerate men, once the laws of property had been altered, would somehow muddle their way to a harmonious result. Both ignored the chief lesson of human experience, which is the insight of high religion, that unregenerate men can only muddle into muddle.

A dim recognition of this truth has helped to inspire the procedure of the two most recent manifestations of the revolutionary spirit. I refer to bolshevism and to fascism. It is proper, I believe, to talk of them as one phenomenon, for their fundamental similarities, as most everyone but the bolshevists and the fascists themselves has noted, are much greater than their superficial differences. They were attempts to cure the evils resulting from the breakdown of a somewhat primitive form of capitalism. In neither Russia nor Italy had modern industrialism passed beyond its adolescent phase. In both countries the prevailing social order for the great mass of people was still pre-machine and pre-industrial. In both countries the acids of modernity had not yet eaten deeply into the religious disposition of the people. In both countries the natural pattern of all government was still the primitive pattern of the hierarchy with an absolute sovereign at the top. The bolshevik dictatorship and the fascist dictatorship, underneath all their modernist labels and theories, are feudal military organizations attempting to subdue and administer the machine technology.

The theorists of the two dictatorships are, however, men educated under modern influences, and the result is that their theories are an attempt to explain the primitive behavior of the two dictatorships in terms which are consistent with modern ideas. The formula reached in both instances is the same one. The dictatorships are said to be temporary. Their purpose, we are told, is to put the new social order into effect, and to keep it going long enough by dictation from on top to give time for a new generation to grow up which will be purged of those vices which would make the new order unworkable. The bolshevists and fascists regard themselves as ever so much more realistic than the old democratic socialists and the *laissez-faire* liberals whom they have executed, exiled, or dosed with castor oil. In an important sense they are more realistic. They have recognized that a substitute for primitive capitalism cannot be inaugurated or administered by a generation which has been schooled in the ways of primitive capitalism. And therefore the oligarchy of dictators, as a conscious, enlightened, superior, and heavily armed minority, propose to administer the industrial machine as trustees until there is a generation ready to accept the responsibilities.

It would be idle to predict that they will not succeed. But it is reasonable, I believe, to predict that if they succeed it will be because they are administering relatively simple industrial arrangements. It is precisely because the economic system of Russia is still fundamentally pre-capitalist and pre-mechanical that the feudal organization of the bolshevists is most likely to survive. Because the economic system of Italy is more modern than Russia's, the future of the fascist dictatorship is much less assured. For insofar as the machine technology is advanced, it becomes complex, delicate, and difficult to manage by commands from the top.

## 6. THE DIFFUSION OF THE ACQUISITIVE INSTINCT

While both the bolshevists and the fascists look upon themselves as pathfinders of progress, it is fairly clear, I think, that they are, in the literal meaning of the term, reactionary. They have won their victories among the people to whom modern large-scale industrial organization is still an unnatural and alien thing. It is no accident that fascism or bolshevism took root in Italy and Spain, but not in Germany and England, in Hungary but not in Austria, in Poland but not in Czechoslovakia, in Russia but not in Scandinavia, in China but not in Japan, in Central America but not in Canada or the United States. Dictatorship, based on a military hierarchy, administering the affairs of the community on behalf of the "nation" or of the "proletariat," is nothing but a return to the natural organization of society in the pre-machine age. Some countries, like Russia, Mexico, and China, for example, are still living in the pre-machine age. Others, like Italy, had become only partially industrialized when they were subjected to such strains by the War that they reverted to the feudal pattern of behavior. Unable to master the industrial process by methods which are appropriate to it, the fascists and the bolshevists are attempting to master it by methods which antedate it. That is why military dictatorship in a country like Mexico may be looked upon as the normal type of social control, whereas in Italy it is regressive and neurotic. Feudal habits are appropriate to a feudal society; in a semi-industrialized nation they are a social disease. It is the disease of frightened and despairing men who, having failed to adjust themselves to the reality of the industrial process, try, by main force and awkwardness, to adjust the machine process to a pre-machine mentality.

The more primitive the machine process is—that is, the more nearly it resembles the petty handicrafts of earlier days—the better are the chances for survival of a bolshevist or fascist dictatorship. Where the machine technology is really established and advanced it is simply unmanageable by militarized functionaries. For when the process has become infinitely complicated, the subdivision of function is carried so far, the internal adjustments are so numerous and so varied that no collection of oligarchs in a capital city, however much they may look like supermen, can possibly direct the industrial system. In its advanced stages, as it now exists in England, Germany, or the United States, nobody comprehends the system as a whole. One has only to glance over the financial pages of an American newspaper, to look at the list of corporations doing business, to try and imagine the myriad daily decisions at a thousand points which their business involves, in order to realize the bewildering complexity of modern industrial society. To suppose that all that can be administered, or even directed, from any central point by any human brain, by any cabinet of office holders or cabal of revolutionists, is simply to have failed to take it in. Here is the essential reason why bolshevism and fascism are, as we say, un-American. They are no less un-Belgian, un-German, un-English. For they are unindustrial.

The same reasons which make dictatorship unworkable are rapidly rendering obsolete the attempts to reform industry by policing it. Every year as the machine technology becomes more elaborated, the legislative control for which the pre-war progressives fought becomes less effective. It becomes more and more difficult for legislatures to make laws to protect the workers which really fit the rapidly changing conditions of work. Hence the tendency to put the real lawmaking power in the hands of administrative officials and judges who can adjust the general purpose of the law to the unclassifiable facts of industry. The whole attempt to regulate public utilities in the interest of the consumer is chaotic, for these organizations, by their intricacies, their scale, and their constant revolutions in technology, tend to escape the jurisdiction of officials exercising a local jurisdiction. The current outcry against the multiplication of laws and the meddling of legislatures is in part, but not wholly, the outcry of old-fashioned business men demanding their old natural liberty to pursue their own interest their own way. The outcry is due no less to a recognition that the industrial process is becoming too subtly organized to be policed successfully by the wholesale, uninformed enactments of legislatures.

Yet the very thing which makes an advanced industrial organization too complex to be directed by a dictatorship, or to be policed by democratic politicians, is forcing the leaders of industry to evolve forms of self-control. When I say that they are being forced to do this I am not referring to those ostentatiously benevolent things which are done now and then as sops to Cerberus. There is a certain amount of reform undertaken voluntarily by men who profess to fear 'bolshevism,' and if not bolshevism, then Congress. That is relatively unimportant. So also is the discovery that it pays to cultivate the good will of the public. What I am referring to is the fact that the sheer complexity of the industrial system would make it unmanageable to business men, no less than to politicians or dictators, if business men were not learning to organize its control.

It is the necessity of stabilizing their own business, of directing technical processes which are beyond the understanding of stockholders, of adjusting the supply and demand of the multitudinous elements they deal in, which is the compelling force behind that divorce between management and ownership, that growing use of experts and of statistical measurements, and that development of trade associations, of conferences, committees, and councils, with which modern industry is honeycombed. The captain of industry in the romantic sense tends to disappear in highly evolved industrial organizations. His thundering commands are replaced by the decisions of executives who consult with representatives of the interests involved and check their opinions by the findings of experts. The greater the corporation the more the shareholders and the directors lose the actual direction of the institution. They cannot direct the corporation because they do not really know what it is and what it is doing. That knowledge is subdivided among the executives and bureau chiefs and consultants, all of them on salary; each of them is so relatively small a factor in the whole that his personal success is in very large degree bound up with the success of the institution. A certain amount of jealousy, intrigue, and destructive pushing, of office politics, in short, naturally prevails, men being what they are. But as compared with the old-style business man, the ordinary executive in a great corporation is something quite strange. He is so little the monarch of all he surveys, his experience is so continually with stubborn and irreducible facts, he is so much compelled to adjust his own preferences to the preferences of others, that he becomes a relatively disinterested person. The more clearly he realizes the nature of his position in industry, the more he tends to submit his desires to the discipline of objective information. And the more he does this the less dominated he is by the acquisitiveness of immaturity. He may on the side gamble acquisitively in the stock market or at the race track, but in relation to his business his acquisitive instinct tends to become diffused and to be absorbed in the job itself.


7. IDEALS

It is my impression that when machine industry reaches a certain scale of complexity it exerts such pressure upon the men who run it that they cannot help socializing it. They are subject to a kind of economic selection under which only those men survive who are capable of taking a somewhat disinterested view of their work. A mature industry, because it is too subtly organized to be run by naively passionate men, puts a premium upon men whose characters are sufficiently matured to make them respect reality and to discount their own prejudices.

When the machine technology is really advanced, that is to say when it has drawn great masses of men within the orbit of its influence, when a corporation has become really great, the old distinction between public and private interest becomes very dim. I think it is destined largely to disappear. It is difficult even to-day to say whether the great railways, the General Electric Company, the United States Steel Corporation, the bigger insurance companies and banks are public or private institutions. When institutions reach a point where the legal owners are virtually disfranchised, when the direction is in the hands of salaried executives, technicians, and experts who hold themselves more or less accountable in standards of conduct to their fellow professionals, when the ultimate control is looked upon by the directors not as "business" but as a trust, it is not fanciful to say, as Mr. Keynes has said, that "the battle of socialism against unlimited private profit is being won in detail hour by hour."

Insofar as industry itself evolves its own control, it will regain its liberty from external interference. To say that is to say simply that the "natural liberty" of the early business man was unworkable because the early business man was unregenerate: he was immature, and he was therefore acquisitive. The only kind of liberty which is workable in the real world is the liberty of the disinterested man, of the man who has transformed his passions by an understanding of necessity. He can, as Confucius said, follow what his heart desires without transgressing what is right. For he has learned to desire what is right.

The more perfectly we understand the implications of the machine technology upon which our civilization is based, the easier it will be for us to live with it. We shall discern the ideals of our industry in the necessities of industry itself. They are the direction in which it must evolve if it is to fulfill itself. That is what ideals are. They are not hallucinations. They are not a collection of pretty and casual preferences. Ideals are an imaginative understanding of that which is desirable in that which is possible. As we discern the ideals of the machine technology we can consciously pursue them, knowing that we are not vainly trying to impose our casual prejudices, but that we are in harmony with the age we live in.

# XIII Government
## in the
## Great
## Society

## 1. LOYALTY

The difficulty of discovering an industrial philosophy which fits machine industry on a large scale has proved less trying than the discovery of a political philosophy which fits the modern state. I do not know why this should be so unless it be that, as compared with politicians, business men have had a closer opportunity to observe and more pressing reasons for trying to understand the transformation wrought by machinery and scientific invention. Certainly even the best political thinking is notably inferior in realism and in pertinence to the economic thinking which now plays so important a part in the direction of industry. To a very considerable degree the writer on politics to-day is about where the economist was when all economic theory began and for all practical purposes seemed to end with Robinson Crusoe and his man Friday. Nobody takes political science very seriously, for nobody is convinced that it is a science or that it has any important bearing on politics.

In very considerable measure political theory in the

modern world is sterilized by its own ideas. There have been passed down from generation to generation a collection of concepts which are so hallowed and so dense that their only use is to excite emotions and to obscure insight. How many of us really know what we are talking about when we use words like the state, sovereignty, independence, democracy, representative government, national honor, liberty, and loyalty? Very few of us, I think, could define any of these terms under cross-examination, though we are prepared to shed blood, or at least ink, in their behalf. These terms have ceased to be intellectual instruments for apprehending the facts we have to deal with and have become push buttons which touch off emotional reflexes.

As good a way as any to raise the temperature of political debate is to talk about loyalty. Everybody regards himself as loyal and resents any imputation upon his loyalty, yet even a cursory inspection of this term will show, I think, that it may mean any number of different things. It is clearest when used in a military sense. A loyal soldier is one who obeys his superior officer. A loyal officer is one who obeys his commander-in-chief. But just exactly what is a loyal commander-in-chief cannot be told so easily. He is loyal to the nation. He is loyal to the best interests of the nation. But what those best interests may be, whether they mean making peace or carrying the war into the enemy's country, is an exceedingly debatable question. When the citizen's loyalty is in question the whole matter becomes immensely subtle. Must he be loyal to every law and every command issued by the established authorities, kings, legislators, and aldermen? There are many who would say that this is the definition of civic loyalty, to obey the law without qualifications while it is a law. But such definition puts the taint of disloyalty on almost all citizens of the modern state. For the fact is that all the laws on the books are not even known, and that a considerable portion are entirely disregarded, and many it is impossible to obey. The definition, moreover, places outside the pale many who rank as great patriots, men who defied the law out of loyalty to some principle which the lawmakers have rejected. But what makes matters even more complicated is the fact that in modern communities the principle is accepted that the commands of the established authorities not only may be criticized but that they ought to be.

At this stage of political development the military element in loyalty has virtually disappeared. The idea of toleration, of freedom of speech, and above all the idea of organized opposition, alters radically the attributes of the sovereign. For a sovereign who has to be obeyed but not believed in, whose decisions are legitimate matters of dispute, who may be displaced by his bitterest opponents, has lost all semblance of omnipotence and omniscience. "He has sovereignty," wrote Jean Bodin, "who, after God, acknowledges no one greater than himself." Our governors command only for the time being—and within strict limits. Their authority is only such as they can win and hold. Political loyalty under these conditions, whatever else it may be, is certainly not unqualified allegiance to those who hold office, to the policies they pursue, or even to the laws they enact. Neither the government as it exists, nor its conduct, nor even the constitution by which it operates, exercises any ultimate claim upon the loyalty of the citizen. The most one can say, I think, is that the loyal citizen is one who loves his country and regards the status quo as an arrangement which he is at liberty to modify only by argument, according to well-understood rules, without violence, and with due regard for the interests and opinions of his fellow men. If he is loyal to this ideal of political conduct he is as loyal as the modern state can force him to be, or as it is desirable that he should be.

## 2. THE EVOLUTION OF LOYALTY

Broadly speaking, the evolution of political loyalty passes through three phases. In the earliest, the most primitive, and for almost all men the most natural, loyalty is allegiance to a chieftain; in the middle phase it tends to become allegiance to an institution—that is to say, to a corporate, rather than to a human, personality; and in the last phase it becomes allegiance to a pattern of conduct. The kind of government which any community is capable of operating is very largely determined by the kind of loyalty of which its members are capable.

It is plain, for example, that among a people who are capable only of loyalty to another human being the political system is bound to take the shape of a hierarchy, in which each man is loyal to his superior, and the man at the top is loyal to God alone. Such a society will be feudal, military, theocratic. If it is successfully organized it will be an ordered despotism, culminating, as the feudal system did, in God's Vice-gerent on earth. If it is unsuccessfully organized, as for example, in the more backward countries of Central America to-day, the system of personal allegiances will produce little factions each with its chief, all of them contending for, without quite achieving, absolute power. This type of organization is so fundamentally human that it prevails even in communities which think they have outgrown it. Thus it appears in what Americans call a political machine, which is nothing but a hierarchy of

professional politicians held together by profitable personal loyalties. The political boss is a demilitarized chieftain
in the direct line of descent from his prototypes.

The modern world has come to regard organization on
the basis of human allegiances as alien and dangerous.
Yet the political machine exists even in the most advanced
communities. The reason for that is obvious. With the en-
franchisement of virtually the whole adult population,
political power has passed into the hands of a great mass
of people most of whom are altogether incapable of loyalty
to institutions, much less to ideas. They do not understand
them. For these voters the only kind of political behavior
is through allegiance to a human superior, and modern de-
mocracies are considered fortunate if the political leaders
and bosses on whom these human allegiances converge are
relatively loyal to the institutions of the country. This, for
example, is the meaning of the dramatic speech in which
President Calles on September 1, 1928, voluntarily renounced the continuation of his own dictatorship. "For
the first time in Mexican history," he said, "the Republic
faces a situation (owing to the assassination of General
Obregon) whose dominant note is the lack of a military
leader, which is going to make it finally possible for us to
direct the policy of the country into truly institutional
channels, striving to pass once for all from our historical
condition of one-man rule to the higher, more dignified,
more useful, and more civilized condition of a nation of
laws and institutions." It is hardly to be supposed that
President Calles thought that the Mexican people as a
whole could pass once for all from their historical condition
of one-man rule. What he meant was that the political
chieftains to whom the people were loyal ought thereafter
to arrange the succession and to exercise power not as

seemed desirable to them, or as they might imagine that God had privately commanded them, but in accordance with objective rules of political conduct.

The conceptions of sovereignty which we inherit are derived from the primitive system of personal allegiances. That is why the conception of sovereignty has become increasingly confused as modern civilization has become more complex. In the Middle Ages the theory reached its symmetrical perfection. Mankind was conceived as a great organism in which the spiritual and temporal hierarchies were united as the soul is united with the body in "an inseverable connection and an unbroken interaction which must display itself in every part and also throughout the whole." But of course even in the Middle Ages the symmetry of this conception was marred by the fierce disputes between the Emperors and the Popes. After the Sixteenth Century the whole conception began to disintegrate. There appeared a congeries of monarchs each claiming to rule in his territory by divine right. But obviously when there are many agents of the Lord ruling men, and when they do not agree, the theory of sovereignty in its moral aspects is in grave difficulties.

As time went on, limitations of all kinds began to be imposed upon sovereigns. The existence at the same time of many sovereigns produced the need of international law, for obviously there could have been no international law in a world where all of mankind, barring infidels who did not have to be considered, were under one sovereign power. The limitations imposed by international law from without were accompanied by limitations imposed from within.

These limitations from within were based on quite practical considerations. There grew up slowly in the Middle Ages the idea that the State originated "in a contract of Subjection made between People and Ruler." The first modern writer to argue effectively that government was based not on a warrant from the Lord, but on a "social compact" is said to have been Richard Hooker, a clergyman of the Established Church, who held, in 1594, that the royal authority was derived from a contract between the king and the people. This idea soon became popular, for it suited the needs of all those who did not participate in the privileges of the absolute monarchy. It suited not only the Church of England, when as in Hooker's time it was assailed, but also the dissenting churches, and then the rising middle class whose ambitions were frustrated by the landed nobles with the king at their head. The doctrine of the social compact was expounded in many different forms in the Seventeenth and Eighteenth Centuries by men like Milton, Spinoza, Hobbes, Locke, and Rousseau.

As an historical theory to explain the origin of human society it is of course demonstrably false, but as a weapon for breaking up the concentration of sovereign power and distributing it, the idea has played a mighty role in history. It is almost certain to appear wherever there is an absolutism which men feel the need of checking. But the theory of the social compact disappears when power has become so widely diffused that no one can any longer locate the sovereign. That is what is happening in the advanced modern communities. The sovereign, whom it was once desirable to put under contract, has become so anonymous and diffuse that his very existence to-day is a legal fiction rather than a political fact. And loyalty by the same token is no longer provided with a personal superior of indubitable prestige to which it can be attached.

## 3 PLURALISM

The relationship between lord and vassals in which each man attaches himself for better or worse to some superior person tends gradually to disappear in the modern world. Its passing was somewhat prematurely announced by the Declaration of the Rights of Man; it did not wholly disappear by the dissolution of the bonds which bound one man to another, for the psychological bonds are stronger than the legal. Nevertheless the effect of modern civilization is to dissolve these psychological bonds, to break up clannishness and personal dependence. Men and women alike tend to become more or less independent persons rather than to remain members of a social organism.

The reason for this lies in the diversification of their interests. Life in the ancestral order was not only simpler and contained within narrower limits than it is to-day, but there was a far greater unity in the activity of each individual. Working the land, fighting, raising a family, worshipping, were so closely related that they could be governed by a very simple allegiance to the chief of the tribe or the lord of the manor. In the modern world this synthesis has disintegrated and the activities of a man cannot be directed by a simple allegiance. Each man finds himself the center of a complex of loyalties. He is loyal to his government, he is loyal to his state, he is loyal to his village, he is loyal to his neighborhood. He has his own family. He has his wife's family. His wife has her family. He has his church. His wife may have a different church. He may be an employer of thousands of men. He may be an employee. He must be loyal to his corporation, to his trade union, or his professional society. He is a buyer in many different markets. He is a seller in many different markets. He is a creditor and a debtor. He owns shares in several industries. He belongs to a political party, to clubs, to a social set. The multiplicity of his interests makes it impossible for him to give his whole allegiance to any person or to any institution.

It may be, in fact for most men it must be, that in each of these associations he follows a leader. In any considerable number of people it is certain that they will group themselves in hierarchical form. In every club, in every social circle, in every trade union, in every stockholders' meeting there are leaders and their lieutenants and the led. But these allegiances are partial. Because a man has so many loyalties each loyalty commands only a segment of himself. They are not, therefore, wholehearted loyalties like that of a good soldier to his captain. They are qualified, calculated, debatable, and they are sanctioned not by inherent authority but by expediency or inertia.

The outward manifestation of these complex loyalties of the modern man is the multitude of institutions through which the affairs of mankind are directed. Now since each of these corporate entities represents only a part of any man's interest, except perhaps in the case of the paid executive secretary, none of these institutions can count to the bitter end upon the undivided loyalty of all its members. The conflicts between institutions are in considerable measure conflicts of interest within the same individuals. There is a point where the activity of a man's trade union may so seriously affect the value of the securities he owns that he does not know which way his interest lies. The criss-crossing of loyalties is so great in an advanced community that no grouping is self-contained. No grouping, therefore, can maintain a military discipline or a military character. For when men strive too fiercely as members of any one group they soon find that they are at war with themselves as members of another group.

The statement that modern society is pluralistic cannot, then, be dismissed as a newfangled notion invented by theorists. It is a sober description of the actual facts. Each man has countless interests through which he is attached to a very complex social situation. The complexity of his allegiance cannot fail to be reflected in his political conduct.

## 4. LIVE AND LET LIVE

One of the inevitable effects of being attached to many different, somewhat conflicting, interdependent groupings is to blunt the edges of partisanship. It is possible to be fiercely partisan only as against those who are wholly alien. It is a fair generalization to say that the fiercest Democrats are to be found where there are the fewest Republicans, the most bloodthirsty patriots in the safest swivel chairs. Where men are personally entangled with the groups that are in potential conflict, where Democrats and Republicans belong to the same country club and where Protestants and Catholics marry each other, it is psychologically impossible to be sharply intolerant. That is why astute directors of corporations adopt the policy of distributing their securities as widely as they can; they know quite well that even the most modest shareholder is in some measure insulated against anti-corporate agitation. It is inherent in the complex pluralism of the modern world that men should behave moderately, and experience amply confirms this conclusion.

There is little doubt that in the great metropolitan centers there exists a disposition to live and let live, to give and take, to agree and to agree to differ, which is not to be found in simple homogeneous communities. In complex communities life quickly becomes intolerable if men are intolerant. For they are in daily contact with almost everybody and everything they could conceivably wish to persecute. Their victims would be their customers, their employees, their landlords, their tenants and perhaps their wives' relations. But in a simple community a kind of pastoral intolerance for everything alien adds a quaint flavor to living. For the most part it vents itself in the open air. The terrible indictments drawn up in a Mississippi village against the Pope in Rome, the Russian nation, the vices of Paris, and the enormities of New York are in the main quite lyrical. The Pope may never even know what the Mississippi preacher thinks of him and New York continues to go to, but never apparently to reach, hell.

When an agitator wishes to start a crusade, a religious revival, an inquisition, or some sort of jingo excitement, the further he goes from the centers of modern civilization the more following he can attract. It is in the backwoods and in the hill country, in kitchens and in old men's clubs, that fanaticism can be kindled. The urban crowd, if it has been urban for any length of time and has become used to its environment, may be fickle, faddish, nervous, unstable, but it lacks the concentration of energy to become fiercely excited for any length of time about anything. At its worst it is a raging mob, but it is not persistently fanatical. There are too many things to attract its attention for it to remain preoccupied for long with any one thing.

To responsible men of affairs the complexity of modern civilization is a daily lesson in the necessity of not pressing any claim too far, of understanding opposing points of view, of seeking to reconcile them, of conducting matters so that there is some kind of harmony in a plural society. This accounts, I think, for the increasing use of political devices which are wholly unknown in simpler societies. There is, for example, the ideal of a civil service. It is wholly modern and it is quite revolutionary. For it assumes that a great deal of the business of the state can and must be carried on by a class of men who have no personal and no party allegiance, who are in fact neutral in politics and concerned only with the execution of a task. I know how imperfectly the civil service works, but that it should exist at all, and that the ideal it embodies should be generally acknowledged, is profound testimony as to how inherent in the modern situation is the concept of disinterestedness. The theory of an independent judiciary arises out of the same need for disinterested judgment. Even more significant, perhaps, is the use in all political debates of the evidence of technicians, experts, and neutral investigators. The statesman who imagined he had thought up a solution for a social problem while he was in his bath would be a good deal of a joke; even if he had stumbled on a good idea, he would not dare to commit himself to it without elaborate preliminary surveys, investigations, hearings, conferences, and the like.

Men occupying responsible posts in the Great Society have become aware, in short, that their guesses and their prejudices are untrustworthy, and that successful decisions can be made only in a neutral spirit by comparing their hypotheses with their understanding of reality.

## 5. GOVERNMENT IN THE PEOPLE

It has been the cause of considerable wonder to many persons that the most complex modern communities, where the old loyalties are most completely dissolved, where authority has so little prestige, where moral codes are held in such small esteem, should nevertheless have proved to be far more impervious to the strain of war and revolution than the older and simpler types of civilization. It has been Russia, China, Poland, Italy, Spain, rather than England, Germany, Belgium, and the United States which have been most disorderly in the post-war period. The contrary might have been expected. It might well have been anticipated that the highly organized, delicately poised social mechanisms would disintegrate the most easily.

Yet it is now evident why modern civilization is so durable. Its strength lies in its sensitiveness. The effect of bad decisions is so quickly felt, the consequences are so inescapably serious, that corrective action is almost immediately set in motion. A simple society like Russia can let its railroads go gradually to wrack and ruin, but a complex society like London or New York is instantly disorganized if the railroads do not run on schedule. So many persons are at once affected in so many vitally important ways that remedies have to be found immediately. This does not mean that modern states are governed as wisely as they should be, or that they do not neglect much that they cannot really afford to neglect. They blunder along badly enough in all conscience. There is nevertheless a minimum of order and of necessary services which they have to provide for themselves. They have to keep going. They cannot afford the luxury of prolonged disorder or of a general paralysis. Their own necessities are dependent on such fragile structures, and everyone is so much affected, that when a modern state is in trouble it can draw upon incomparable reserves of public spirit.

"I made ninety-one local committees in ninety-one

local communities to look after the Mississippi flood," Mr. Hoover once explained, "that's what I principally did. . . . You say: 'a couple of thousand refugees are coming. They've got to have accommodations. Huts. Water-mains. Sewers. Streets. Dining-halls. Meals. Doctors. Everything.' . . . So you go away and they go ahead and just simply do it. Of all those ninety-one committees there was just one that fell down." Mr. Hard, who reports these remarks, goes on to make Mr. Hoover say that: "No other Main Street in the world could have done what the American Main Street did in the Mississippi flood; and Europe may jeer as it pleases at our mass production and our mass organization and our mass education. The safety of the United States is its multitudinous mass leadership." Allowing for the fact that these remarks appeared in a campaign biography at a time when Mr. Hoover's friends were rather concerned about demonstrating the intensity of his patriotism, there is nevertheless substantial truth in them. I am inclined to believe that "multitudinous mass leadership" will be found wherever industrial society is firmly established, that is to say, wherever a people has lived with the machine process long enough to acquire the aptitudes that it calls for. This capacity to organize, to administer affairs, to deal realistically with necessity, can hardly be due to some congenital superiority in the American people. They are, after all, only transplanted Europeans. That their aptitudes may be somewhat more highly developed is not, however, inconceivable: the new civilization may have developed more freely in a land where it did not have to contend with the institutions of a military, feudal, and clerical society.

The essential point is that as the machine technology makes social relations complex, it dissolves the habits of

obedience and dependence; it disintegrates the centraliza-
tion of power and of leadership; it diffuses the experience
of responsible decision throughout the population, compelling each man to acquire the habit of making judgments
instead of looking for orders, of adjusting his will to the
wills of others instead of trusting to custom and organic
loyalties. The real law under which modern society is administered is neither the accumulated precedents of tradition nor a set of commands originating on high which are
imposed like orders in an army upon the rank and file below. The real law in the modern state is the multitude of little decisions made daily by millions of men.

Because this is so, the character of government is
changing radically. This change is obscured for us in our
theorizing by the fact that our political ideas derive from
a different kind of social experience. We think of governing
as the act of a person; for the actual king we have tried to
substitute a corporate king, which we call the nation, the
people, the majority, public opinion, or the general will.
But none of these entities has the attributes of a king, and
the failure of political thinking to lay the ghosts of monarchy leads to endless misunderstanding. The crucial difference between modern politics and that to which mankind has been accustomed is that the power to act and to
compel obedience is almost never sufficiently centralized
nowadays to be exercised by one will. The power is distrib-
uted and qualified so that power is exerted not by command but by interaction.

The prime business of government, therefore, is not to
direct the affairs of the community, but to harmonize the
direction which the community gives to its affairs. The Congress of the United States, for example, does not consult the
conscience and its God and then decree a tariff law. It

enacts the kind of tariff which at the moment represents the most stable compromise among the interests which have made themselves heard. The law may be outrageously unfair. But if it is, that is because those whose interests are neglected did not at that time have the power to make themselves felt. If the law favors manufacturers rather than farmers, it is because the manufacturers at that time have greater weight in the social equilibrium than the farmers. That may sound hard. But it is doubtful whether a modern legislature can make laws effective if those laws are not the formal expression of what the persons actually affected can and wish to do.

The amount of law is relatively small which a modern legislature can successfully impose. The reason for this is that unless the enforcement of the law is taken in hand by the citizenry, the officials as such are quite helpless. It is possible to enforce the law of contracts, because the injured party will sue; it is possible to enforce the law against burglary, because almost everybody will report a burglary to the police. But it is not possible to enforce the old-fashioned speed laws on the highways because the police are too few and far between, the pedestrians are uninterested, and motorists like to speed. There is here a very fundamental principle of modern lawmaking: insofar as a law depends upon the initiative of officials in detecting violations and in prosecuting, that law will almost certainly be difficult to enforce. If a considerable part of the population is hostile to the law, and if the majority has only a platonic belief in it, the law will surely break down. For what gives law reality is not that it is commanded by the sovereign but that it brings the organized force of the state to the aid of those citizens who believe in the law.

What the government really does is not to rule men,

but to add overwhelming force to men when they rule their affairs. The passage of a law is in effect a promise that the police, the courts, and the officials will defend and enforce certain rights when citizens choose to exercise them. For all practical purposes this is just as true when what was once a private wrong to be redressed by private action in law courts on proof of specific injury has been made by statute a public wrong which is preventable and punishable by administrative action. When the citizens are no longer interested in preventing or punishing specific instances of what the statute declares is a public wrong, the statute becomes a dead letter. The principle is most obviously true in the case of a sumptuary law like prohibition. The reason prohibition is unenforceable in the great cities is that the citizens will not report the names and addresses of their bootleggers to the prohibition officials. But the principle is no less true in less obvious cases, as, for example, in tariffs or laws to regulate railroads. Thus it is difficult to enforce the tariff law on jewels, for they are easily smuggled. Insofar as the law is enforced it is because jewelers find it profitable to maintain an organization which detects smuggling. Because they know the ins and outs of the trade, and have men in all the jewelry markets of the world who have an interest in catching smugglers, it is possible for the United States Government to make a fair showing in administering the law. The government cannot from hour to hour inspect all the transactions of its people, and any law which rests on the premise that government can do this is a foolish law. The railroad laws are enforced because shippers are vigilant. The criminal laws depend upon how earnestly citizens object to certain kinds of crime. In fact it may be said that laws which make certain kinds of conduct illicit are effective insofar as the breach of these laws arouses the citizenry to call in the police and to take the trouble to help the police. It is not enough that the mass of the population should be law-abiding. A minority can stultify the law if the population as a whole is not also law-enforcing.

This is the real sense in which it can be said that power in the modern state resides not in the government but in the people. As that phrase is usually employed it alleges that 'the people,' as articulated by elected officials, can govern by command as the monarch or tribal chieftain once governed. In this sense government by the people is a delusion. What we have among advanced communities is something that might perhaps be described as government in the people. The naively democratic theory was that out of the mass of the voters there arose a cloud of wills which ascended to heaven, condensed into a thunderbolt, and then smote the people. It was supposed that the opinion of masses of persons somehow became the opinion of a corporate person called The People, and that this corporate person then directed human affairs like a monarch. But that is not what happens. Government is in the people and stays there. Government is their multitudinous decisions in concrete situations, and what officials do is to assist and facilitate this process of governing. Effective laws may be said to register an understanding among those concerned by which the law-abiding know what to expect and what is expected of them; they are insured with all the force that the state commands against the disruption of this understanding by the recalcitrant minority. In the modern state a law which does not register the inward assent of most of those who are affected will have very little force as against the breakers of that law. For it is only by that inward assent that power becomes mobilized to enforce the law. The government in the person of its officials, its paltry inspectors and policemen, has relatively little power of its own. It derives its power from the people in amounts which vary with the circumstances of each law. That is why the same government may act with invincible majesty in one place and with ludicrous futility in another.

## 6. POLITICIANS AND STATESMEN

The role of the leader would be easier to define if it were agreed to give separate meanings to two very common words. I mean the words 'politician' and 'statesman.' In popular usage a vague distinction is recognized: to call a man a statesman is eulogy, to call him a politician is to be, however faintly, disparaging. The dictionary, in fact, defines a politician as one who seeks to subserve the interests of a political party *merely;* as an afterthought it defines him as one skilled in political science: a statesman. And in defining a statesman the dictionary says that he is a political leader of distinguished ability.

These definitions can, I think, be improved upon by clarifying the meanings which are vaguely intended in popular usage. When we think offhand of a politician we think of a man who works for a partial interest. At the worst it is his own pocket. At the best it may be his party, his class, or an institution with which he is identified. We never feel that he can or will take into account all the interests concerned, and because bias and partisanship are the qualities of his conduct, we feel, unless we are naively afflicted with the same bias, that he is not to be trusted too far. Now the word 'statesman,' when it is not mere pomposity, connotes a man whose mind is elevated sufficiently above the conflict of contending parties to enable him to adopt a course of action which takes into account a greater number of interests in the perspective of a longer period of time. It is some such conception as this that Edmund Burke had in mind when he wrote that the state "ought not to be considered as nothing better than a partnership in a trade of pepper and coffee, calico or tobacco, or some other such low concern, to be taken up for a little temporary interest and to be dissolved by the fancy of the parties. . . . It is a partnership in a higher and more permanent sense—a partnership in all science; a partnership in all art; a partnership in every virtue and in all perfection. As the ends of such a partnership cannot be obtained in many generations it becomes a partnership not only between those who are living, but between those who are dead and those who are to be born."

The politician, then, is a man who seeks to attain the special objects of particular interests. If he is the leader of a political party he will try either to purchase the support of particular interests by specific pledges, or if that is impracticable, he will employ some form of deception. I include under the term 'deception' the whole art of propaganda, whether it consists of half-truths, lies, ambiguities, evasions, calculated silence, red herrings, unresponsiveness, slogans, catchwords, showmanship, bathos, hokum, and buncombe. They are, one and all, methods of preventing a disinterested inquiry into the situation. I do not say that any one can be elected to office without employing deception, though I am inclined to think that there is a new school of political reporters in the land who with a kind of beautiful cruelty are making it rather embarrassing for politicians to employ their old tricks. A man may have to be a politician to be elected when there is adult suffrage, and it may be that statesmanship, in the sense in which I am using the term, cannot occupy the whole attention of any public man. It is true at least that it never does.

The reason for this is that in order to hold office a man must array in his support a varied assortment of persons with all sorts of confused and conflicting purposes. When then, it may be asked, does he begin to be a statesman? He begins whenever he stops trying merely to satisfy or to obfuscate the momentary wishes of his constituents, and sets out to make them realize and assent to those hidden interests of theirs which are permanent because they fit the facts and can be harmonized with the interests of their neighbors. The politician says: "I will give you what you want." The statesman says: "What you think you want is this. What it is possible for you to get is that. What you really want, therefore, is the following." The politician stirs up a following; the statesman leads it. The politician, in brief, accepts unregenerate desire at its face value and either fulfills it or perpetrates a fraud; the statesman reeducates desire by confronting it with the reality, and so makes possible an enduring adjustment of interests within the community.

The chief element in the art of statesmanship under modern conditions is the ability to elucidate the confused and clamorous interests which converge upon the seat of government. It is an ability to penetrate from the naive self-interest of each group to its permanent and real interest. It is a difficult art which requires great courage, deep sympathy, and a vast amount of information. That is why it is so rare. But when a statesman is successful in converting his constituents from a childlike pursuit of what seems interesting to a realistic view of their interests, he receives a kind of support which the ordinary glib politician can never hope for. Candor is a bitter pill when first it is tasted but it is full of health, and once a man becomes established in the public mind as a person who deals habitually and successfully with real things, he acquires an eminence of a wholly different quality from that of even the most celebrated caterer to the popular favor. His hold on the people is enduring because he promises nothing which he cannot achieve; he proposes nothing which turns out to be a fake. Sooner or later the politician, because he deals in unrealities, is found out. Then he either goes to jail, or he is tolerated cynically as a picturesque and amiable scoundrel; or he retires and ceases to meddle with the destinies of men. The words of a statesman prove to have value because they express not the desires of the moment but the conditions under which desires can actually be adjusted to reality. His projects are policies which lay down an ordered plan of action in which all the elements affected will, after they have had some experience of it, find it profitable to co-operate. His laws register what the people really desire when they have clarified their wants. His laws have force because they mobilize the energies which alone can make laws effective.

It is not necessary, nor is it probable, that a statesmanlike policy will win such assent when it is first proposed. Nor is it necessary for the statesman to wait until he has won complete assent. There are many things which people cannot understand until they have lived with them for a while. Often, therefore, the great statesman is bound to act boldly in advance of his constituents. When he does this he stakes his judgment as to what the people will in the end find to be good against what the people happen ardently to desire. This capacity to act upon the hidden realities of a situation in spite of appearances is the essence of statesmanship. It consists in giving the people not what they want but what they will learn to want. It requires the courage which is possible only in a mind that is detached from the agitations of the moment. It requires the insight which comes only from an objective and discerning knowledge of the facts, and a high and imperturbable disinterestedness.

# XIV Love
in the
Great
Society

## 1. THE EXTERNAL CONTROL OF SEXUAL CONDUCT

While the changes which modernity implies affect the premises of all human conduct, the problem as a whole engages the attention of relatively few persons. The larger number of men and women living within the orbit of the Great Society are no doubt aware that their inherited beliefs about religion, politics, business, and sex do not square entirely with the actual beliefs upon which they feel compelled to act. But the fundamental alterations in political and economic ideals which the machine technology is inducing come home to each man only indirectly and partially. The consequences are subtle, delayed, and what is even more important, they are outside the scope of the ordinary man's personal decision. There is little that is urgent, immediate, or decisive which he can do, even if he understands them, about the changes in the structure and purpose of industry and the state. Most men can manage, therefore, to live without ever attempting to decide for themselves any fundamental question about business or politics. But they can neither ignore changes in sexual relations nor do they wish to. It is possible for a man to be a socialist or an individualist without ever having to make one responsible decision in which his theories play any part. But what he thinks about divorce and contraception, continence and license, monogamy, prostitution, and sexual experience outside of marriage, are matters that are bound at some point in his life to affect his own happiness immediately and directly. It is possible to be hypocritical about sex. But it is not possible for any adult who is not anaesthetic to be indifferent. The affairs of state may be regulated by leaders. But the affairs of a man and a woman are inescapably their own.

That obviously is the reason why in the popular mind it is immediately assumed that when morals are discussed it is sexual morals that are meant. The morals of the politician and the voter, of the shareholder and executive and employee, are only moderately interesting to the general public: thus they almost never supply the main theme of popular fiction. But the relation between boy and girl, man and woman, husband and wife, mistress and lover, parents and children, are themes which no amount of repetition makes stale. The explanation is obvious. The modern audience is composed of persons among whom only a comparatively negligible few are serenely happy in their personal lives. Popular fiction responds to their longings: to the unappeased it offers some measure of vicarious satisfaction, to the prurient an indulgence, to the worried, if not a way out, then at least the comfort of knowing that their secret despair is a common, and not a unique, experience.

Yet in spite of this immense preoccupation with sex it is extraordinarily difficult to arrive at any reliable knowledge of what actual change in human behavior it reflects. This is not surprising. In fact this is the very essence of the matter. The reason it is difficult to know the actual facts about sexual behavior in modern society is that sexual behavior eludes observation and control. We know that the old conventions have lost most of their authority because we cannot know about, and therefore can no longer regulate, the sexual behavior of others. It may be that there is, as some optimists believe, a fine but candid restraint practiced among modern men and women. It may be that incredible licentiousness exists all about us, as the gloomier prophets insist. It may be that there is just about as much unconventional conduct and no more than there has always been. Nobody, I think, really knows. Nobody knows whether the conversation about sex reflects more promiscuity or less hypocrisy. But what everybody must know is that sexual conduct, whatever it may be, is regulated personally and not publicly in modern society. If there is restraint it is, in the last analysis, voluntary; if there is promiscuity, it can be quite secret.

The circumstances which have wrought this change are inherent in modern ways of living. Until quite recently the main conventions of sex were enforced first by the parents and then by the husband through their control over the life of the woman. The main conventions were: first, that she must not encourage or display any amorous inclinations except where there was practical certainty that the young man's intentions were serious; second, that when she was married to the young man she submitted to his embraces only because the Lord somehow failed to contrive a less vile method of perpetuating the species. All the minor conventions were subsidiary to these; the whole system was organized on the premise that procreation was the woman's only sanction for sexual intercourse. Such control as was exercised over the conduct of men was subordinate to this control over the conduct of women. The chastity of women before marriage was guarded; that meant that seduction was a crime, but that relations with 'lost' or unchaste women were tolerated. The virtuous man, by popular standards, was one who before his marriage did not have sexual relations with a virtuous woman. There is ample testimony in the outcries of moralists that even in the olden days these conventions were not perfectly administered. But they were sufficiently well administered to remain the accepted conventions, honored even in the breach. It was possible, because of the way people lived, to administer them.

The woman lived a sheltered life. That is another way of saying that she lived under the constant inspection of her family. She lived at home. She worked at home. She met young men under the zealous chaperonage of practically the whole community. No doubt, couples slipped away occasionally and more went on than was known or acknowledged. But even then there was a very powerful deterrent against an illicit relationship. This deterrent was the fear of pregnancy. That in the end made it almost certain that if a secret affair were consummated it could not be kept secret and that terrible penalties would be exacted. In the modern world effective chaperonage has become impracticable and the fear of pregnancy has been virtually eliminated by the very general knowledge of contraceptive methods.

The whole revolution in the field of sexual morals turns upon the fact that external control of the chastity of women is becoming impossible.

## 2. BIRTH CONTROL

The Biblical account of how Jehovah slew Onan for disobeying his father's commandment to go to his brother's widow, Tamar, and "perform the duty of an husband's brother," shows that the deliberate prevention of conception is not a new discovery. Mr. Harold Cox must be right when he says "it is fairly certain that in all ages and in all countries men and women have practiced various devices to prevent conception while continuing to indulge in sexual intercourse." For while I know of no positive evidence to support this, it appears to be self-evident that the human race within historical times has not multiplied up to the limits of human fecundity. Since it is hardly probable that this has been due to the continence of husbands, nor wholly to infanticide, abortion, infant mortality, and postponement of marriage, it is safe to conclude that birth control is an ancient practice.

Nevertheless, it was not until the Nineteenth Century that the practice of contraception began to be publicly advocated on grounds of public policy. Until the industrial age the weight of opinion was overwhelmingly in favor of very large families. Kings and nobles needed soldiers and retainers: "As arrows in the hand of a mighty man, so are the children of youth. Happy is the man that hath his quiver full of them. They shall not be ashamed, but they shall speak with the enemies in the gate." Fathers of families desired many sons. The early factory-owners could use abundant cheap labor. There had been men from Plato's time who had their doubts about the value of an indefinitely growing population. But the substantial opinion down to the end of the Eighteenth Century was Adam Smith's that: "the most decisive mark of the prosperity of any country is the increase of the number of its inhabitants."

Apparently it was the sinister character of the early factory system, and the ominous unrest which pervaded

Europe after the French Revolution, which rather suddenly changed into pessimism this bland optimism about an ever growing population. Malthus published the first edition of his *Essay on Population* in 1798. This book is undoubtedly one of the great landmarks of human culture, for it focussed the attention of Europe on the necessity of regulating the growth of population. Malthus himself, it seems, hoped that this regulation could be achieved by the postponement of marriage and by continence. It is not clear whether he disapproved of what is now called neo-Malthusianism, or whether he did not regard it as practicable. Nevertheless, within less than twenty-five years James Mill in the *Encyclopaedia Britannica* had in guarded fashion put forward the neo-Malthusian principle, and shortly thereafter, that is in 1823, an active public propaganda was set on foot, most probably by Francis Place, by means of what were known as the 'diabolical handbills.' These leaflets were addressed to the working classes and contained descriptions of methods for preventing conception. Some of them were sent to a good lady named Mrs. Fildes, who indignantly, but mistakenly from her point of view, assisted the nefarious propaganda by exposing it in the public prints. Fifty years later Mr. Bradlaugh and Mrs. Besant had themselves indicted and tried for selling an illustrated edition of Knowlton's *Fruits of Philosophy*. After that advertisement, neo-Malthusian principles and practices were known and were, therefore, available to all but the poorest and most illiterate.

No propaganda so threatening to the established moral order ever encountered such an ineffective opposition. I do not know how much money has been spent on the propaganda nor how many martyrs have had to coerce reluctant judges to try them. But it is evident that once it was known that fairly dependable methods of contraception exist, the people took the matter into their own hands. For the public reasons by which neo-Malthusianism was justified were also private reasons. The social philosopher said that population must be adjusted to the means of subsistence. Man and wife said that they must have only as many children as they could afford to rear. The eugenist said that certain stocks ought not to multiply. Individual women decided that too many children, or even any children, were bad for their health. But these were not the only reasons which explain the demand for neo-Malthusian knowledge. There was also the very plain demand due to a desire to enjoy sexual intercourse without social consequences.

On this aspect of birth control the liberal reformers have, I think, been until recently more than a little disingenuous. They have been arguing for the removal of the prohibitory laws, and they have built their case on two main theses. They have argued, first, that the limitation of births was sound public policy for economic and eugenic reasons; and second, that it was necessary to the happiness of families, the health of mothers, and the welfare of children. All these reasons may be unimpeachable. I think they are. But it was idle to pretend that the dissemination of this knowledge, even if legally confined to the instruction of married women by licensed physicians, could be kept from the rest of the adult population. Obviously that which all married couples are permitted to know every one is bound to know. Human curiosity will make that certain. Now this is what the Christian churches, especially the Roman Catholic, which oppose contraception on principle, instantly recognized. They were quite right. They were quite right, too, in recognizing that whether or not birth control is eugenic, hygienic, and economic, it is the most revolutionary practice in the history of sexual morals.

For when conception could be prevented, there was an end to the theory that woman submits to the embrace of the male only for purposes of procreation. She had to be persuaded to cooperate, and no possible reason could be advanced except that the pleasure was reciprocal. She had to understand and inwardly assent to the principle that it is proper to have sexual intercourse with her husband and to prevent conception. She had, therefore, to give up the whole traditional theory which she may have only half-believed anyway, that sexual intercourse was an impure means to a noble end. She could no longer believe that procreation alone mitigated the vileness of cohabiting with a man, and so she had to change her valuation and accept it as inherently delightful. Thus by an inevitable process the practice of contraception led husbands and wives to the conviction that they need not be in the least ashamed of their desires for each other.

But this transvaluation of values within the sancity of the marital chamber could hardly be kept a secret. What had happened was that married couples were indulging in the pleasures of sex because they had learned how to isolate them from the responsibilities of parenthood. When we talk about the unconventional theories of the younger generation we might in all honesty take this fact into account. They have had it demonstrated to them by their own parents, by those in whom the administering of the conventions is vested, that under certain circumstances it is legitimate and proper to gratify sexual desire apart from any obligation to the family or to the race. They have been taught that it is possible to do this, and that it may be proper. Therefore, the older generation could no longer argue that sexual intercourse as such was evil. It could no longer argue that it was obviously dangerous. It could only maintain that the psychological consequences are serious if sexual gratification is not made incidental to the enduring partnership of marriage and a home. That may be, in fact, I think it can be shown to be, the real wisdom of the matter. Yet if it is the wisdom of the matter, it is a kind of wisdom which men and women can acquire by experience alone. They do not have it instinctively. They cannot be compelled to adopt it. They can only learn to believe it.

That is a very different thing from submitting to a convention upheld by all human and divine authority.

## 3. THE LOGIC OF BIRTH CONTROL

With contraception established as a more or less legitimate idea in modern society, a vast discussion has ensued as to how the practice of it can be rationalized. In this discussion the pace is set by those who accept the apparent logic of contraception and are prepared boldly to revise the sexual conventions accordingly. They take as their major premise the obvious fact that by contraception it is possible to dissociate procreation from gratification, and therefore to pursue independently what Mr. Havelock Ellis calls the primary and secondary objects of the sexual impulse. They propose, therefore, to sanction two distinct sets of conventions: one designed to protect the interests of the offspring by promoting intelligent, secure, and cheerful parenthood; the other designed to permit the freest and fullest expression of the erotic personality. They propose, in other words, to distinguish between parenthood as a vocation involving public responsibility, and love as an art, pursued privately for the sake of happiness.

As a preparation for the vocation of parenthood it is proposed to educate both men and women in the care, both physical and psychological, of children. It is proposed further that mating for parenthood shall become an altogether deliberate and voluntary choice: the argument here is that the duties of parenthood cannot be successfully fulfilled except where both parents cheerfully and knowingly assume them. Therefore, it is proposed, in order to avert the dangers of love at first sight and of mating under the blind compulsion of instinct, that a period of free experimentation be allowed to precede the solemn engagement to produce and rear children. This engagement is regarded as so much a public responsibility that it is even proposed, and to some extent has been embodied in the law of certain jurisdictions, that marriages for parenthood must be sanctioned by medical authority. In order, too, that no compulsive considerations may determine what ought to be a free and intelligent choice, it is argued that women should be economically independent before and during marriage. As this may not be possible for women without property of their own during the years when they are bearing and rearing children, it is proposed in some form or other to endow motherhood. This endowment may take the form of a legal claim upon the earnings of the father, or it may mean a subsidy from the state through mothers' pensions, free medical attention, day nurseries, and kindergartens. The principle that successful parenthood must be voluntary is maintained as consistently as possible. Therefore, among those who follow the logic of their idea, it is proposed that even marriages deliberately entered into for procreation shall be dissoluble at the will of either party, the state intervening only to insure the economic security of the offspring. It is proposed, furthermore, that where women find the vocation of motherhood impracticable for one reason or another, they may be relieved of the duty of rearing their children.

Not all of the advanced reformers adopt the whole of

this program, but the whole of this program is logically inherent in the conception of parenthood as a vocation deliberately undertaken, publicly pursued, and motivated solely by the parental instincts.

The separate set of conventions which it is proposed to adopt for the development of love as an art have a logic of their own. Their function is not to protect the welfare of the child but the happiness of lovers. It is very easy to misunderstand this conception. Mr. Havelock Ellis, in fact, describes it as a "divine and elusive mystery," a description which threatens to provide a rather elusive standard by which to fix a new set of sexual conventions. But baffling as this sounds, it is not wholly inscrutable, and a sufficient understanding of what is meant can be attained by clearing up the dangerous ambiguity in the phrase "love as an art."

There are two arts of love and it makes a considerable difference which one is meant. There is the art of love as Casanova, for example, practiced it. It is the art of seduction, courtship, and sexual gratification: it is an art which culminates in the sexual act. It can be repeated with the same lover and with other lovers, but it exhausts itself in the moment of ecstasy. When that moment is reached, the work of art is done, and the lover as artist "after an interval, perhaps of stupor and vital recuperation" must start all over again, until at last the rhythm is so stale it is a weariness to start at all; or the lover must find new lovers and new resistances to conquer. The aftermath of romantic love—that is, of love that is consummated in sexual ecstasy —is either tedium in middle age or the compulsive adventurousness of the libertine.

Now this is not what Mr. Ellis means when he talks about love as an art. "The act of intercourse," he says, "is only an incident, and not an essential in love." Incident to what? His answer is that it is an incident to an "exquisitely and variously and harmoniously blended" activity of "all the finer activities of the organism, physical and psychic." I take this to mean that when a man and woman are successfully in love, their whole activity is energized and victorious. They walk better, their digestion improves, they think more clearly, their secret worries drop away, the world is fresh and interesting, and they can do more than they dreamed that they could do. In love of this kind sexual intimacy is not the dead end of desire as it is in romantic or promiscuous love, but periodic affirmation of the inward delight of desire pervading an active life. Love of this sort can grow: it is not, like youth itself, a moment that comes and is gone and remains only a memory of something which cannot be recovered. It can grow because it has something to grow upon and to grow with; it is not contracted and stale because it has for its object, not the mere relief of physical tension, but all the objects with which the two lovers are concerned. They desire their worlds in each other, and therefore their love is as interesting as their worlds and their worlds are as interesting as their love.

It is to promote unions of this sort that the older liberals are proposing a new set of sexual conventions. There are, however, reformers in the field who take a much less exalted view of the sexual act, who regard it, indeed, not only as without biological or social significance, but also as without any very impressive psychological significance. "The practice of birth control," says Mr. C.E.M. Joad, for example, "will profoundly modify our sexual habits. It will enable the pleasures of sex to be tasted without its penalties, and it will remove the most formidable deterrent to irregular intercourse." For birth control "offers to the young . . . the prospect of shameless, harmless, and unlimited pleasure." But whether the reformers agree with Mr. Ellis that sexual intimacy is, as he says, a sacrament signifying some great spiritual reality, or with Mr. Joad that it is a harmless pleasure, they are agreed that the sexual conventions should be revised to permit such unions without penalties and without any sense of shame.

They ask public opinion to sanction what contraception has made feasible. They point out that "a large number of the men and women of to-day form sexual relationships outside marriage—whether or not they ultimately lead to marriage—which they conceal or seek to conceal from the world." These relationships, says Mr. Ellis, differ from the extra-marital manifestations of the sexual life of the past in that they do not derive from prostitution or seduction. Both of these ancient practices, he adds, are diminishing, for prostitution is becoming less attractive and, with the education of women, seduction is becoming less possible. The novelty of these new relations, the prevalence of which is conceded though it cannot be measured, lies in the fact that they are entered into voluntarily, have no obvious social consequences, and are altogether beyond the power of law or opinion to control. The argument, therefore, is that they should be approved, the chief point made being that by removing all stigma from such unions, they will become candid, wholesome, and delightful. The objection of the reformers to the existing conventions is that the sense of sin poisons the spontaneous goodness of such relationships.

The actual proposals go by a great variety of fancy names such as free love, trial marriage, companionate marriage. When these proposals are examined it is evident they all take birth control as their major premise, and then deduce from it some part or all of the logical consequences. Companionate marriage, for example, is from the point of view of the law, whatever it may be subjectively, nothing but a somewhat roundabout way of saying that childless couples may be divorced by mutual consent. It is a proposal, if not to control, then at least to register, publicly all sexual unions, the theory being that this public registration will abolish shame and furtiveness and give them a certain permanence. Companionate marriage is frankly an attempt at a compromise between marriages that are difficult to dissolve and clandestine relationships which have no sanction whatever.

The uncompromising logic of birth control has been stated more clearly, I think, by Mr. Bertrand Russell than by anyone else. Writing to Judge Lindsey during the uproar about companionate marriage, Mr. Russell said:

> I go further than you do: the things which your enemies say about you would be largely true of me. My own view is that the state and the law should take no notice of sexual relations apart from children, and that no marriage ceremony should be valid unless accompanied by a medical certificate of the woman's pregnancy. But when once there are children, I think that divorce should be avoided except for very grave cause. I should not regard physical infidelity as a very grave cause and should teach people that it is to be expected and tolerated, but should not involve the begetting of illegitimate children—not because illegitimacy is bad in itself, but because a home with two parents is best for children. I do not feel that the main thing in marriage is the feeling of the parents for each other; the main thing is cooperation in bearing children.

In this admirably clear statement there is set forth a plan for that complete separation between the primary and secondary function of sexual intercourse which contraception makes possible.

## 4. THE USE OF CONVENTION

It is one thing, however, to recognize the full logic of birth control and quite another thing to say that convention ought to be determined by that logic. One might as well argue that because automobiles can be driven at a hundred miles an hour the laws should sanction driving at the rate of a hundred miles an hour. Birth control is a device like the automobile, and its inherent possibilities do not fix the best uses to be made of it.

What an understanding of the logic of birth control does is to set before us the limits of coercive control of sexual relations. The law can, for example, make divorce very difficult where there are children. It could, as Mr. Bertrand Russell suggests, refuse divorce on the ground of infidelity. On the other hand the law cannot effectively prohibit infidelity, and as a matter of fact does not do so to-day. It cannot effectively prohibit fornication though there are statutes against it. Therefore, what Mr. Russell has done is to describe accurately enough the actual limits of effective legal control.

But sexual conventions are not statutes, and it is important to define quite clearly just what they are. In the older world they were rules of conduct enforceable by the family and the community through habit, coercion, and authority. In this sense of the word, convention tends to lose force and effect in modern civilization. Yet a conven-

tion is essentially a theory of conduct and all human conduct implies some theory of conduct. Therefore, although
it may be that no convention is any longer coercive, conventions remain, are adopted, revised, and debated. They
embody the considered results of experience: perhaps the
experience of a lonely pioneer or perhaps the collective experience of the dominant members of a community. In any
event they are as necessary to a society which recognizes
no authority as to one which does. For the inexperienced
must be offered some kind of hypothesis when they are confronted with the necessity of making choices: they cannot be
so utterly open-minded that they stand inert until something
collides with them. In the modern world, therefore, the
function of conventions is to declare the meaning of experience. A good convention is one which will most probably
show the inexperienced the way to happy experience.

Just because the rule of sexual conduct by authority is
dissolving, the need of conventions which will guide conduct is increasing. That, in fact, is the reason for the immense and urgent discussion of sex throughout the modern
world. It is an attempt to attain an understanding of the
bewilderingly new experiences to which few men or women
know how to adjust themselves. The true business of the
moralist in the midst of all this is not to denounce this and
to advocate that, but to see as clearly as he can into the
meaning of it, so that out of the chaos of pain and happiness and worry he may help to deliver a usable insight.

It is, I think, to the separation of parenthood as a vocation from love as an end in itself that the moralist must
address himself. For this is the heart of the problem: to
determine whether this separation, which birth control has
made feasible and which law can no longer prevent, is in
harmony with the conditions of human happiness.

## 5. THE NEW HEDONISM

Among those who hold that the separation of the primary and secondary functions of the sexual impulse is good and should constitute the major premise of modern sexual conventions, there are, as I have already pointed out, two schools of thought. There are the transcendentalists who believe with Mr. Havelock Ellis that "sexual pleasure, wisely used and not abused, may prove the stimulus and liberator of our finest and most exalted activities," and there are the unpretentious hedonists who believe that sexual pleasure is pleasure and not the stimulus or liberator of anything important. Both are, as we say, emancipated: neither recognizes the legitimacy of objective control unless a child is born, and both reject as an evil the traditional subjective control exercised by the sense of sin. Where they differ is in their valuation of love.

Hedonism as an attitude toward life is, of course, not a new thing in the world, but it has never before been tested out under such favorable conditions. To be a successful hedonist a man must have the opportunity to seek his pleasures without fear of any kind. Theodorus of Cyrene, who taught about 310 B.C., saw that clearly, and therefore to release men from fear openly denied the Olympian gods. But the newest hedonism has had an even better prospect than the classical: it finds men emancipated not only of all fear of divine authority and human custom but of physical and social consequences as well. If the pursuit of pleasure by carefree men were the way to happiness, hedonism ought, then, to be proving itself triumphantly in the modern world. Possibly it is too early to judge, but the fact is nevertheless highly significant, I think, that the new hedonists should already have arrived at the same conclusion as the later hedonists in the classical world. Hegesias, for example, wrote when hedonism had already had a great vogue: he was called, rather significantly, the "persuader to die." For having started from the premise that pleasure is the end of life, he concluded that, since life affords at least as much pain as pleasure, the end of life cannot be realized. There is now a generation in the world which is approaching middle age. They have exercised the privileges which were won by the iconoclasts who attacked what was usually called the Puritan or Victorian tradition. They have exercised the privileges without external restraint and without inhibition. Their conclusions are reported in the latest works of fiction. Do they report that they have found happiness in their freedom? Well, hardly. Instead of the gladness which they were promised, they seem, like Hegesias, to have found the wasteland.

"If love has come to be less often a sin," says that very discerning critic of life and letters, Mr. Joseph Wood Krutch, "it has come also to be less often a supreme privilege. If one turns to the smarter of those novelists who describe the doings of the more advanced set of those who are experimenting with life—to, for example, Mr. Aldous Huxley or Mr. Ernest Hemingway,—one will discover in their tragic farces the picture of a society which is at bottom in despair because, though it is more completely absorbed in the pursuit of love than in anything else, it has lost the sense of any ultimate importance inherent in the experience which preoccupies it; and if one turns to the graver of the intellectual writers,—to, for example, Mr. D. H. Lawrence, Mr. T. S. Eliot, or Mr. James Joyce,—one will find both explicitly and implicitly a similar sense that the transcendental value of love has become somehow attenuated, and that, to take a perfectly concrete example, a conclusion which does no more than bring a man and woman into complete possession of one another is a mere bathos which does nothing except legitimately provoke the comment, 'Well, what of it?' One can hardly imagine them concerned with what used to be called, in a phrase which they have helped to make faintly ridiculous, 'the right to love.' Individual freedom they have inherited and assumed as a right, but they are concerned with something which their more restricted forefathers assumed—with, that is to say, the value of love itself. No inhibitions either within or without restrain them, but they are asking themselves, 'What is it worth?' and they are certainly no longer feeling that it is obviously and in itself something which makes life worth the living.

"To Huxley and Hemingway—I take them as the most conspicuous exemplars of a whole school—love is at times only a sort of obscene joke. The former in particular has delighted to mock sentiment with physiology, to place the emotions of the lover in comic juxtaposition with quaint biological lore, and to picture a romantic pair 'quietly sweating palm to palm.' But the joke is one which turns quickly bitter upon the tongue, for a great and gratifying illusion has passed away, leaving the need for it still there. His characters still feel the psychological urge, and, since they have no sense of sin in connection with it, they yield easily and continually to that urge; but they have also the human need to respect their chief preoccupation, and it is the capacity to do this that they have lost. Absorbed in the pursuit of sexual satisfaction, they never find love and they are scarcely aware that they are seeking it, but they are far from content with themselves. In a generally devaluated world they are eagerly endeavoring to get what they can in the pursuit of satisfactions which are sufficiently instinctive to retain inevitably a modicum of animal pleasure, but they cannot transmute that simple animal pleasure into anything else. They themselves not infrequently share the contempt with which their creator regards them, and nothing could be less seductive, because nothing could be less glamorous, than the description of the debaucheries born of nothing except a sense of the emptiness of life."

This "generally devaluated world," of which Mr. Krutch speaks, what is it after all, but a world in which nothing connects itself very much with anything else? If you start with the belief that love is the pleasure of a moment, is it really surprising that it yields only a momentary pleasure? For it is the most ironical of all illusions to suppose that one is free of illusions in contracting any human desire to its primary physiological satisfaction. Does a man dine well because he ingests the requisite number of calories? Is he freer from illusions about his appetite than the man who creates an interesting dinner party out of the underlying fact that his guests and he have the need to fill their stomachs? Would it really be a mark of enlightenment if each of them filled his stomach in the solitary and solemn conviction that good conversation and pleasant companionship are one thing and nutrition is another?

This much the transcendentalists understand well enough. They do not wish to isolate the satisfaction of desire from our "finest and most exalted activities." They would make it "the stimulus and the liberator" of these activities. They would use it to arouse to "wholesome activity all the complex and interrelated systems of the organism." But what are these finest and most exalted activities which are to be stimulated and liberated? The discovery of truth, the making of works of art, meditation and insight? Mr. Ellis does not specify. If these are the activities that are meant, then the discussion applies to a very few of the men and women on earth. For the activities of most of them are necessarily concerned with earning a living and managing a household and rearing children and finding recreation. If the art of love is to stimulate and liberate activities, it is these prosaic activities which it must stimulate and liberate. But if you idealize the logic of birth control, make parenthood a separate vocation, isolate love from work and the hard realities of living, and say that it must be spontaneous and carefree, what have you done? You have separated it from all the important activities which it might stimulate and liberate. You have made love spontaneous but empty, and you have made home-building and parenthood efficient, responsible, and dull.

What has happened, I believe, is what so often happens in the first enthusiasm for a revolutionary invention. Its possibilities are so dazzling that men forget that inventions belong to man and not man to his inventions. In the discussion which has ensued since birth control became generally feasible, the central confusion has been that the reformers have tried to fix their sexual ideals in accordance with the logic of birth control instead of the logic of human nature. Birth control does make feasible this dissociation of interests which were once organically united. There are undoubtedly the best of reasons for dissociating them up to a point. But how completely it is wise to dissociate them is a matter to be determined not by saying how completely it is possible to dissociate them, but how much it is desirable to dissociate them.

All the varieties of the modern doctrine that man is a collection of separate impulses, each of which can attain its private satisfaction, are in fundamental contradiction not only with the traditional body of human wisdom but with the modern conception of the human character. Thus in one breath it is said in advanced circles that love is a series of casual episodes, and in the next it transpires that the speaker is in process of having himself elaborately psychoanalyzed in order to disengage his soul from the effects of apparently trivial episodes in his childhood. On the one hand it is asserted that sex pervades everything and on the other that sexual behavior is inconsequential. It is taught that experience is cumulative, that we are what our past has made us and shall be what we are making of ourselves now, and then with bland indifference to the significance of this we are told that all experiences are free, equal, and independent.

## 6. MARRIAGE AND AFFINITY

It is not hard to see why those who are concerned in revising sexual conventions should have taken the logic of birth control rather than knowledge of human nature as their major premise. Birth control is an immensely beneficent invention which can and does relieve men and women of some of the most tragic sorrows which afflict them: the tragedies of the unwanted child, the tragedies of insupportable economic burdens, the tragedies of excessive child-bearing and the destruction of youth and the necessity of living in an unrelenting series of pregnancies. It offers them freedom from intolerable mismating, from sterile virtue, from withering denials of happiness. These are the facts which the reformers saw, and in birth control they saw the instrument by which such freedom could be obtained.

The sexual conventions which they have proposed are really designed to cure notorious evils. They do not define the good life in sex; they point out ways of escape from the bad life. Thus companionate marriage is proposed by Judge Lindsey not as a type of union which is inherently desirable, but as an avenue of escape from corrupt marriages on the one hand and furtive promiscuity on the other. The movement for free divorce comes down to this: it is necessary because so many marriages are a failure. The whole theory that love is separate from parenthood and home-building is supported by the evidence in those cases where married couples are not lovers. It is the pathology of sexual relations which inspires the reformers of sexual conventions.

There is no need to quarrel with them because they insist upon remedies for manifest evils. Deep confusion results when they forget that these remedies are only remedies, and go on to institute them as ideals. It is better, without any doubt, that incompatible couples should be divorced and that each should then be free to find a mate who is compatible. But the frequency with which men and women have to resort to divorce because they are incompatible will be greatly influenced by the notions they have before and during marriage of what compatibility is, and what it involves. The remedies for failure are important. But what is central is the conception of sexual relations by which they expect to live successfully.

They cannot—I am, of course, speaking broadly—expect to live successfully by the conception that the primary and secondary functions of sex are in separate compartments of the soul. I have indicated why this conception is self-defeating and why, since human nature is organic and experience cumulative, our activities must, so to speak, engage and imply each other. Mates who are not lovers will not really cooperate, as Mr. Bertrand Russell thinks they should, in bearing children; they will be distracted, insufficient, and worst of all they will be merely dutiful. Lovers who have nothing to do but love each other are not really to be envied; love and nothing else very soon is nothing else. The emotion of love, in spite of the romantics, is not self-sustaining; it endures only when the lovers love many things together, and not merely each other. It is this understanding that love cannot successfully be isolated from the business of living which is the enduring wisdom of the institution of marriage. Let the law be what it may be as to what constitutes a marriage contract and how and when it may be dissolved. Let public opinion be as tolerant as it can be toward any and every kind of irregular and experimental relationship. When all the criticisms have been made, when all supernatural sanctions have been discarded, all subjective inhibitions erased, all compulsions abolished, the convention of marriage still remains to be considered as an interpretation of human experience. It is by the test of how genuinely it interprets human experience that the convention of marriage will ultimately be judged.

The wisdom of marriage rests upon an extremely unsentimental view of lovers and their passions. Its assumptions, when they are frankly exposed, are horrifying to those who have been brought up in the popular romantic tradition of the Nineteenth Century. These assumptions are that, given an initial attraction, a common social background, common responsibilities, and the conviction that the relationship is permanent, compatibility in marriage can normally be achieved. It is precisely this that the prevailing sentimentality about love denies. It assumes that marriages are made in heaven, that compatibility is instinctive, a mere coincidence, that happy unions are, in the last analysis, lucky accidents in which two people who happen to suit each other happen to have met. The convention of marriage rests on an interpretation of human nature which does not confuse the subjective feeling of the lovers that their passion is unique, with the brutal but objective fact that, had they never met, each of them would in all probability have found a lover who was just as unique. "Love," says Mr. Santayana, "is indeed much less exacting than it thinks itself. Nine-tenths of its cause are in the lover, for one-tenth that may be in the object. Were the latter not accidentally at hand, an almost identical passion would probably have been felt for some one else; for, although with acquaintance the quality of an attachment naturally adapts itself to the person loved, and makes that person its standard and ideal, the first assault and mysterious glow of the passion is much the same for every object."

This is the reason why the popular conception of romantic love as the meeting of two affinities produces so much unhappiness. The mysterious glow of passion is accepted as a sign that the great coincidence has occurred; there is a wedding and soon, as the glow of passion cools, it is discovered that no instinctive and preordained affinity is present. At this point the wisdom of popular romantic marriage is exhausted. For it proceeds on the assumption that love is a mysterious visitation. There is nothing left, then, but to grin and bear a miserably dull and nagging fate, or to break off and try again. The deep fallacy of the conception is in the failure to realize that compatibility is a process and not an accident, that it depends upon the maturing of instinctive desire by adaptation to the whole nature of the other person and to the common concerns of the pair of lovers.

The romantic theory of affinities rests upon an immature theory of desire. It springs from an infantile belief that the success of love is in the satisfactions which the other person provides. What this really means is that in childlike fashion the lover expects his mistress to supply him with happiness. But in the adult world that expectation is false. Because nine-tenths of the cause, as Mr. Santayana says, are in the lover for one-tenth that may be in the object, it is what the lover does about that nine-tenths which is decisive for his happiness. It is the claim, therefore, of those who uphold the ideal of marriage as a full partnership, and reject the ideal which would separate love as an art from parenthood as a vocation, that in the home made by a couple who propose to see it through, there are provided the essential conditions under which the passions of men and women are most likely to become mature, and therefore harmonious and disinterested.

## 7. THE SCHOOLING OF DESIRE

They need not deny, indeed it would be foolish as well as cruel for them to underestimate, the enormous difficulty of achieving successful marriages under modern conditions. For with the dissolution of authority and compulsion, a successful marriage depends wholly upon the capacity of the man and the woman to make it successful. They have to accomplish wholly by understanding and sympathy and disinterestedness of purpose what was once in a very large measure achieved by habit, necessity, and the absence of any practicable alternative. It takes two persons to make a successful marriage in the modern world, and that fact more than doubles its difficulty. For these reasons alone the modern state ought to do what it would none the less be compelled to do: it ought to provide decent ways of retreat in case of failure.

But if it is the truth that the convention of marriage correctly interprets human experience, whereas the separatist conventions are self-defeating, then the convention of marriage will prove to be the conclusion which emerges out of all this immense experimenting. It will survive not as a rule of law imposed by force, for that is now, I think, become impossible. It will not survive as a moral commandment with which the elderly can threaten the young. They will not listen. It will survive as the dominant insight into the reality of love and happiness, or it will not survive at all. That does not mean that all persons will live under the convention of marriage. As a matter of fact in civilized ages all persons never have. It means that the convention of marriage, when it is clarified by insight into reality, is likely to be the hypothesis upon which men and women will ordinarily proceed. There will be no compulsion behind it except the compulsion in each man and woman to reach a true adjustment of his life.

It is in this necessity of clarifying their love for those who are closest to them that the moral problems of the new age come to a personal issue. It is in the realm of sexual relations that mankind is being schooled amidst pain and worry for the novel conditions which modernity imposes. It is there, rather than in politics, business, or even in religion, that the issues are urgent, vivid, and inescapable. It is there that they touch most poignantly and most radically the organic roots of human personality. And it is there, in the ordering of their personal attachments, that for most men the process of salvation must necessarily begin.

For disinterestedness in all things, as Dean Inge says, is a mountain track which the many are likely in the future as in the past to find cold, bleak, and bare: that is why "the road of ascent is by personal affection for man." By the happy ordering of their personal affections they may establish the type and the quality and the direction of their desires for all things. It is in the hidden issues between lovers, more than anywhere else, that modern men and women are compelled, by personal anguish rather than by laws and preachments or even by the persuasions of abstract philosophy, to transcend naive desire and to reach out towards a mature and disinterested partnership with their world.

# XV The Moralist in an Unbelieving World

## 1. THE DECLARATION OF IDEALS

Of all the bewilderments of the present age none is greater than that of the conscientious and candid moralist himself. The very name of moralist seems to have become a term of disparagement and to suggest a somewhat pretentious and a somewhat stupid, perhaps even a somewhat hypocritical, meddler in other men's lives. In the minds of very many in the modern generation moralists are set down as persons who, in the words of Dean Inge, fancy themselves attracted by God when they are really only repelled by man.

The disesteem into which moralists have fallen is an historical accident. It so happens that those who administered the affairs of the established churches have, by and large, failed utterly to comprehend how deep and how inexorable was the dissolution of the ancestral order. They imagined either that this change in human affairs was a kind of temporary corruption, or that, like the eighty propositions listed in the Syllabus of Pope Pius IX, it could be regarded as due to "errors" of the human mind.

There were, of course, churchmen who knew better, but on the whole those who prevailed in the great ecclesiastical establishments could not believe that the skepticism of mind and the freedom of action which modern men exercise were due to inexorable historic causes. They declined to acknowledge that modern freedom was not merely a wilful iconoclasm, but the liquidation of an older order of human life.

Because they could not comprehend the magnitude of the revolution in which they were involved, they set themselves the task of impeding its progress by chastising the rebels and refuting their rationalizations. This was described as a vindication of morals. The effect was to associate morality with the vindication of the habits and dispositions of those who were most thoroughly out of sympathy with the genuine needs of modern men.

The difficulties of the new age were much more urgent than those which the orthodox moralists were concerned with. The moralists insisted that conduct must conform to the established code; what really worried men was how to adjust their conduct to the novel circumstances which confronted them. When they discovered that those who professed to be moralists were continuing to deny that the novelty of modern things had any bearing upon human conduct, and that morality was a word signifying a return to usages which it was impossible to follow, even if it were desirable, there was a kind of tacit agreement to let the moralists be moral and to find other language in which to describe the difference between good and bad, right and wrong. Mr. Joad is not unrepresentative of this reaction into contempt when he speaks of "the dowagers, the aunts, the old maids, the parsons, the town councillors, the clerks, the members of vigilance committees and purity leagues,

all those who are themselves too old to enjoy sex, too un-
attractive to obtain what they would wish to enjoy, or too
respectable to prefer enjoyment to respectability." Thus
for many the name of moralist came to be very nearly
synonymous with antipathy to the genius and the vitality
of the modern age.

But it is idle for moralists to ascribe the decline of
their influence to the perversity of their fellow creatures.
The phenomenon is world-wide. Moreover, it is most intensely present at precisely those points where the effect of
science and the machine technology have been most thoroughly manifested. The moralists are not confronted with a
scandal but with history. They have to come to terms with
a process in the life of mankind which is working upon the
inner springs of being and altering inevitably the premises
of conduct. They need not suppose that their pews are empty and that their exhortations are ignored because modern
men are really as wilful as the manners of the younger generation lead them to conclude. Much of what appears to
be a tough self-sufficiency is protective: it is a brittle crust
covering depths of uncertainty. If the advice of moralists
is ignored, it is not because this generation is too proud to
listen, or unaware that it has anything to learn. On the
contrary there is such curiosity and questioning as never
before engaged so large a number of men. The audience to
which a genuine moralist might speak is there. If it is inat-
tentive when the orthodox moralist speaks, it is because he
seems to speak irrelevantly.

The trouble with the moralists is in the moralists
themselves: they have failed to understand their times.
They think they are dealing with a generation that refuses
to believe in ancient authority. They are, in fact, dealing
with a generation that cannot believe in it. They think
they are confronted with men who have an irrational pref-

erence for immorality, whereas the men and women about
them are ridden by doubts because they do not know what
they prefer, nor why. The moralists fancy that they are
standing upon the rock of eternal truth, surveying the
chaos about them. They are greatly mistaken. Nothing in
the modern world is more chaotic—not its politics, its business, or its sexual relations—than the minds of orthodox
moralists who suppose that the problem of morals is somehow to find a way of reinforcing the sanctions which are
dissolving. How can we, they say in effect, find formulas
and rhetoric potent enough to make men behave? How
can we revive in them that love and fear of God, that sense
of the creature's dependence upon his creator, that obedience to the commands of a heavenly king, which once gave
force and effect to the moral code?

They have misconceived the moral problem, and therefore they misconceive the function of the moralist. An authoritative code of morals has force and effect when it expresses the settled customs of a stable society: the pharisee
can impose upon the minority only such conventions as the
majority find appropriate and necessary. But when customs are unsettled, as they are in the modern world, by
continual change in the circumstances of life, the pharisee
is helpless. He cannot command with authority because
his commands no longer imply the usages of the community: they express the prejudices of the moralist rather
than the practices of men. When that happens, it is presumptuous to issue moral commandments, for in fact nobody has authority to command. It is useless to command
when nobody has the disposition to obey. It is futile when
nobody really knows exactly what to command. In such
societies, wherever they have appeared among civilized
men, the moralist has ceased to be an administrator of
usages and has had to become an interpreter of human

needs. For ages when custom is unsettled are necessarily ages of prophecy. The moralist cannot teach what is revealed; he must reveal what can be taught. He has to seek insight rather than to preach.

The disesteem into which moralists have fallen is due at bottom to their failure to see that in an age like this one the function of the moralist is not to exhort men to be good but to elucidate what the good is. The problem of sanctions is secondary. For sanctions cannot be artificially constructed: they are a product of agreement and usage. Where no agreement exists, where no usages are established, where ideals are not clarified and where conventions are not followed comfortably by the mass of men, there are not, and cannot be, sanctions. It is possible to command where most men are already obedient. But even the greatest general cannot discipline a whole army at once. It is only when the greater part of his army is with him that he can quell the mutiny of a faction.

The acids of modernity are dissolving the usages and the sanctions to which men once habitually conformed. It is therefore impossible for the moralist to command. He can only persuade. To persuade he must show that the course of conduct he advocates is not an arbitrary pattern to which vitality must submit, but that which vitality itself would choose if it were clearly understood. He must be able to show that goodness is victorious vitality and badness defeated vitality; that sin is the denial and virtue the fulfilment of the promise inherent in the purposes of men. The good, said the Greek moralist, is "that which all things aim at"; we may perhaps take this to mean that the good is that which men would wish to do if they knew what they were doing.

If the morality of the naive hedonist who blindly seeks

the gratification of his instincts is irrational in that he trusts immature desire, disregards intelligence and damns the consequences, the morality of the pharisee is no less irrational. It reduces itself to the wholly arbitrary proposition that the best life for man would be some other kind of life than that which satisfies his nature. The true function of the moralist in an age when usage is unsettled is what Aristotle who lived in such an age described it to be: to promote good conduct by discovering and explaining the mark at which things aim. The moralist is irrelevant, if not meddlesome and dangerous, unless in his teaching he strives to give a true account, imaginatively conceived, of that which experience would show is desirable among the choices that are possible and necessary. If he is to be listened to, and if he is to deserve a hearing among his fellows, he must set himself this task which is so much humbler than to command and so much more difficult than to exhort: he must seek to anticipate and to supplement the insight of his fellow men into the problems of their adjustment to reality. He must find ways to make clear and ordered and expressive those concerns which are latent but overlaid and confused by their preoccupations and misunderstandings.

Could he do that with perfect lucidity he would not need to summon the police nor evoke the fear of hell: hell would be what it really is, and what in all inspired moralities it has always been understood to be, the very quality of evil itself. Nor would he find himself in the absurd predicament of seeming to argue that virtue is highly desirable but intensely unpleasant. It would not be necessary to praise goodness, for it would be that which men most ardently desired. Were the nature of good and evil really made plain by moralists, their teachings would appear to the modern listener not like exhortations from without, but as Keats said of poetry: "a wording of his own highest thoughts and . . . almost a remembrance."

## 2. THE CHOICE OF A WAY

What modernity requires of the moralist is that he should see with an innocent eye how men must reform their wants in a world which is not concerned to make them happy. The problem, as I have tried to show, is not a new one. It has been faced and solved by the masters of wisdom. What is new is the scale on which the problem is presented—in that so many must face it now—and its radical character in that the organic bonds of custom and belief are dissolving. There ensues a continual necessity of adjusting their lives to complex novelty. In such a world simple customs are unsuitable and authoritative commandments incredible. No prescription can now be written which men can naively and obediently follow. They have, therefore, to re-educate their wants by an understanding of their own relation to a world which is unconcerned with their hopes and fears. From the moralists they can get only hypotheses —distillations of experience carefully examined—probabilities, that is to say, upon which they may begin to act, but which they themselves must constantly correct by their own insight.

It is difficult for the orthodox moralists to believe that amidst the ruins of authority men will ever learn to do this. They can point to the urban crowds and ask whether anyone supposes that such persons are capable of ordering their lives by so subtle an instrument as the human understanding. They can insist with unanswerable force that this is absurd: that the great mass of men must be guided by rules and moved by the symbols of hope and fear. And they can ask what there is in the conception of the moralist as I have outlined it which takes the character of the populace into account.

What I take into account first of all is the fact, which it seems to me is indisputable, that for the modern populace the old rules are becoming progressively unsuitable and the old symbols of hope and fear progressively unreal. I ascribe that to the inherent character of the modern ways of living. I conclude from this that if the populace must be led, if it must have easily comprehended rules, if it must have common symbols of hope and fear, the question is how are its leaders to be developed, rules to be worked out, symbols created. The ultimate question is not how the populace is to be ruled, but what the teachers are to think. That is the question that has to be settled first: it is the preface to everything else.

For while moralists are at sixes and sevens in their own souls, not much can be done about morality, however high or low may be our estimates of the popular intelligence and character. If it were necessary to assume that ideals are relevant only if they are universally attainable, it would be a waste of time to discuss them. For it is evident enough that many, if not most men, must fail to comprehend what modern morality implies. But to recognize this is not to prophesy that the world is doomed unless men perform the miracle of reverting to their ancestral tradition. This is not the first time in the history of mankind when a revolution in the affairs of men has produced chaos in the human spirit. The world can endure a good deal of chaos. It always has. The ideal inherent in any age is never realized completely: Greece, which we like to idealize as an oasis of rationality, was only in some respects Hellenic; the Ages of Faith were only somewhat Christian. The processes of nature and of society go on somehow none the less. Men are born and they live and die with some happiness and some sorrow though they neither envisage wholly nor nearly approximate the ideals they pursue.

But if civilization is to be coherent and confident it must be *known* in that civilization what its ideals are. There must exist in the form of clearly available ideas an understanding of what the fulfilment of the promise of that civilization might mean, an imaginative conception of the good at which it might, and, if it is to flourish, at which it must aim. That knowledge, though no one has it perfectly, and though relatively few have it at all, is the principle of all order and certainty in the life of that people. By it they can clarify the practical conduct of life in some measure, and add immeasurably to its dignity.

To elucidate the ideals with which the modern world is pregnant is the original business of the moralist. Insofar as he succeeds in disentangling that which men think they believe from that which it is appropriate for them to believe, he is opening his mind to a true vision of the good life. The vision itself we can discern only faintly, for we have as yet only the occasional and fragmentary testimony of sages and saints and heroes, dim anticipations here and there, a most imperfect science of human behavior, and our own obscure endeavor to make explicit and rational the stresses of the modern world within our own souls. But we can begin to see, I think, that the evidence converges upon the theory that what the sages have prophesied as high religion, what psychologists delineate as matured personality, and the disinterestedness which the Great Society requires for its practical fulfilment, are all of a piece, and are the basic elements of a modern morality. I think the truth lies in this theory.

If it does, experience will enrich and refine it, and what is now an abstract principle arrived at by intuition and dialectic will engender ideas that marshal, illuminate, and anticipate the subtle and intricate detail of our actual experience. That at least can be our belief. In the meantime, the modern moralist cannot expect soon to construct a systematic and harmonious moral edifice like that which St. Thomas Aquinas and Dante constructed to house the aspirations of the mediaeval world. He is in a much earlier phase in the evolution of his world, in the phase of inquiry and prophecy rather than of ordering and harmonizing, and he is under the necessity of remaining close to the elements of experience in order to apprehend them freshly. He cannot, therefore, permit the old symbols of faith and the old formulations of right and wrong to prejudice his insight. Insofar as they contain wisdom for him or can become its vehicles, he will return to them. But he cannot return to them with honor or with sincerity until he has himself gone and drunk deeply at the sources of experience from which they originated.

Only when he has done that can he again in any honest sense take possession of the wisdom which he inherits. It requires wisdom to understand wisdom; the music is nothing if the audience is deaf. In the great moral systems and the great religions of mankind are embedded the record of how men have dealt with destiny, and only the thoughtless will argue that that record is obsolete and insignificant. But it is overlaid with much that is obsolete and for that reason it is undeciphered and inexpressive. The wisdom it contains has to be discovered anew before the old symbols will yield up their meaning. That is the only way in which Bacon's aphorism can be fulfilled, that "a little philosophy inclineth man's mind to atheism, but depth in philosophy bringeth men's minds about to religion." The depth in philosophy which can bring them about is a much deeper and more poignant experience than complacent churchmen suppose.

It can be no mere settling back into that from which men in the ardor of their youth escaped. This man and that may settle back, to be sure; he may cease to inquire though his questions are unanswered. But such conformity is sterile, and due to mere weariness of mind and body. The inquiry goes on because it has to go on, and while the vitality of our race is unimpaired, there will be men who feel with Mr. Whitehead that "to acquiesce in discrepancy is destructive of candor and of moral cleanliness," and that "it belongs to the self-respect of intellect to pursue every tangle of thought to its final unravelment." The crisis in the religious loyalties of mankind cannot be resolved by weariness and good nature, or by the invention of little intellectual devices for straightening out the dilemmas of biology and Genesis, history and the Gospels with which so many churchmen busy themselves. Beneath these little conflicts there is a real dilemma which modern men cannot successfully evade. "Where is the way where light dwelleth?" They are compelled to choose consciously, clearly, and with full realization of what the choice implies, between religion as a system of cosmic government and religion as insight into a cleansed and matured personality: between God conceived as the master of that fate, creator, providence, and king, and God conceived as the highest good at which they might aim. For God is the supreme symbol in which man expresses his destiny, and if that symbol is confused, his life is confused.

Men have not, hitherto, had to make that choice, for the historic churches have sheltered both kinds of religious experience, and the same mysteries have been the symbols of both. That confusion is no longer benign because men are no longer unconscious of it. They are aware that it is a confusion, and they are stultified by it. Because the popular religion of supernatural governments is undermined, the symbols of religion do not provide clear channels for religious experience. They are choked with the debris of dead notions in which men are unable to believe and unwilling to disbelieve. The result is a frustration in the inner life which will persist as long as the leaders of thought speak of God in more senses than one, and thus render all faith invalid, insincere, and faltering.

## 3. THE RELIGION OF THE SPIRIT

The choice is at last a personal one. The decision is rendered not by argument but by feeling. Those who believe that their salvation lies in obedience to, and communion with, the King of Creation can know how wholehearted their faith is by the confidence of their own hearts. If they are at peace, they need inquire no further. There are, however, those who do not find a principle of order in the belief that they are related to a supernatural power. They cannot be argued into the ancient belief, for it has been dissolved by the circumstances of their lives. They are deeply perplexed. They have learned that the absence of belief is vacancy; they know, from disillusionment and anxiety, that there is no freedom in mere freedom. They must find, then, some other principle which will give coherence and direction to their lives.

If the argument in these pages is sound, they need not look for and, in fact, cannot hope for, some new and unexpected revelation. Since they are unable to find a principle of order in the authority of a will outside themselves, there is no place they can find it except in an ideal of the human personality. But they do not have to invent such an ideal out of hand. The ideal way of life for men who must make their own terms with experience and find their own happiness has been stated again and again. It is that only the regenerate, the disinterested, the mature, can make use of freedom. This is the central insight of the teachers of wisdom. We can see now, I think, that it is also the mark at which the modern study of human nature points. We can see, too, that it is the pattern of successful conduct in the most advanced phases of the development of modern civilization. The ideal, then, is an old one, but its confirmation and its practical pertinence are new. The world is able at last to take seriously what its greatest teachers have said. And since all things need a name, if they are to be talked about, devotion to this ideal may properly be called by the name which these greatest teachers gave it; it may be called the religion of the spirit. At the heart of it is the knowledge that the goal of human effort is to be able, in the words I have so often quoted from Confucius, to follow what the heart desires without transgressing what is right.

In an age when custom is dissolved and authority is broken, the religion of the spirit is not merely a possible way of life. In principle it is the only way which transcends the difficulties. It alone is perfectly neutral about the constitution of the universe, in that it has no expectation that the universe will justify naive desire. Therefore, the progress of science cannot upset it. Its indifference to what the facts may be is indeed the very spirit of scientific inquiry.

A religion which rests upon particular conclusions in astronomy, biology, and history may be fatally injured by the discovery of new truths. But the religion of the spirit does not depend upon creeds and cosmologies; it has no vested interest in any particular truth. It is concerned not with the organization of matter, but with the quality of human desire.

It alone can endure the variety and complexity of things, for the religion of the spirit has no thesis to defend. It seeks excellence wherever it may appear, and finds it in anything which is inwardly understood; its motive is not acquisition but sympathy. Whatever is completely understood with sympathy for its own logic and purposes ceases to be external and stubborn and is wholly tamed. To understand is not only to pardon, but in the end to love. There is no itch in the religion of the spirit to make men good by bearing down upon them with righteousness and making them conform to a pattern. Its social principle is to live and let live. It has the only tolerable code of manners for a society in which men and women have become freely-moving individuals, no longer held in the grooves of custom by their ancestral ways. It is the only disposition of the soul which meets the moral difficulties of an anarchical age, for its principle is to civilize the passions, not by regulating them imperiously, but by transforming them with a mature understanding of their place in an adult environment. It is the only possible hygiene of the soul for men whose selves have become disjointed by the loss of their central certainties, because it counsels them to draw the sting of possessiveness out of their passions, and thus by removing anxiety to render them harmonious and serene.

The philosophy of the spirit is an almost exact reversal of the worldling's philosophy. The ordinary man believes that he will be blessed if he is virtuous, and therefore virtue seems to him a price he pays now for a blessedness he will some day enjoy. While he is waiting for his reward, therefore, virtue seems to him drab, arbitrary, and meaningless. For the reward is deferred, and there is really no instant proof that virtue really leads to the happiness he has been promised. Because the reward is deferred, it too becomes vague and dubious, for that which we never experience, we cannot truly understand. In the realm of the spirit, blessedness is not deferred: there is no future which is more auspicious than the present; there are no compensations later for evils now. Evil is to be overcome now and happiness is to be achieved now, for the kingdom of God is within you. The life of the spirit is not a commercial transaction in which the profit has to be anticipated; it is a kind of experience which is inherently profitable.

And so the mature man would take the world as it comes, and within himself remain quite unperturbed. When he acted, he would know that he was only testing an hypothesis, and if he failed, he would know that he had made a mistake. He would be quite prepared for the discovery that he might make mistakes, for his intelligence would be disentangled from his hopes. The failure of his experiment could not, therefore, involve the failure of his life. For the aspect of life which implicated his soul would be his understanding of life, and, to the understanding, defeat is no less interesting than victory. It would be no effort, therefore, for him to be tolerant, and no annoyance to be skeptical. He would face pain with fortitude, for he would have put it away from the inner chambers of his soul. Fear would not haunt him, for he would be without compulsion to seize anything and without anxiety as to its fate. He would be strong, not with the strength of hard resolves, but because he was free of that tension which vain expectations beget. Would his life be uninteresting because he was disinterested? He would have the whole universe, rather than the prison of his own hopes and fears, for his habitation, and in imagination all possible forms of being. How could that be dull unless he brought the dullness with him? He might dwell with all beauty and all knowledge, and they are inexhaustible. Would he, then, dream idle dreams? Only if he chose to. For he might go quite simply about the business of the world, a good deal more effectively perhaps than the worldling, in that he did not place an absolute value upon it, and deceive himself. Would he be hopeful? Not if to be hopeful was to expect the world to submit rather soon to his vanity. Would he be hopeless? Hope is an expectation of favors to come, and he would take his delights here and now. Since nothing gnawed at his vitals, neither doubt nor ambition, nor frustration, nor fear, he would move easily through life. And so whether he saw the thing as comedy, or high tragedy, or plain farce, he would affirm that it is what it is, and that the wise man can enjoy it.

# Acknowledgments

At the suggestion of the publishers, the references which follow have been segregated in an appendix instead of being scattered as footnotes through the text. They felt, rightly enough, I think, that in a book of this character the purpose of the notes was to acknowledge indebtedness for the material cited rather than to support the argument, and that the reader would prefer not to have the text encumbered by the apparatus of a kind of scholarship to which the author makes no pretensions.

While these notes, except in a few instances, refer only to matter actually used in the text, they are also an approximate bibliography of the works which I have consulted. I wish I could adequately acknowledge the obligation I owe to my teachers, William James, George Santayana, and Graham Wallas, though that perhaps is self-evident. I should like to thank Miss Jane Mather and Miss Orrie Lashin for help in the preparation of the manuscript. I am under special obligation to my wife, Faye Lippmann, without whose assistance I could not have completed the book.

W. L.

NEW YORK CITY, JANUARY, 1929.

# Notes

PAGE LINE

23   21   William James, *The Varieties of Religious Experience*, p. 518.

24   5   James, op. cit., p. 519.

24   30   Alfred North Whitehead, *Science and the Modern World*, pp. 249-250.

25   33   Bertrand Russell, *A Free Man's Worship*, in *Mysticism and Logic*, p. 54.

26   14   Kirsopp Lake, *The Religion of Yesterday and Tomorrow.*

28   15   W. R. Inge, *Science, Religion and Reality*, p. 388.

29   16   Cf. W. B. Riley, *The Faith of the Fundamentalists*, Times Current History, June, 1927.

32   20   *Fundamentalism and the Faith*, Commonweal, Aug. 19, 1925.

33   28   George Santayana, *Reason in Religion*, p. 97.

35   27   The material in this section is taken from Harry Emerson Fosdick, *The Modern Use of the Bible.*

37   31   Fosdick, op. cit., p. 83.

39   30   Fosdick, *The Desire for Immortality*, in *Adventurous Religion.*

41   29   W. R. Inge, *The Philosophy of Plotinus*, Vol. II, p. 166.

42   7   W. R. Inge, *The Platonic Tradition in English Religious Thought.*

45   4   Fosdick, *The Modern Use of the Bible.*

48   28   Cf. Rudolf Otto, *Chrysostom on the Inconceivable in God*, in *The Idea of the Holy.* Appendix I; cf. also the *Catholic Encyclopedia*, Vol. VIII, p. 452; cf. also William James, *The Varieties of Religious Experience*, Lecture III.

53   11   Lord Acton, inaugural *Lecture on the Study of History*, in *Lectures on Modern History.*

65   32   Otto Gierke, *Political Theories of the Middle Ages*—Translated by F. W. Maitland, p. 7.

66   15   From the Song of Roland, cited, Henry Adams, *Mont-Saint-Michel and Chartres*, p. 29.

67   17   For an analysis of the texts on which this claim was based, cf. James T. Shotwell and Louise Ropes Loomis, *The See of Peter.*

68   17   Cited in A. C. M'Giffert, *Protestant Thought Before Kant*, p. 44.

69   3   For a comprehensive condemnation by the Holy See of modern opinions which undermine the authority of the Roman Catholic Church, see the Syllabus of Pius IX (1864) and the Syllabus of Pius X (1907). The Syllabus of 1864 lists and condemns eighty principal errors of our time, and is described by the Catholic Encyclopedia (Vol. XIV, p. 369) as opposition "to the high tide of that intellectual movement of the Nineteenth Century which strove to sweep away the foundations of all human and Divine order." The Syllabus of 1907 condemns

sixty-five propositions of the Modernists which would "destroy the foundations of all natural and supernatural knowledge." (Catholic Encyclopedia, Vol. XIV, p. 370.) It should be noted that there is difference of opinion among Catholic scholars as to the binding power of these two pronouncements, and also that their meaning is open to elaborate interpretation.

69  31  *Catholic Encyclopedia,* Vol. XIV, p. 766.

71  13  J. N. Figgis, *Political Thought in the Sixteenth Century,* Cambridge Modern History, Vol. III, p. 743.

73  26  Cf. J. N. Figgis, op. cit., p. 742.

75  4  For an able recent exposition by an American of this theory of absolutism, cf. Charles C. Marshall, *The Roman Catholic Church in the Modern State.*

79  28  Cited R. H. Tawney, *Religion and the Rise of Capitalism,* p. 44.

80  13  Cited Tawney, op. cit., p. 243.

91  20  The facts cited in this section are from: E. Mâle, *L'Art Religieux du XIIIème Siècle en France,* and *L'Art Religieux de la Fin du Moyen-Age en France.* But cf. G. G. Coulton, *Art and the Reformation.*

96  7  *Prometheus Unbound,* cited A. N. Whitehead, *Science and the Modern World,* p. 119.

97  32  R. H. Wilenski, *The Modern Movement in Art,* p. 5.

102  4  Cf. Diego Rivera, *The Revolution in Painting,* in Creative Art, Vol. IV, No. 1. "And there is absolutely no reason to be frightened because the subject is so essential. On the contrary, precisely because the subject is admitted as a prime necessity, the artist is absolutely free to create a thoroughly plastic form of art. The subject is to the painter what the rails are to a locomotive. He cannot do without it. In fact, when he refuses to seek or accept a subject, his own plastic methods and his own esthetic theories become his subject instead. And even if he escapes them, he himself becomes the subject of his work. He becomes nothing but an illustrator of his own state of mind, and in trying to liberate himself he falls into the worst form of slavery. That is the cause of all the boredom which emanates from so many of the large expositions of modern art, a fact testified to again and again by the most different temperaments."

102  12  Bernard Berenson, *The Florentine Painters of the Renaissance,* p. 19.

103  25  Cf. R. H. Wilenski, *The Modern Movement in Art,* p. 119.

108  29  Cf. George Santayana, *Reason in Religion,* pp. 92 et seq.

112  16  Cf. *Catholic Encyclopedia,* Vol. X, p. 342.

115  27  Whitehead, *Science and the Modern World,* p. 257.

119  10  A. S. Eddington, *Stars and Atoms,* p. 121.

PAGE   LINE

120   8   John Herman Randall Jr., *The Making of the Modern Mind*, p. 100.
120   15   *Epist. ad Can Grand,* cited in footnote to *Paradiso* in the Temple Classics.
121   9   Cf. P. W. Bridgman, *The Logic of Modern Physics*, p. 45.
121   28   C. S. Peirce, *How to Make Our Ideas Clear in Chance, Love and Logic,* edited by Morris R. Cohen.
122   8   Bridgman, op. cit., p. 38.
126   25   Cited L. R. Farnell, *The Attributes of God*, p. 275.
129   12   Cf. M. C. Otto, *Natural Laws and Human Hopes,* pp. 32 et seq.
136   33   The *Catholic Encyclopedia*, Vol. XII, p. 345.
137   29   Cf. B. L. Manning, *The People's Faith in the Time of Wyclif.*
138   2   Fosdick, *Adventurous Religion*, p. 85 et seq.
138   7   Santayana, *Reason in Religion*, p. 43.
138   14   L. R. Farnell, *The Attributes of God*, p. 15.
139   10   Manning, op. cit.
148   28   Herbert Asbury, *A Methodist Saint, The Life of Bishop Asbury,* p. 265.
150   10   Cf. *Encyclopaedia Britannica,* "Asceticism."
151   4   Cf. *Catholic Encyclopedia,* Vol. I, p. 768.
151   22   Quoted in Irving Babbitt, *Rousseau and Romanticism,* p. 45.
152   3   *Rabelais,* Book II, Chapter 34.
152   20   Cited Henry Osborn Taylor, *Thought and Expression in the Sixteenth Century,* Vol. I, p. 330.
153   6   Babbitt, op. cit., p. 161.
153   10   Cf. Dora Russell, *The Right to be Happy.*
153   18   Cf. Bertrand Russell, *Political Ideals.*
154   29   T. W. Rhys Davids, *Buddhism*, p. 111.
155   33   *Ethics,* Book II, Chapter 9.
165   22   S. Freud, *Formulierung über die zwei Prinzipien des psychischen Geschehens,* 1911, Jahrb, Bd., I, s. 411.
165   29   S. Ferenczi, *Stages in the Development of the Sense of Reality,* 1913. In *Contributions to Psychoanalysis,* translated by Dr. Ernest Jones.
179   25   Spinoza, *Ethics*, Part V, Prop. XLII.
180   1   Cf. T. W. Rhys Davids, *Buddhism*, p. 110.
180   11   *Confucian Analects,* Book II, Chapter 4.
182   27   A. N. Whitehead, *Religion in the Making,* pp. 15-16.
183   19   *Analects* VII, XX.
184   25   *Ethics*, Part V, Prop. XLII.
186   12   Cf. T. W. Rhys Davids, *Buddhism*, p. 84.
186   23   C. Snouck Hurgronje, *Mohammedanism*, p. 82.
187   8   *Republic,* VI, 495, 504.

PAGE  LINE

191  16  Cf. J. Burnet, *Philosophy* in *The Legacy of Greece*, edited by R. W. Livingstone, p. 67.

203  32  Lucretius, *On the Nature of Things*, Book Third, Translation by H.A.J. Munro.

205  19  Spinoza, *Ethics*, Part V, Prop. III.

205  21  Id., Part V, Prop. VI.

210  2  Aristotle, *Ethics*, Book IV, Chapter III.

217  24  Oswald Spengler, *The Decline of the West*.

218  29  C. A. Beard, *Is Western Civilization in Peril?* Harper's Magazine, August, 1928.

219  19  H. G. Wells, *The Outline of History*, Vol. II, pp. 394-5.

220  31  A. N. Whitehead, *Science and the Modern World*, p. 4.

221  9  W. T. Sedgwick and H. W. Tyler, *A Short History of Science*, p. 269. Cf. Martha Ornstein, *The Role of Scientific Societies in the Seventeenth Century*.

222  2  J. B. Bury, *The Idea of Progress*, p. 330.

223  7  For a most illuminating description of the behavior of a great scientific investigator, cf. Claude Bernard, *An Introduction to the Study of Experimental Medicine*.

223  17  Bertrand Russell, *Mysticism and Logic*, p. 42.

225  4  Cf. Graham Wallas, *Our Social Heritage*, Chapter I.

225  30  John Herman Randall Jr., *The Making of the Modern Mind*, p. 279.

227  6  Adam Smith, *The Wealth of Nations*, Book IV, Chapter 9.

229  13  Cited In R. H. Tawney, *Religion and the Rise of Capitalism*, p. 286.

243  14  Otto Gierke, *Political Theories of the Middle Age*, Translated by F. W. Maitland, p. 23.

249  2  Id., p. 88.

249  5  Cf. J. W. Garner, *Introduction to Political Science*, p. 92.

249  31  For a discussion of the concept of sovereignty in the modern world, cf. Otto Gierke, *Political Theories of the Middle Ages;* J. N. Figgis, *Churches in the Modern State;* Lord Acton, *History of Freedom and Other Essays;* H. J. Laski, *A Grammar of Politics;* Kung Chuan Hsiao, *Political Pluralism*.

256  14  William Hard, *Who's Hoover?* p. 193.

262  15  *Reflections on the French Revolution*, cf. Garner, op. cit., p. 112.

269  34  Genesis XXXVIII; cf. Harold Cox, *The Problem of Population*, pp. 208-211, for an interpretation of the story of Onan in the light of Deut. XXV, which shows that the crime of Onan was not the spilling of his seed, but a breach of Jewish tribal law in refusing "to perform the duty of a husband's brother" with his brother's widow.

270  24  Psalm 127, cf. Cox, op. cit.

PAGE  LINE

270   32   The historical data are from A. M. Carr-Saunders, *The Population Problem*, Chapter I.

276   10   Havelock Ellis, *Love as an Art*, in Count Hermann Keyserling's *The Book of Marriage*, p. 388.

277   25   Santayana, *The Life of Reason*, Vol. II, p. 10.

278   3    C.E.M. Joad, *Thrasymachus, or The Future of Morals*, pp. 54-55.

278   15   Havelock Ellis, *The Family*, in *Whither Mankind*, p. 216.

279   34   Quoted in Judge Ben B. Lindsey and Wainwright Evans, *The Companionate Marriage*, p. 210.

283   7    Cf. Alfred Weber, *History of Philosophy*, p. 72.

285   7    *Love—Or the Life and Death of a Value*, Atlantic Monthly, August, 1928.

290   14   *Reason in Society*, p. 22.

293   1    W. R. Inge, *The Philosophy of Plotinus*, Vol. II, p. 161.

300   3    John Keats, Letters to John Taylor, Feb. 27, 1818—in *Oxford Book of English Prose*, No. 379.

# Index

**A note about
the production
of this book**

The typeface for the text of this special edition of *A Preface to Morals* is Book-
man, a contemporary face designed in 1903. The text was photocomposed at
Time Inc. under the direction of Albert J. Dunn and Arthur J. Dunn, and print-
ed by W. R. Bean & Son, Inc., Atlanta, Georgia. The binding was done by J. W.
Clement Co., Buffalo, New York. The cover was printed by Livermore and
Knight Co., a division of Printing Corporation of America, in Providence,
Rhode Island.

✗

The paper, TIME Reading Text, is from The Mead Corporation, Dayton, Ohio.
The cover stock is from The Plastic Coating Corporation, Holyoke, Massa-
chusetts.